GATHERING
THE
WINDS

GATHERING
THE
WINDS

Visionary Imagination and Radical Transformation of Self and Society

ELEANOR WILNER

THE JOHNS HOPKINS UNIVERSITY PRESS

Baltimore and London

This book has been brought to publication with
the generous assistance of the Andrew W. Mellon Foundation.

The Johns Hopkins University Press, Baltimore, Maryland 21218
The Johns Hopkins University Press Ltd., London

Library of Congress Catalog Card Number 75–9846
ISBN 0-8018-1670-X

Library of Congress Cataloging in Publication data
will be found on the last printed page of this book.

CONTENTS

The centre of the self, the self
Of the future, of future man
And future place, when these are known,
A freedom at last from the mystical,
The beginning of a final order,
The order of man's right to be
As he is, the discipline of his scope
Observed as an absolute, himself.

       Wallace Stevens, "The Sail of Ulysses"

                 Doubtless
It would be better to be always right, refraining
From those millennial expectations, but strangely,
Rising sometimes from hatred and wrong,
The song sings itself out to the end,
And like a running stream which purifies itself
It leaves behind the mortality of its maker,
Who has the skill of his art, and a trembling hand.

       Howard Nemerov, "Maestria"

To be radical is to grasp the matter by the root.
But for man the root is man himself.

       Karl Marx

INTRODUCTION

This study attempts to discover the structural constants in imagination, especially in response to a breakdown of personal and social order, and to understand the role of imagination in maintaining human order and mediating social and personal change. The recurrence of radical visionary experience in crisis situations is considered across a wide range of minds and societies, in order to show, not only that a patterned response does recur, but also to suggest the transformative and potentially curative power of such vision both for individuals and for societies.

In its most general sense the term "imagination" refers simply to the mind's ability to form images or concepts in the absence of the actual objects. More specifically, imagination (called by psychology, creative imagination) denotes the synthesizing power of the human mind, its ability to solve problems by recombining former experience in the creation of new images and .image patterns. The term "imagination," as it is used throughout this study, will refer to a particular kind of creative imagination which has been called variously poetic, mythic, or visionary imagination and whose special nature is to generate *humanly* significant syntheses whose shapes are not merely a mirror of experienced life but also an implicit valuation of a particular human condition in a specific time and place. When that condition is one of extremity and crisis—of oppression, disorder, and disharmony—a special kind of visionary imagination, the apocalyptic-millennial, may intervene, revealing and resolving seemingly irreconcilable conflicts in a new vision of man and society.

The first chapter studies the occurrence of this apocalyptic vision among the prophets of some preliterate societies, using anthropological data to confirm that such visions are produced out of deep social crises of order; that they are the product of individual imaginations that share in a collective experience of disorder, and are often radically transformative and regenerative both for the individual psyches in which they occur and for the collectivities in which they find a communal resonance and assent; and further, that they often lead to radical realignments in actual socio-political structures which have become inadequate and oppressive. These visions, which involve inspired recombinations of heretofore conflicting systems, examined through comparisons with historical instances of similar phenomena spontaneously erupting in response to social dislocation, will suggest the common origin of all religions in such imaginative reconstitution of a cosmos out of crisis—uniting past and present, real and ideal, individual and society

1

in the image of a perfected future on the far side of a creative heightening of conflict—through its destruction to a new resolution.

The second chapter contains a reading of the poets William Blake, Thomas Lovell Beddoes, and William Butler Yeats, who span a century when social change was outgrowing cultural forms, a reading against the imaginative paradigm of apocalyptic vision as response to social and personal malaise of order, suggesting the common imaginative source of both religious and poetic vision as well as the interpenetration of personal and social realities. Working on the assumption drawn from the evidence of the previous chapter that imagination has a diagnostic and curative human purpose, this section attempts to show how Blake's imagination, fed by the revolutionary currents of his time and freed by his confidence in its saving power, evolves a full apocalyptic-millennial vision. Beddoes, on the other hand, will be discussed as a negative instance of apocalyptic or "doomsday" vision, his role likened to that of sorcery in preliterate societies, which kills where it cannot cure. Finally, the poetry of Yeats will be seen as a contrived or willed apocalypse, not a radically transformative vision but an accommodation which perpetuates a dualistic, split reality—a construction of unity which is revealed as both tragic and artificial by an imagination working as rebellious subversive agent in the fundamentally conservative system it is forced to serve.

The final chapter focuses primarily on another nineteenth century visionary, Karl Marx, whose new world view, embodying both social critique and prospective vision, is seen in terms of its power as an apocalyptic-millennial prophecy in perhaps its most fully developed modern form. With this vision, and a review of the others with which it shares a family relationship, this study concludes by attempting to point to the kind of human order which all these visions, through the agency of the mythic imagination, are designed to defend.

Any study of the visionary imagination demands by the very nature of its subject an interdisciplinary approach, for vision is the embodied nexus of the particular human being and his social matrix. Imaginative vision is the unification of the two seemingly opposing but actually interconnected and reciprocally determined states of particularity and collectivity: the king dreams for the community, the hero's mythic journey ends with his return to and renewal of his society, the poet "purifies the dialect of the tribe"; in each case a psychological quest for individual wholeness leads inevitably to a social vision. As the very form of the myth suggests, vision is conceived in an individual mind and may be embraced by a community; visions once embraced are changed in that very act, altered by the work of other minds and other times on them, homogenized, recreated or transformed in their transmission until they have a collective life which is itself not single but various as the members of the collectivity who embrace them. And in speaking of individual visions in the first place, the language misleads, for the examination of any "individual" vision will show its roots in a common experience, in inherited images, shared language and beliefs, an inheritance whose depth in time can only be guessed at, and whose carriers, genetic or cultural, cannot be finally sorted out or separately determined. The imagination can only begin to reveal its nature, and our own, through an active encounter, by changing the mind that regards it, by demanding a method as concrete and holistic as its subject. This demands the crossing of disciplinary lines which tend to segment the experience that imaginative action unifies. Drawing, then, as it must, on a variety of disciplines, in particular on the complementary insights offered by anthropology, depth psychology, and literary criticism, this study is inevitably limited in knowledge in each of the separate disciplines and constantly encounters the frustration of not knowing nearly enough. It should be considered, however, for what it is—the preliminary investigation of a vast and inexhaustible subject.

Finally, the development of the argument that follows also takes its form from its subject; a number of visions, in all their concrete detail, are allowed to reflect on each other for their mutual illumination and clarification, avoiding as far as possible their reduction into another and inappropriate set of terms. The imagination is the rebel of those subjects on which a detached analytic eye throws its light; it is often hidden, digging its tunnel to freedom, while the detached eye circles the prison yard with its cold white light. But escape requires cunning and a knowledge of the more limited—even if ruling—order it must outsmart; imagination is integrated intelligence, intellect attached to rather than detached from the totality of human life. Reason *alone* is helpless to bring the rebellious imagination to light precisely because it forgets that it is itself only a part, that the part cannot comprehend the whole, and that it is imagination, which contains intellect but is not exhausted by it, that therefore has true dominion. Thus, even as only equals are capable of anything approaching mutual understanding, the contemplation of imagination must itself be an imaginative act. The reader's forbearance is asked, therefore, for what must be a somewhat internal argument; it is hoped that—with a little companionable patience—its intention may, as we proceed, reveal and justify itself.

1/THE
COLLECTIVE
EYE

Vision as an Agent
of Recurrent and Radical Change
in Preliterate Societies

> . . . the process of higher cultural formation
> may indeed be regarded as the dream life of society.
> What an individual's most significant and
> revealing dreams are to him personally,
> the symbolism of a culture is collectively to
> the society that produces it.[1]

The dream has all the characteristics which belong to the arts of mankind: it has the transformations of magic, the disproportionate emotions of religion, the demons of sorcery, the condensed images of poetry. It is the prototype for its more conscious cousins of ritual, myth and poetry, because it springs, though more darkly, from the same source—the human imagination.

There are before us a bewildering diversity of the works of human imagination—of collective myths from all the various cultures of mankind, formulated dreams which communities share and which compel belief, myths whose origins, though variously explained, are shrouded in prehistory. There are, however, myths at whose birth modern investigators have been in attendance, and it is these new myths, born out of a clash of cultures and the resultant dislocation of an old system of values and relations, that begin to throw light on the relation between individual and collective vision, the connection between myth and social order, and finally, the origins of collective myths and, thereby, the structure, function, purpose—and not least, the power—of the human imagination. These new myths, appearing in widely separated societies but under similar conditions, indicate by their common characteristics that there is a special imaginative state common to and potentially

---

1. Walter Abell, *The Collective Dream in Art* (New York: Schocken Books, 1957), p. 276.

curative of deep crisis of order which shall be called the apocalyptic or prophetic imagination.

Based on what emerges as demonstrably similar in these crisis visions, it will be argued with Jung and his anthropological descendants like Radin, Wallace, and others that the apocalyptic imagination, unleashed in visions, dreams, and trance, is the response of an innate integrative function, a kind of "voice of human nature," if such an expression may be justified by the unbidden and seemingly spontaneous appearance of this strange phenomenon; and that the voice of this partly unconscious life-affirming and ordering force is loudest when integrity is most deeply threatened, when the conflicting forces in men and society are most at odds and the need for synthesis most acute. If the vision misfires, if the dream of redemption ends in suicidal actions, then we must look to the circumstances and accidents of history; the response of other, often dominant, groups; the exploitation of the vision by the cynical and the opportunistic; the particular pathology of certain prophets; and the veiled and sometimes misunderstood tongues in which the language of imagination speaks. It is, nevertheless, hard to miss something like the struggle of health (i.e., harmonious psycho-biological-social order) against the forces of entropy and rigidity and not to find, whatever its eventual success or failure, at least the movement toward unity and integrity in the midst of complexity and division, and even, at the furthest extreme, amid anomie and chaos.

> History's going to save us—we were thinking.
> Going to save us—were we dreaming?
> It wasn't all just uprisings, barricades, bonfires;
> in our heads it was a dress of bubbling foam, a
> Rhine maiden with clear eyes, smiling, standing
> at the door, hand outstretched
> toward a hungry and waiting people.[2]

The study of what Wallace calls "revitalization cults," and La Barre, "crisis cults," the imaginative vision of unnumbered "hungry and waiting people," will be of central concern. The primacy of this consideration is based on several justifications: (1) the relative contemporaneity and widespread occurrence of these cults; (2) the large amount of available and reliable data and the consequent possibility of assessing the forces which produced the cults; (3) the light which these cults throw on the role of the imagination as an integrative force in society, on the origins of religion in general, and on the relation of religion to visionary art; (4) the way in which these cults embody and

2. Heberto Padilla, "Important Occasions," trans. Paul Blackburn, *The New York Review of Books* 16, no. 10 (June 3, 1971): 5.

make change (and thereby innovation of order) visible, as they enable a new man and a new society to emerge from the rubble of the old; and finally, (5) the imaginative patterns which appear among diverse peoples faced with similar crisis situations, patterns which also appear at the center of art that responds to personal and cultural crisis.

There is an expression among the people of Russia, who fear their dreams with a holy fear, that "the dream is a fool." There is also a tradition in the literature of that people, typified by Dostoyevsky's Idiot, of the holy fool, a figure who, on the borderline between madness and profundity, is depicted both as an affront to common sense and as a kind of lightning rod for the powers considered most sacred. Ambivalence to dream phenomena is widespread in human society; dreams have been alternately regarded as the work of gods or the voice of devils, as the deepest wisdom or as symptoms of madness. The same figure, the prophet or visionary, is sometimes considered a savior, sometimes a psychotic. The dream may be viewed as the protector of man and of social order; equally, it may be seen as destructive of that order. What then may resolve such a fundamental contradiction: that the highest value (sacredness) and the lowest (madness or foolishness) are attached to the same phenomena—the dream and the dreamer?

Man has feelings, related to his basic psycho-biological needs, whose satisfaction is fundamental to his well-being as an organism. He has, in addition, an adaptive structure of social regulations which pattern the way in which, with others, he goes about the satisfaction of these needs. The more adaptive the order—that is, the more it serves the basic needs for food, for affection, for security, for sex, for natural expression—the less potency the dream life has. The less that conscious order serves these basic emotional and bodily needs, the more power the dream assumes, the more it invades the waking life. But since these basic needs may at times be in opposition to each other, or may be at odds with the prescribed order, and since no social order, however well arranged, can satisfactorily serve all our needs nor resolve all the conflicts that individuals have with one another, every mind produces and depends on some dream life. Furthermore, the changes from one stage of life to another inevitably involve conflicts that the dream life embodies and attempts to solve. Shamanism, as will be shown, is the institutionalization of these phenomena within the social order, as are other prescribed ways of regarding or acting on dream material. Since the operation of the imagination is not purely "mental" but involves bodily processes and the discharge of feeling, the dream serves in part to allow expression of feelings which relieve the tension of the organism. But if dream were only wish-fulfillment, its relationship to reality would be purely conservative; it could not be, as it often is, an agent of change. For the dream, besides liberating certain suppressed feelings, accompanied by the images which embody them, also creatively suggests ways in which the conflict may be resolved. Thus the dream imagines a way out of the tension producing conflict, and if it is taken seriously may serve to alter relationships in the real world, an alteration which is in the interest of the harmony of inner need and social order. It thus corrects order in the direction of such harmony, adding emotional certainty, often interpreted as divine validation, to its proposed solution.

One man, for instance, may have an excess of wealth and excite jealousy among his kin; this envy, expressed in covert ways, may disturb him and even make him ill, and guilt feelings may compound his discomfort. In his social context he may experience these feelings as fears of sorcery, and believing himself bewitched may call upon a shaman to restore his health and his confidence. The shaman, in trance, may identify the injured parties as the source of the trouble and may suggest the gift of some of his wealth to induce them to undo their destructive magic. Thus a minor redistribution of wealth may take place which restores the balance of power among kin and resolves the conflict which its imbalance aroused.

As another instance of imaginative interference in real action, a Plains Indian in his maturation vision sees a mythic animal or natural protector who indicates to him the direction his life should take. He may, for example, be visited by the moon, a feminine archetype, and choose as a result the role of *berdache*, a transvestite role permitted within the social order which allows a function for the deviant male personality whose sensitivity or physical make-up precludes his functioning as a normally aggressive male hunter. This role often includes certain shamanistic functions which utilize his extraordinary sensitivity for social ends, and give him status in the tribe, a special sort of power which compensates him for his inability to compete as a hunter and assures him an income as recompense for his special magical powers. Again, the dream served to resolve a conflict between individual need and social prescription, providing for both in a way to insure maximum harmony.[3]

In the above situations, the social order provides for sufficient

3. George Devereux in his anthropological psychotherapy of a Plains Indian makes it clear that dreams have a functional utility, heightened by the seriousness with which they are regarded, representing "a kind of defense mechanism . . . for the purpose of ego defense and ego gratification in Plains Indian society." (*Reality and Dream: Psychotherapy of a Plains Indian* [Garden City, N. Y.: Doubleday and Company, 1969], p. 150.)

accommodation to materially reduce the conflict. In these instances, the dream, as manifestation of a harmonious principle, is, in a sense, a result of cultural patterning of particular need and is basically compatible with the given order. However, the degree to which social order is adaptive differs, and it is this difference which determines the intensity of dream and the degree to which it may disagree with the given external order. At times when the social order is felt as extremely inimical to instinctual life, the dream may invade waking life and end by radically re-structuring the conscious order which it overthrows. If this experience is reserved for an isolated individual here and there, his imaginative rejection of the going order may be adjudged insane or evil by his peers; if, on the other hand, there is a widespread feeling that the present order is oppressive or inadequate, such a vision may be experienced in the individual and his community alike as renewed harmony and restored self-esteem, and the visionary thereby assumes the mantle of the prophet. Thus the first kind of dream is basically adjustive to order; the second subversive to it. A central paradox is here resolved: imaginative vision or religious solution of conflict may be either conservative or radical, both being equally authentic. It depends entirely on the social situation, and whether, as it exists, it promotes harmony. Where it does, religious vision tends to be conservative; where it does not, authentic vision is radically subversive. The test of which is authentic "religious truth" at the moment lies in communal response to the myth-dream. "The truth," as the Marxists say, "is with the people."

These introductory speculations put into perspective the various theories of mythico-religious function by allowing them to appear as complementary and partial descriptions of what is, by its very nature, a multi-functional phenomenon. If it is the function of religion to assure that individual needs and social prescriptions are mutually supportive, then it is to be expected that any adequate description of religion would account for both sides of the equation, with the interrelation of the two seen as central. Thus, partial views are the insightful ingredients of a fuller understanding; but insofar as they are partial they are falsifying. What is sought here is the most inclusive description, which is not to be confused with a true explanation. How so many elements combine in the imagination to produce a vision with such functional economy is now, and may always be, beyond the understanding of the minds in which this order-making activity takes place. Awe, which is aroused by the workings of human imagination, is not displaced by enquiry into its function. On the contrary.

The earliest anthropological theorists of religion like Tylor and Frazer, because of their own rationalist bias, tended to stress the intellectual needs of men, describing religion in terms of a kind of erroneous logic. Similarly, Radcliffe-Brown, neglecting the irrational, offers a jural and rationalistic description of religion as the explanation for natural phenomena on the basis of social order, which suggests the way in which religion, while offering this mentally satisfying explanation, also strengthens the social bonds. He bows to feeling only insofar as he sees the communal acting out of the explanatory myth in rite as emotional reinforcement of the communal order.

Following or departing from Freud, later students of myths and religion tend to account primarily for the biological-emotional side of the religious function. Róheim's Freudian view sees religion and magic as symptomatic expression of or ego-defense mechanisms against unconscious, repressed infantile sexual wishes and conflicts, forced under by the socially enforced superego. Malinowski, less self-consciously Freudian, is nevertheless psychologically oriented in viewing religion and magic as the psychological safety valves for the fears and tensions of men in society, and as builders of confidence in the face of the unknown and the unpredictable in nature. La Barre, essentially Freudian in his view, sees religion as a kind of collective neurosis and infantile autism. Jung, while considering religious archetypes as expressions of a repressed collective unconscious, tends to see religious symbolism more positively as the symbolic key which unlocks the maturational process in individuals, and collectively, in social history. Basically compatible with this view is that of Van Gennep, whose view of religious rituals as rites of passage also suggests the central role of religion in the ongoing process of life within society, though his view is set within a fundamentally cyclical view of social life in its general outlines, while Jung's view suggests the possibility of continuous social and psychic evolution.

There are, in addition, those theorists, drawing their intellectual ancestry from Radcliffe-Brown and Durkheim, who see the sociological function, i.e., providing for society's cohesion and continuity, as central. Durkheim and his followers see society as the "hidden god" of religion, the gods being but personifications of the institutions of society, which are the real objects of worship. Swanson, less theoretical and more statistical than Durkheim in his approach, attempts to show the concordance between certain kinds of social institutions and specific varieties of religious belief, supporting the thesis that particular religious forms owe their origins to the social arrangements of the societies molding them: gods tend to be the personifications of sovereign groups which are relatively numerous, spirits of the dead of strong kinship arrangements, with private magic intervening in areas where juridical institutions are missing or inadequate. The Marxist theory of religion also sees it as the reflection and validator of production relations and class structures of a society, and therefore as the effective, if often unconscious, manipulative tool of the ruling class. Recent anthropologists like Firth and Leach also define religion in basically sociological terms, but their more fluid concept of society alters their view of religion's function. Refusing a static reification of society, they tend to view society as process within structure, a process consisting of the interplay of deviating and choosing individuals who manipulate myths and produce variants that tend to promote their individual interests. Thus religion becomes the agent not only of continuity but of change, whose normative power aids individuals in alterations of the social order, changes whose slow statistical drift results in a constantly changing larger social structure.

Lévi-Strauss, who somewhat eludes classification, views religion as the mediator of contradictory impulses and values in the social order, serving to validate that order by playing out its possible alternatives in symbolic forms. While taking account of the unconscious determinants of mythic structure, a structure he sees as complementary to social structure, he makes the myth-producing unconscious "logic of the mind" a kind of binary computer, and thereby detracts from his original insights by his application of an ingenious but often arbitrary and rigid kind of logic.

Some contemporary theorists like Spiro tend to a syncretic view of religion, which sees the normative and prescriptive function of the collective interaction with superhuman beings but does not neglect the other insights into religious function. Spiro combines the psychological, intellectualist, and sociological descriptions of religion by postulating, in somewhat slippery terminology, the satisfaction of cognitive, pragmatic, and expressive needs in what he calls the "adjustive, adaptive, and integrative" functions of religion.[4] The pairs of terms don't quite match, but the syncretic attempt is clear.

All of these thinkers illuminate the central importance of religion for man as a social being, whether by stressing the way in which religion reflects and validates social order, or the way in which it drains off or offers substitute satisfaction to the libidinal drives which are potentially destructive of that order. But none of them, with the exception of La Barre, Wallace, and Jung, satisfactorily begins to account for the role of religion in abrupt and gross social change. Yet it is precisely here that the relation between religious imagination and the continuum of psychological and social order becomes most explicit. It is precisely in the examination of the spontaneously erupting apocalyptic-millennial myth-dream, of its dreamers, its basic constituents, and of its relation

4. Melford E. Spiro, "Religion: A Definition," *Anthropological Approaches to the Study of Religion* (New York: F. A. Praeger, 1966), pp. 109–10.

to a particular social situation that it is possible to see how individual and collective, past and future, intellect and emotion, dynamically interrelate in the highly charged imagination, that transformer of consciousness on which so much depends. "One can ask," writes Wallace, the anthropologist who gives perhaps the most convincing account of religious functions,

> whether a large proportion of religious phenomena have not originated in personality transformation dreams or visions characteristic of the revitalization process. Myths, legends, and rituals may be relics, either of the manifest content of vision-dreams or of the doctrines and history of revival and import cults, the circumstances of whose origin have been distorted and forgotten, and whose connection with dream states is now ignored. . . . In fact it can be argued that all organized religions are relics of old revitalization movements, surviving in routinized form in stabilized cultures, and that religious phenomena per se originated (if it is permissible still in this day and age to talk about the "origins" of major elements of culture) in the revitalization process—i.e., in visions of a new life by individuals under extreme stress.[5]

Thus whether religion is seen as conservative or radical force depends upon the social moment. Since religion is intended to insure the satisfaction of instincts within social order, the overwhelming denial of those instincts by a given order, or its inability to arbitrate deep conflicts, puts that order in question, and the visionary imagination becomes subversive. The human organism seems able to tolerate great amounts of stress and to attempt to go on regulating itself in habitual patterns. But there is a limit, a degree of conflict and tension, when no more disorder can be borne, at which point the adaptive mechanism of the crisis imagination may intervene. Self-esteem (identity, integrity, or narcissism, as it is variously named) is a sense of place in an adequately rewarding order; when that order is no longer sufficiently rewarding, self-esteem breaks down, and it is this loss of center, the loss of "home valence," that imperils the organism. Then volcanic forces may be unleashed and a creative act take place in the imagination which overthrows by force an oppressive internalized order and creates a new order in which once again self and world are felt as a harmonious whole.

It will not be any surprise then that such visions offer an image of violent destruction and of a paradisiacal aftermath; this is, among other things, a projection of what has already transpired in the individual. Since imagination is a nexus of body and mind which works its

5. Anthony F. C. Wallace, "Revitalization Movements," *American Anthropologist* 58, no. 2 (April 1956): 267–68.

transformations through objectified feeling states, it is no wonder that what is expected to happen is empowered by the deep sense that it has, somehow, already happened. This begins to explain the mystical certainty that accompanies the vision, the sense of magical power that resides in those possessed by this deadly serious dream.

It is well to remember here, lest the emotional side of the dream overshadow the fact that its insights involve the whole being, that these visions, which often come in "a waking state as hallucinatory experience, or in an ecstatic trance rather than in normal sleep," have content often highly rational and intellectually argued, with attendant "cogent moral exhortation," which, along with the mythic images of divinity and vivid prophecies, are remembered in "unusually rich detail."[6]

In the contemporary play *Marat-Sade*, by Peter Weiss, the insane asylum becomes the setting for a replaying of the French Revolution, the madness of revolutionary hopes incarcerated by the conservative outer order which is represented by the asylum's director who watches the proceedings with a smug incomprehension. Sade, author of the play within the play and real director of this elegant irony, is the vehicle for Weiss's ambivalence about revolution, but also for his sense that the asylum is history and that the asylum's present director stands fair to be its principal dupe. It is clear that intelligence, passion, and vision are the possession of the mad inmates, and that the complacent bourgeoisie (both the eighteenth-century Frenchman and his family and the twentieth-century audience) who are watching are being treated to a play which coincides with their view of radical mentality, at the same time that is thoroughly subversive of that view. The character of the mad priest in the strait jacket (one is reminded of the number of New Guinea prophets who were committed to asylums) is the bearer of humanity's profoundest ethical ideals and of the real sanity that lies at the heart of the radical vision. For this vision, as it intrudes on a conservative order, is always seen as madness; yet, when circumstances have altered and the old solutions no longer serve, it is these figures adjudged mad by the conventional who move to society's center and unleash the irresistible forces of hope for a new future.

Thus to view the prophet as "psychotic," as some students of society wish to do, is to miss the fact of public affirmation which totally alters the definition of what is unreasonable. When society itself is sick, the member most sensitive to the powerful disintegration in the air often becomes the carrier of that tension and the agent through which its resolution may be effected. Such vision often follows what Wallace calls a state of "cultural distortion," and thus must be seen, not

6. *Ibid.*, p. 271.

as merely another symptom, but as a possible cure for the malaise which produced it. This is not simplistically to state that health is automatically assured, nor that some societies may not be more fortunate in their prophets than others, but only to suggest that it is in an act of individual imaginative vision from the depths of disorientation that a new orientation, a new synthesis, and a new man *may* emerge. Failing that, there may be the drowning of the Children's Crusade on its sad pilgrimage to the New Jerusalem, the death of the Kickapoo Indians who tried to wake their prophet Kanakuk from the dead on the third day and died from the pox he carried, or the massacre of the Sioux Indians at Wounded Knee who believed themselves invulnerable to white men's bullets. Cult vision, however, may evolve, with a tendency to correct its own excesses. The Ghost Dance, given the Indian's hopeless military situation, was too autistic in its belief in invulnerability in battle; it gave way to the more adaptive and quietistic Peyote Cult.

Another case in point, with an opposite progression—from accommodation to open defiance—was the development of the Cargo myths of New Guinea, which had in common a belief in a dramatic overturning of the present condition of society, when, through the return of the New Guinea culture hero, the New Guineans would magically receive "cargo" (i.e., Western goods) and their subjugation by white masters would be at an end. Some early versions of these myths considered the white man's ancestor to be their own lost culture hero who had departed and taken his magical ability to make "cargo" with him; following the Christian religion (believed to be the road to "cargo") or propitiating the white man would give them the white man's magic power to make "cargo" appear, or, alternately, induce him to forgive them for the wrong they had done to their departed ancestor, recognize the obligations of kin, and share "cargo" with them. These early Cargo myths were too accommodative in seeing the whites as more fortunate brothers descended from a common ancestor, the New Guinea culture hero, or, in another version showing Christian influence, from the common ancestor Adam; brothers whose kin obligation could therefore be appealed to, to make them share "cargo." Thus dependency on the Europeans was reinforced by the hopeless task of trying to conciliate a power so unequal that it did not have to take them into account. Later evolutions of Cargo myth redirected this demeaning guilt, this time seeing the whites as deceitful, illegitimate possessors of a cargo stolen from its rightful owners in New Guinea whose gods had made it, and thus devising nativistic rites which would destroy white power and return the gods and "cargo"; this led to anti-mission, anti-white actions and attitudes which the government had to notice and contend with.

The Collective Eye 13

In a situation as unreasonable as the seemingly hopeless domination and exploitation of one people by another, the "irrational" forces which are unleashed by the "crisis dreams" of the prophets seem· as natural and inevitable as they are volatile and ultimately unpredictable as to outcome. The imagination, at the extreme, does not measure the risks. It merely does what it must. In a situation where a great mass of people feel, at some deep and unintelligible level, that there is nothing to lose and a world to gain, then invocations to reason ·are themselves unreasonable. When "the rush hour of the gods" is at hand, reason alone is powerless to do anything but describe.

The anthropologist Marwick, who collected data on sorcery among the Cewa, wrote:

> Whenever someone died—and the death-rate was high—I found it relatively easy, if only as a means of detecting social tensions, to change from the Western thought, "What disease or accident caused his death?", to the more typically Cewa one, "What wrong has he committed; with whom has he quarrelled; who was jealous of him; in short, who has killed him?" So ingrained did this cultivated habit become that I sometimes had to remind myself that notorious "sorcerers" in the local community were not in fact responsible for others' misfortunes, but were unfortunate people whose social positions or eccentric personalities made them unpopular.[7]

This quotation goes by way of underlining the obvious and yet often underestimated power of collective apprehensions of reality, which by their persuasive effect even on a mind so differently oriented and so aware of the mechanisms at work may serve as a reminder of how naturally a collective vision, drawn from a collective store of highly cathected images, empowered by a common, underlying set of emotional needs, and strengthened by the resulting communal consent, may sweep everything and everyone before it.

Before turning to the content of the revelation of the crisis cult prophet, it may be useful to consider first the little brother of the prophet, the carrier and curer of society's more routine tensions—the shaman. Since the prophet is the shaman writ large, the nature of shamanistic practice and its relation to the social whole may offer a way of relating the more routine ritual with the ritual of crisis in a mutually illuminating way. Like the monks and saints of the Middle Ages, who were his disguised heirs, the shaman is a healer and a diviner, an extremely sensitive personality, strongly imaginative, susceptible to trances and self-induced twilight states, whose visionary and dissociative

7. M. G. Marwick, *Sorcery in Its Social Setting: A Study of the Northern Rhodesian Ceŵa* (Manchester, England: Manchester University Press, 1965), pp. 13–14.

powers enable him to divine and act out the unconscious conflicts of the afflicted, and to act as an intermediary in returning them to health. The shaman is often a master psychologist and student of interpersonal tensions, so that his divination of the source of a problem is an involved combination of intuitive vision and careful observation, not to mention a flair for the dramatic and symbolic, which may be as much a learned technique of social manipulation as a manifestation of an hysterical personality. The shaman may be called in to diagnose and treat an individual illness, or to relieve a great social anxiety before an impending event, such as a war or a period of famine, or to reduce the stresses of a present disaster, such as widespread disease.

All societies, however stable, face recurrent crises and tensions. The shaman is a kind of social safety valve who dramatizes the disequilibrium and employs techniques to reduce it, not the least of which is the dramatization itself. Like all imaginative acts, the shamanistic seance and ritual make the unknown visible and palpable, transforming anxiety into something manageable by giving it form—a name, a shape, and a way of acting as a consequence of this embodiment. Devereux has suggested that the shaman is a basically neurotic[8] personality who through the institution of shamanism is given a socially acceptable and useful channel for his own unconscious conflicts. Needless to say, he also needs talent. Like the poets of more individualistic societies, he often produces, in trance, original variations of the culture's myths, sings his own songs, and adds to the mythological store of the community his own stock of personalized creations, some of which may find their way into the general stock, and outlive him. He often sets great store, in a compulsive way, on his own idiosyncratic variations of myth and ritual, adding the shape of his own obsessions to the magical mask entrusted to him by the community.[9] The shaman, according to La Barre, "often of unstable or abnormal type, often transvestite, sometimes even psychotic in our society's terms though not necessarily in his own . . . may be seen as the individual most threatened by the uncertainties of life, and perhaps also the most unable to meet them on practical secular grounds or in ordinary male terms. But at the same time it was the shaman whose autistic defenses against those threats and anxieties obtained 'solutions' of which his society stood in dire need."[10]

---

8. The term "neurotic" here is highly questionable. The creative individual who, as Jungians suggest, feels conflict more tangibly is not necessarily neurotic. Devereux's use of this term is itself a socially conditioned judgment.

9. George Devereux, "Dream Learning and Individual Ritual Differences in Mohave Shamanism," *American Anthropologist* 59, no. 6 (December 1957): 1042.

10. Weston La Barre, *The Ghost Dance: Origins of Religion* (Garden City, N.Y.: Doubleday and Company, 1970), p. 138.

In preparation for his role the shaman often undergoes long periods of training or ordeals, of isolation, fasting, self-mutilation. In addition to these universal methods of inducing the mental concentration necessary to trance states or dissociation, he may use drugs, tobacco, rhythmic or hypnotic devices—any of the many techniques which suppress the conscious mind and raise the hallucinatory spectres of the unconscious dream world, or, for the animist, the world of spirits, of that other but parallel world of gods, spirits, ancestors, or souls, which has somehow come into conflict with the daylight world. The intuitive recognition of these societies that there is such a realm, which discloses itself in dreams and visions, which somehow holds the key to renewed harmony between self and world, is in fact similar to the recognition by modern Westerners of the so-called unconscious, expressed symbolically in dreams, whose forces can disorder behavior despite their denial by the waking man. One of the most striking examples of this prior and intuitive understanding of the psychoanalytic tenet of the compensatory nature of dreamwork is the Iroquois belief that every dream must be interpreted and its wishes performed in reality—or symbolically if the wish is too destructive.[11]

The typical shamanistic healing ceremony involves an act of regression to so-called primary processes and situations, embodied here in mythical landscapes and figures, to which the shaman imaginatively journeys, a journey sometimes pictured as an ascent to the realm of the gods on a mountain or in the sky, sometimes in a descent to a subterranean world of spirits or of the departed. Various spirits appear to him, some helpful, some threatening; a struggle often ensues with hostile spirits and he returns at last, bearing the now liberated soul of the afflicted, who then feels psychologically whole and physically relieved. The seance may include persistent questioning of the patient, demands for public confession—all aimed at obtaining release from the tension that accompanies hidden guilt. The belief that such rituals will affect the physical world—either the body of the diseased or the unfavorable conditions in the natural world—does, in fact, make psychosomatic cures possible, and, where the cause lies outside the psychic sphere, may still enable a society to attack its pragmatic difficulties with renewed determination and confidence. Devereux points to the high incidence of somatization reactions and conversion phenomena in these peoples; "the best proof of the tendency of primitives to develop somatization reactions is . . . the proven efficacy of shamanistic

11. Anthony F. C. Wallace, "Dreams and the Wishes of the Soul: A Type of Psychoanalytic Theory among the Seventeenth-Century Iroquois," in *Magic, Witchcraft and Curing*, ed. John Middleton (Garden City, N. Y.: Natural History Press, 1967), pp. 171–90.

treatments, whose impact upon the patient is a purely psychological one."[12] Lévi-Strauss's description of the shamanistic cure of an unsuccessfully laboring woman by transforming her uterine environment into a mythic world, presenting her pain to her in tangible forms available to her imagination, is a striking illustration of this phenomenon in reverse, when symbolic parallels of somatic symptoms help the patient to mobilize her body's forces, resulting in her "cure" and the delivery of the child.[13]

The typical shamanistic journey from despair through disorder to health or renewed order has obvious parallels to the mythic journeys of the culture hero (see Frazer's *Golden Bough*; Campbell's *Hero with a Thousand Faces*; Jung's archetypes), that pattern repeated in so many cultures of the hero's journey, his ordeal, his struggle with powerful, non-human forces, his symbolic death and rebirth, his return with the golden fleece, the sacred branch, the holy grail—talisman of his journey and symbol of his redeemed and hard-won manhood. This central myth of maturation is also mirrored in the puberty rites of many societies, and, in its most amplified and cosmic manifestation, in the rites of spring celebrating the apotheosis of the dying and reviving god. All these are rites of renewal through process, the descent through dismemberment and chaos and the return to a newly created cosmos, that replay the time of origin when the creation took shape out of original chaos. As Eliade suggests in *The Sacred and the Profane* and *The Myth of the Eternal Return*, this action, which purifies and reorders the world of profane time, takes place in a timeless and eternal space which is related to this world as the symbol to the emotion, the sign to the thing, the paradigm to the imperfect patterns of human order. The division of these terms is, however, misleading; the viability of vision is precisely in the inseparability of the terms which analysis divides: the symbol is the emotion, the word is made flesh, the timeless world of the imagination invades and becomes the present. The shaman, who plays out a drama similar to this myth in a more modest form, shares, in trance, this timeless sphere of the imagination and in similar if more restricted fashion than the seasonal rites that renew the cosmos and society, moves through it to renew the creation of the particular, the symbolic expression of which is the reunion of the suffering man with his wandering or stolen soul.

These shamanistic practices are an active and integral part of religious function in these societies. Essentially the difference between

12. Devereux, *Reality and Dream*, p. 109.
13. Claude Lévi-Strauss, *Structural Anthropology*, trans. Claire Jacobson and Brooke G. Schoepf (Garden City, N.Y.: Doubleday and Company, 1967), pp. 181–92.

priest and shaman is not the difference between religion and magic (a distinction so variously drawn, so hotly argued, and so riddled with particular religious and philosophic bias as to be rendered practically useless); it is, more properly, the difference between institution and inspiration. The priest performs inherited rites and keeps the vision of past prophets; the shaman is himself susceptible to visions, produces his own, and carries the live tradition of the supercharged imagination. His visions, while marked with his own idiosyncrasies and touched by the vagaries of the present moment in which he lives, are, nonetheless, peopled with the mythic stock figures of his tribal religion and play variations on an inherited theme. Thus it is the priest who preserves the old forms while the shaman continually elaborates them. The shaman, it would seem, is a figure who helps provide process within tradition, and who, by reacting at an often unconscious level to the inherent malaise in his, as in all, societies, mutates in minor ways the inherited stock of magico-mythical (i.e., imaginative) responses to human ills.

The shaman, then, can be seen as a genuinely religious (i.e., restorative) figure, one who, as magician, is the bearer of divine powers attested to by religious beliefs, the live and personal carrier of the religious tradition at work in the psychic life of the individual and the community. And when the tensions generated by the traditional order outrun its ability to cope with them, or when some disaster or change in outward circumstances calls into question the efficacy of traditional solutions, the shamanistic figure, no longer able to work his magic within the traditional framework, may be magnified into the figure of the prophet. As the shaman is called upon to heal the sick man and make him whole again, so the prophet is called to heal the sick society and remake it in a new image. Thus, because it is the larger order itself which is to be envisioned in new form, the term "shamanistic" will be replaced here by the word "prophetic" as we see a quest akin to that of the culture hero in the beginning—a quest for the soul of the society that has gone astray, a struggle with and identification of those forces which carried it off, an ordeal that results in the dying of the old and initiation of the new, which projects an image of the society made new, cleansed and once again whole—its soul returned. Thus the visionary experience of the prophet can be seen as a set of symbols—made flesh in dream—that answers to the extreme psychic situation of the people in the same way that the shaman's answered to the less radical tensions of the everyday.

It is thus that new social configurations are born, through the birth of a new religious vision, which is the act of the human imagination working with the dissonant symbols of its own disorientation until it produces a new synthesis of symbols, a new explanation which suggests a new set of actions, an altered set of reciprocal relations, and a new set of social obligations. The vision is, in a sense, the precipitate of the *prima materia* of society in imaginative solution, a process similar to that symbolically represented in the alchemical attempt to produce the Philosopher's Stone—a new wholeness, purified and perfected, out of the separation of the elements, their return to original chaos, and their reconstitution in the golden stone—matter and spirit made one. If, as Eliade suggests,[14] the alchemical formula is the material analogue to the psychic quest for rebirth, whose counterpart is the dismemberment, death, and resurrection of the god, the same pattern emerges in all these imaginative projections, their various forms but reflections of the peculiar historical situations and inherited cultural and psychic symbols which gives each its distinctive form.

The general pattern of crisis cult vision has elements, repeatedly found, which, though varying in their emphasis of certain elements, tend to an impressive similarity. It has been argued that the Judeo-Christian influence is responsible for these congruencies; however, it is clear that the selection of apocalyptic elements from that tradition is symptomatic of a repetition of the cultural situation which produced them in the first place, and furthermore there is evidence of spontaneous cult formation in peoples who have had little or no contact with Christianity. Burridge, for instance, cites "one example of millennarian type activities that took place among a New Guinea people when they sighted an aircraft—this before they had seen or heard of Christians, Europeans, or any other sophisticated people."[15] Furthermore, elements of millennial thought are clear reworkings of indigenous mythic material widely found—the expected return of a culture hero some day, and myths of the origin of the creation when a great cataclysm turned the world upside down and the present order emerged. These origin myths, as will be seen, are replayed in the millennial myth, when once again the creation must be made anew.

When a number of crisis cult visions are compared, the following common traits emerge: (1) the imminent expectation of a great cataclysm or apocalypse which will destroy the world as it is; (2) an accompanying return of the dead, the ancestors, and/or the man-god or culture hero; (3) an inversion of the present state of affairs, involving often both nature and culture, with particular focus on the power arrangements of the society; (4) a belief in the invulnerability of the "elect" cultists through the period of destruction, their redemptive

14. In Mircea Eliade, *The Forge and the Crucible: The Origins and Structure of Alchemy*, trans. Stephen Corrin (New York: Harper and Row, 1971).
15. Kenelm Burridge, *New Heaven, New Earth* (New York: Schocken Books, 1969), p. 35.

power, and their inheritance of a new world; (5) a redemptive millennial vision of the new world, which often promises eternal youth, perfect amity, and material plenty, as well as release from inhibitions and obligations; (6) techniques for the expediting of the apocalypse-millennium which usually involve both a return to certain nativistic customs and rites and an assimilation and transvaluation of alien cultural elements.

This last point indicates that both those students of crisis cult, like Lawrence, who see the cults as preservative of old patterns of thought and social interaction in a changed situation, and those, like Burridge, who see them as fundamentally productive of a "new man," are right; the new is transvalued in terms of the old, so that whether one sees the cult as a reversion or a progression depends partly on one's own cultural assumptions and partly on how much change one expects from humans at any one historical moment. Lawrence's sense that the cults are "too" conservative seems to result from unrealistic expectations which fail to recognize the limitations in even the most radical mental realignments.

The inversion element of cult reveals not only a desire for power that is presently denied but also seems to be a spontaneous neurophysiological reaction to trauma, more radical but not unlike the socially prescribed role among Plains Indians of the "Crazy-Dog-Wishes-to-Die: a warrior who, for a season, pledges himself to seek death in battle, and, in the meantime, behaves in a socially standardized negativistic manner, saying the opposite of what he means, and doing the opposite of what he is told to do."[16] This is, as Devereux points out, the reaction to severe trauma—in the case he cites, of a warrior whose sudden laming precluded his accomplishment of the last feat that would make him a chief. One is reminded here of Sargant's experimental dogs, who, following a brush with drowning when water flooded the laboratory, showed a complete inversion of previously learned behavior, including vicious attacks on those who had heretofore been their trusted masters.

Thus the new is the precipitate of the old in two ways: by reaction against it in the inversion syndrome, and by reworking of discordant alien elements in accommodation to it, in the syncretic elements of vision. Since ambivalence marks the emotional climate of cult, it is to be expected that both will transpire simultaneously; in the acculturation situation the cultist both wishes to be like the European and at the same time to be rid of him. In the Mambu movement in New Guinea, native garments were buried as the past was put to earth, while the "claim to European goods and European power [was] dramatically

16. Devereux, *Reality and Dream*, p. 108.

symbolized" by the wearing of European clothes. Yet Mambu's doctrine, while syncretic, "compounded of both pagan and Christian elements, . . . [was] anti-white, anti-mission and anti-Government in its general content."[17] Thus, the inversion transfers the European's mastery to himself; the accommodation permits him to partake of certain European ways, while remaining himself—a feat which before the cult was impossible.

The new, then, is essentially a reorganization of what already exists, the old elements remaining while their relation to one another shifts. That the most truly original visionaries are often the most collectively relevant is an observation which only tends to suggest that originality is in fact the power to reformulate and creatively restructure the symbols already given. The creative act is invention, not *ex nihilo*, but from what already exists; genius is inspired recombination, and thus offers the route by which less energetic minds can be restructured and reoriented, brought to a place familiar because it retains many of the old forms, but familiar, too, because it has changed in a way precisely analogous to the needs of the psyche in a changed situation. Only when a new orientation that feels right, familiar somehow, is imaginatively realized can men begin to take control of a situation in whose grip they already struggle.

Before analyzing further the ingredients of the visionary and ritual response to crisis, it would be well to examine in its broad outlines the psychological situation which precipitates it. There are certain significant elements which may, in individuals and societies, precipitate a kind of crisis of order, one which passes beyond dilemma into radical disorientation. All change is disquieting, and its unquiet is as much a part of the continuum of life as the inertia which opposes it. It is not change per se, then, which is the essential quality of the radical internal crisis; it is a special form of dislocation (quite literally dis-location, a disappearance of center) which has, in both the personal and the social situation, which are often inextricable, a common quality: that of severe damage or overwhelming threat to self-esteem.

One can, in review of culture and personality, admit a million forms of "adjustment" and recognize the supreme adaptability and inventiveness of the human mind when confronted with the myriad variabilities of circumstance. There are, however, breakdowns that seem to occur—like the suicidal flight of lemmings or the lethal paroxysms of rabbits, both responses to overpopulation—when the organism at some deep, instinctual level of its being seems to perceive itself as super-

17. Peter Worsley, *The Trumpet Shall Sound: A Study of 'Cargo' Cults in Melanesia* (London: Macgibbon and Kee, 1957), pp. 105–6.

fluous. Now, of all forms of awareness, this one appears the most difficult to sustain, as it is in deepest disagreement with the sense each being has of its own centrality, of its own supreme importance to which all else is subsidiary, a sense of itself on which self-preservation depends. The dislocation of this sense sets at odds the complementary drives, ideally united, of preservation of self and of species; the two drives are set in conflict, and breakdown is the result. This disorientation is at root a refusal to make sense of an order perceived as cancelling identity out, a cause which is revealed when breakdown leads to a re-imagining of order which restores self-esteem. And, however far from reality this new perception of the world seems, it nevertheless seizes the mind with a reality more persuasive than the actual one it imaginatively overturns, for the actual one, it must be remembered, is divided, contradictory—as in the colonial order where the colonialist's description of his actions is at variance with the way the colonized person experiences them.

Before a man picks up a gun and turns it on his master, several steps must intervene. He must first have imagined himself in such an act, an act previously unimaginable, since it is an action which reverses the order of things, which many may consider mad—as he himself must at one time have so considered it. Now before the ego can be empowered to act against its previous notions of what is right in the order of things, it must somehow enlist the approval of the inhibiting superego, or social conscience, and this can only be done by somehow seeing the new actions as approved by the old powers—the parental archetypes, the ancestors, the culture hero, the god or gods of the tribe. This, in part, explains why all forward movements, or radical turns to a different future, involve an imaginative return to the past—a return, as it were, for permission, which is accompanied by a regression to more childlike, primal patterns of behavior, which enable the personality to be reformed much in the same way as it was formed in the beginning. It will not seem surprising, then, that the New Guineans, when imagining a new life more like that of the Europeans, will invoke their ancestors as its cause; or that the Renaissance men, in rejecting the Medieval world and creating the modern one, turned back to the world of classical antiquity; or that the utopian socialists who opened the way to a contemporary vision turned back to the Middle Ages or to the primitive world for their model. It is well to remember that this "nativism" is not a return to a world as it was but as it is imagined to have been, a mystification which quite perfectly fits the needs of a new order trying to be born. When the Renaissance men looked back at the Greek world, they found Apollo; when Nietzsche looked back, he found Dionysius. As the imagination turns back to seek authority for its future, and to empower itself against the terrors of the reversal of things such a new order implies, regressive behavior is aroused—often an excess of obedience, a childish regimentation of behavior to satisfy the powers who promise a great reward, an outpouring of penitence and contrition to propitiate these powers for the guilt of not having obeyed them sooner, and/or an enormous outflow of libidinal energies, the release of energy which accompanies the destruction of old bonds and the recombination of elements in a new compound, and even the feeling that, in a world being made new by the powers of righteousness, the elect have been given a kind of ethical blank check.

The revelation granted the prophet often instructs the visionary that he no longer need obey the old injunctions, that the taxes ought not be paid the Europeans, that the gardens are to be neglected, or large quantities of food eaten in preparation for the great day at hand. There are precedents for this in the traditional order: days when taboos are lifted and the order of things reversed. These days often coincide with the return of the dead; sacred time bursts into the profane, and the original chaos is recreated that order may be reconstituted out of it. The period is limited; emotional steam is discharged and the forbidden given expression, then order is reinstated and the cosmos repeats its cycle. In crisis cult this period is greatly extended and intensified, and with it comes the feeling, not merely of repetition but of real change. The dead are to return for good, the order of things to be permanently reversed, the old taboos to be relieved of their power forever. It is this peculiar "madness" which characterizes crisis cult, a madness born of the deep intuitive sense that the world itself has gone mad and must be set straight.

"In unbearable crisis situations, religious prophets are culture innovators who are able to contrive new social forms and new symbolism to keep all men in the society from going individually insane; but what a monstrous pathology then is the new 'normality.'"[18] Yet the seeming unreasonableness of the cult and its hopes are in exact proportion to the impossibility of the present situation, and the overthrow of normal limits is testimony to the fact that obedience to them brought few rewards. The equation is not so much mad as psychologically exact.

Often, but not always, in cult vision it is the high god who speaks, the "great spirit," the original creator of the world, who in normal times is relatively remote and withdrawn; it is the lesser polytheistic pantheon and the ancestor spirits who are invoked on a daily basis. The high god is often conceived of as intervening only for the poor and helpless,

18. *Ibid.*, p. 46.

those whom the other gods do not help, those gods who are, as Swanson has suggested, personifications of the sovereign groups and institutions that regulate social interaction. Thus the persons left unprovided for by the social order are left to the mercy and protection of the high god who provides the antidote to their powerlessness. In much the same way, when a whole society feels "poor and helpless" and unprovided for by the present social order, the high god or the absent culture hero intervenes; again, the intervention equals the need, and further, the intervening deity stands in a relation to society which somehow transcends the given social order and represents the original creative principle on which the people now call. In a similar fashion the culture hero is appropriate to the moment, since it was he who organized the culture in the first place; so it is he who is called upon to make it anew. At any rate, as this personification of creative force appears, analogous to the large task before the imagination, he sweeps the old limits before him, and as a new unity takes shape, much is permitted which had heretofore been forsworn.

One of the most extreme cases of the strict conscience turned permissive in the apocalyptic moment was among the seventeenth-century ghetto Jews of Europe, followers of the professed messiah Sabbatai Zevi, who believed with him that the apocalypse was at hand and that their political and spiritual liberation would follow in a millennial age which he had come to announce. When Zevi became an apostate to Judaism, converting to the Moslem religion, many of his more fanatic followers, unable to revoke their belief in his saving power and their own internal change, interpreted his apostasy as a religious act, the opposite of what it appeared, a martyrdom designed to raise the level of evil in the world and so to hasten the world's end and the ascendance of the new order. The belief in the holiness of apostasy was further reinforced by the numbers of "Marranos" or "secret Jews" who had fled Spain, Jews who had reason to embrace a doctrine which turned their own earlier conversion to Catholicism from a mark of shame to one of pride. Following what they believed to be Zevi's holy example, many Jews converted or openly flaunted the strict teachings of the Torah, indulging in orgiastic and immoral behavior, all in the belief that they were divinely ordained to act as carriers of the millennium by practicing their "holy sins." The cult took a further step toward nihilism under the monomaniacal leadership of Jacob Frank, who put himself above even Zevi, declaring: "I have to redeem . . . [the world] from all the laws and customs that have ever existed. It is my task to annihilate all this so that the Good God can reveal Himself."[19]

19. Gershom Scholem, "The Holiness of Sin," *Commentary* 51, no. 1 (January 1971): 65.

As this fanatic cult faded out of existence, its demolition work fed into the saner Reform Judaism movement, which did much to adapt the rigidity of an ancient code to an increasingly modern world.

For a moment it would be well to consider further the connection between physical and psychic threat, and to observe how inextricably they run together in human existence. An Indian of the American Northwest, when he falls ill, feels his self-esteem threatened, for he imagines that illness results from sin, from breaking a taboo, from failing in some tribal obligation, or from offending another man who now turns sorcerer. Thus physical threat and psychic guilt are felt together and may indeed even be causally connected, as was shown before, in the somatization of psychic conflict. However that may be, the inability to find food or to function well physically is presented in a man's mind as a failure attaching to himself. Where socially prescribed rites have repeatedly failed to restore self-esteem, a more serious disorientation sets in. Sometimes, as when the customary social defense mechanisms are under attack by the foreign missionaries or new rulers, the defense itself may be seen as contributing to the evil, and when this last buffer against loss of self-esteem is itself seen as either impotent or dangerous, the sickness is at the center.

It is at this extreme that the vision comes—to an exceptional individual whose personal plight mirrors that of the society, in that he is usually himself ill, often beset by sorrows, recent deaths, deprivation, and feelings of hopelessness. Often he is himself at the point of death when the vision visits him, and his success in evangelizing his method gets its most powerful reinforcement from his own miraculous recovery. The Amerindian prophets Handsome Lake, Smohalla, and Wovoka are cases in point. "At this time, then, we would tentatively conclude that the religious vision experience per se is not psychopathological but rather the reverse, being a synthesizing and often therapeutic process performed under extreme stress by individuals already sick." [20] According to Wallace, the prophet "generally . . . shows evidence of a radical change in personality soon after the vision experience: a remission of old and chronic physical complaints, a more active and purposeful way of life, greater confidence in interpersonal relations, the dropping of deep-seated habits like alcoholism. Hence, we may call these visions 'personality transformation dreams.' "[21]

Thus is seen how the individual imagination becomes the crucible for the vision which responds to and attempts to resolve what is also the collective crisis. Just as collective symbols aid the individual in his own mental and physical health, so the individual's manipulation of

20. Wallace, "Revitalization Movements," p. 273.
21. *Ibid.*, p. 271.

them may aid the collective in its time of need, which is, by definition, also his own.[22] There is no need to posit some suprapersonal collective psyche or unconscious to explain how shared archetypes and common experience can permit the vision of one man to stir a whole people in its depths. According to La Barre, the prophet's "*charisma* is only the shared unconscious wishes and symbiotic thought-paradigms in leader and communicants . . . Thus the prophet draws to himself the power which these felt, but heretofore unexpressed, forces have in the individuals of his group; he becomes, as it were, the embodiment of their dreams, and thereby draws to himself and seems to exude their own libidinal energies."[23] This agrees in basic emphasis with Jung's characterization of the "mana-personality," whose magical numinosity is the result of his identification with a projected archetype, which causes his followers to transfer to him the potency of their own unconscious forces. Jung is particularly concerned with the personal danger involved in this too literal transfer, which confuses an individual with an inner, and also collective, force, and thereby robs the individual of the autonomy with which the proper identification of this force would endow him. However, it must be acknowledged that such an error seems endemic to the cult phenomenon, and though it may subvert individuality, it does promote solidarity, although at the price of the prophet's indispensability. The greatest of prophets may be able to keep themselves separate from the collective archetype which speaks through their imagination, but seldom are the followers as perspicacious. And undoubtedly the adoration of his followers may end by leading the prophet into their delusion. Thus the prophet, by a kind of historical necessity, often unwittingly ends by becoming the prisoner of the archetype which empowered him. That this may lead him into increasingly narcissistic betrayals of his own vision, and manipulation of it for his own egotistic ends, is one of the unavoidable dangers of the psychic power of his vision and its resonance in the collectivity.

The question of "social compulsion'" *vs.* "individual initiative" is, for Wallis, an "unreal difficulty. . . . Individual initiative may properly describe an act which is, at the same time, the forwarding of a group purpose. The same act may be designed to serve both the individual and his group: both aims may be co-ordinated in the individual . . . in the person of the prophet does the individual become the point at which the past and the future converge. He gives a creative impulse to a

22. The understanding of this principle enabled Devereux, in his psychotherapy of a Plains Indian, to effect a cure by channeling the patient's transference to him through the traditional figure of the guardian spirit who appears to young Indians in their vision quest.
23. La Barre, *Ghost Dance*, p. 48.

prospective 'moment' of history, and into him, in turn, flows the tradition which is history's moment of retrospection."[24]

This new synthetic vision often requires in its carrier a special experience, one which makes him especially fertile ground for a recombination of old and new elements. He is often the man who has gone away, who is of his culture but who has also served an apprenticeship in an alien world. His experience of that other world, while first hand, is often somewhat superficial and rife with the misunderstandings born of his own cultural conditioning and the very partial inclusion which the alien masters permit him in their world. Still, he is more deeply touched by the alien, and his response to conflicting world views is thereby heightened.

The originator of the Hallelujah cult among the Carib-speaking peoples of South America, the prophet Bichiwung, traveled to England with a minister who was instructing him in the Christian faith. Left alone by his master in a strange house, and slighted by being treated as a servant, his suspicions aroused by an overheard conversation in which the minister said that Bichiwung was not yet ready to be baptized, this uprooted man, isolated in an alien world, had a vision which reinstated his tribal identity and reinterpreted Christian teachings in terms of his own Indian beliefs. "To Bichiwung's way of thinking it was a very real trail which would lead him—his spirit—in a dream or in a prayer to heaven, just in the same way as a path led him from one village to another. In other words, he took his teacher's words more concretely than they had been intended and understood the path to be a reality, having a specific direction, and not a symbolic path of moral conduct sustained by Christian faith. . . . Bichiwung's 'way to God' was the shaman's way."[25] His vision paralleled the traditional shamanistic seance in which the shaman travels to *imawali's* round house in the mountains to bring back the imprisoned spirit of the sick man. In his vision he brings back the heart spirit of his people, a collective cure for a sick society, and with it "an Indian Bible from God," with a revelation for Amerindian benefit only, "or at least, benefits [which] are to be dispensed by Amerindians to the rest of mankind."[26] Explicit in the message of Indian salvation which he brought back was the admonition not to trust the whites or listen to the deceitful missionaries, or all the world would become servants of the whites. As it was, whites would be servants of

24. W. D. Wallis, quoted in Vittorio Lanternari, *The Religions of the Oppressed: A Study of Modern Messianic Cults,* trans. Lisa Sergio (New York: New American Library, 1965), p. 242.

25. Audrey J. Butt, "The Birth of a Religion," in *Gods and Rituals,* ed. John Middleton (Garden City, N. Y.: Natural History Press, 1967), p. 389.

26. *Ibid.,* p. 434.

the Indians, and his people would have all the white man's goods they wanted. Thus the new "path" is accommodated to the old, with the supremacy of the Indian and his integrity assured, along with a promise of plenty to come.

Another case in point is the New Guinea prophet Yali, who was to institute the "pagan revival," a return to and restored respect for certain traditional customs and rites; to write "Yali's laws," which made selective accommodations to European life styles in the context of the new-found respect for New Guinea tradition; and to become the near-divine focus of a powerful nativistic cargo cult. Yali too spent much of his early life working for Europeans and visited Australia as a recruit in the Allied forces. He never lost the basic epistemological bias of his people, the belief in the efficacy of ritual to produce material rewards, but he assimilated to these beliefs many of his new experiences with white men. These experiences he reinterpreted in the light of his own assumptions: Australian zoos with their seeming idolatry of animals and taboo against hunting or eating them—characteristic of the respect given totem animals, and the theory of evolution improperly understood as a white belief in a totem ancestor, the monkey, gave double evidence of the whites' belief in animal totemic ancestry. This exposed for him the deceitfulness of the missionaries who had hidden this fact, and it also relieved him of the Christian-taught belief that whites were kin descended from a common ancestor, Adam, releasing him from any sense of kin obligation between whites and his people. An ethnological museum he interpreted as proof that the whites had stolen the New Guinea gods, and with them the "cargo" that rightfully belonged to the islanders. Thus he negated the need to be concerned with white missions or authorities. This seemingly farfetched logic, understandable, however, in terms of Yali's assumptions and his deep desire to restore his people's damaged pride, led to a cult that cut across tribal lines, and whose identification of the New Guineans as a people vis-à-vis the whites resulted in the transcendence of the old tribal system and the growth of a new sense of pan-tribal identity and a nascent political organization which began to create the vehicle to contain this wider sense of unity and extended sovereignty. This pattern was followed in many places in the world, where cult activity, as it spread across tribal boundaries, provided the first stirrings of a wider allegiance and a dawning nationalism.

Yali's religious evolution from trust in and a desire to accommodate the Europeans to a fierce rejection of white supremacy and a partial return to pagan ways is a microcosm of the evolution of cargo myths in New Guinea; it is, further, a mirror of that almost perfect misunderstanding that may mark two people's relations: the missionaries who thought they were saving souls, the Kanakas who thought they were being initiated into the secrets of obtaining "cargo." Each people continued to work within its own context until mounting frustration resulted in the New Guineans returning to their own beliefs, but transformed by their misunderstood contact with an alien culture.

This type of misunderstanding, promulgated by cultural contact where both parties are closed off from genuine knowledge of each other's assumptions, has often led, paradoxically, to the feeding by Christian missionaries of the very magical practices which they intended to expunge. The missionaries did not teach colonized peoples the scientific basis of Western medicine nor the technological origin of Western goods, and these peoples had no way of knowing that the spiritual concerns of the West had split off from their material existence, and that an alternate description of reality from the Christian one was responsible for the superior powers that the whites had in the material realm. The natives of New Guinea never saw a factory nor men working at the production of goods; what they did see was the occasional and sudden appearance of steamships at their docks bringing "cargo," a seemingly magical appearance which was the germ of their own cargo myths: one day, when the proper rites had been performed, the ship would come for *them*. Thus their attendance at missionary schools had been an attempt to discover "road belong cargo," the magical route by which cargo might be obtained from the gods or ancestors who produced it. Furthermore, besides the inadvertent reinforcement of a mistaken notion, as in the case of "cargo," these early misunderstandings promulgated unknowingly by missionary teachings were often to make the colonized peoples ambivalent—not about magic—but about themselves and their own magic, thereby reducing its ability to relieve their tensions, while leaving unchanged their misapprehensions about the real source of Western goods and the real nature of Western society. As a matter of fact, their increased anxiety often caused them to redouble their protective magic and to suspect malign magic everywhere, to engender, in fact, the "sorcery epidemics" which will be discussed later, or to assimilate Christian myth and ritual into their own magical context in an attempt thereby to co-opt white dominance and the superior cultural goods on which it rested. Out of such misunderstandings the prophets drew their new understanding and attempted to master a disordered world.

It is the extraordinary individual, then, who innovates; as his vision is spread abroad it tends to both subtraction and accretion—subtraction of what is most eccentric, and accretion of what is more acceptable and traditional. Like the sea at work on a sunken hull, the foreign projections are worn away, the oulines blurred, the elements of

The Collective Eye 29

sea life blended with it, until it comes at last to resemble both what it once was and what it is becoming. Further, social myth and individual creation feed each other, since every individual is formed of the patterns and images native to his tribe or nation, and every society is but the slow statistical drift and homogenation of the individual choices and imaginings which comprise it. Even cult vision, which ushers in abrupt change, is subject to this evolution once it is abroad in the land. Needless to say, the fact of literacy is the all important determinant of whether acts of individual creation tend to be preserved in their uniqueness as acts of art or of revealed dogma, or tend to merge into the common store as social myths or folk lore. Even here, preservation of the original, individual act is only relative; once the popular imagination has seized on a work of art, even a written one, it often simplifies and selects to the point where the popular conception of that creation is extremely far from the original work, and has, as it were, a life of its own which is collective. With the *Iliad,* for example, numberless people know Achilles as the personification of the war hero, but how many remember him as the vehicle of perhaps the most eloquent speech in the ancient world on the absurdity of war? The Book of Job, in like manner, has filtered into the collective mind as a parable of the reward of patience, the virtues of the long-suffering and their ultimate victory. The real Book of Job, which is a tough-minded and terrifying dark night of the soul, with its tyrannical and monstrous God, with Job as his questioning, passionate, and morally indignant antagonist who is finally ground down in an unequal struggle with omnipotence, has been almost completely suppressed—because it is so difficult, so filled with a radical despair, and basically so incompatible with the pious hopes of the orthodox (who, by the way, are the human villains of the piece). The ending, in which Job gets his reward, tacked on by later priestly editors, was a master stroke of faith saving, but that it has managed to overbalance the dark poetic vision of the book itself with which it fits so ill is only an indication of how myth tends inevitably to drift in the direction of simplicity, certainty, and desire.

To return from the evolution of myth to its origins, understanding of the myth-dream of the crisis cult requires a closer look at the kind of historical setting which, with innumerable variations, has time and again provoked the psychological situation described earlier which evokes the cult vision. The stress situation must be internal to the society, but its causes are often, though not always, a result of influence external to the society in crisis.

The modern versions of crisis cult appear most commonly in situations of oppressive acculturation, usually the colonization or domination of a non-Western society by a more sophisticated Western one. There are many ancient analogues to this situation which produced similar apocalyptic or mystery cults, most notably the Jewish messianic cult under the oppressive rule of the Romans, which Paul and others transformed into early Christianity, and whose propagation was in direct proportion to the subsequent decay of Roman order. Christianity, besides Jewish eschatology, also assimilated Greek, Persian, and other Eastern mystery cults, whose original appearance dates back to periods of defeat and loss of nerve in the history of those societies.

Crisis cult has also made its appearance throughout history among those who are oppressed within a society: among starving, famine-ridden peasants of the Middle Ages and among the flotsam of city life when the waning of the Middle Ages broke down the protections of serfdom and forced many to leave the farms and end, jobless and hopeless, without social institutions to provide for them, in the newly burgeoning cities. Always the cults were precipitated by extreme situations of deprivation, deprivations widespread and seemingly without social cure.[27] In the Japan of the twentieth century there has been a widespread appearance of minor prophets and "New Religions," syncretist and millennial, most popular among those of lowest status and least resources in society, paralleling the breakdown of the divine assurance of Imperial rule, the encroachment of modern technology and alien mores, and the experience of world war and atomic holocaust.[28]

Always there is the sense of being outcast, oppressed, and denied, the experience of obligations without the usual reward, of status which is undermined, of solutions which no longer explain, and the loss of a fundamental sense of self-worth which almost automatically accompanies a role in an order that provides inadequately for the individual's needs. When the American Indians suffered defeat in war, loss of their lands, and destruction of their hunting animals, the Ghost Dance cult appeared. When New Guinea headmen were passed over for European selected officials, when their lands were seized and their men conscripted for day labor, when their customs were reviled or proscribed by the agents of Western authority, when the inferiority of their own goods made the reciprocal trade relations on which their notion of status rested impossible with Europeans, cargo cults began to erupt among the Kanakas. As Frantz Fanon has said, the "colonial world is a Manichaean world"; the challenge to it is not, therefore, "a rational confrontation of points of view."[29] Because the settler has been all and

27. See Norman Cohn, *The Pursuit of the Millennium* (New York: Harper and Row, 1961).
28. See H. Neill McFarland, *The Rush Hour of the Gods: A Study of the New Religious Movements in Japan* (New York: Harper and Row, 1967).
29. Frantz Fanon, *The Wretched of the Earth*, trans. Constance Farrington (Harmondsworth, England: Penguin Books, 1973), p. 31.

the native nothing, all these movements share the same "untidy affirmation of an original idea propounded as an absolute"[30] which can be described most precisely, says Fanon, "in the well-known words: 'The last shall be first and the first last.'"[31]

In all of these movements, a nascent form of social protest can be discerned; and in most of them, imaginative visions and fantastic rituals tended, in the long run, to produce new political and economic practices. The New Guinea collective farms and the Vietnamese Viet Minh nationalist uprising are two examples of cult activities which evolved into reality oriented movements.

To return to an earlier observation, then, the imagination seems to work here as a catalyst, precipitating, in the long run, not merely escapism and fantasy but a new way of conceiving self and society which contains the sense of certainty that the present order is impermanent and must change in accommodation with this new view, a subjective realignment of powers. Fanon identifies the psychological colonization of a people as the first ground on which a revolution is fought: "Initially subjective, the breaches made in colonialism are the result of a victory of the colonized over their old fear and over the atmosphere of despair distilled day after day by a colonialism that has incrusted itself with the *prospect of* enduring forever."[32] When Elijah Muhammad remade biblical myth, predicting the downfall of the white devils and the reversal of the world order resulting in the dominance of blacks—as it was in the beginning before the evil Big Head Scientist bleached out his race of devils, he was devising a fiction which fit the feelings of his race; the outcome of his myth, however, was real and political in consequence, for the first step in destroying the political dominance of the whites was to destroy the mythological hold it had on the minds of his people. The conversion of Malcolm X in prison and his accompanying transformation of personality from hustler to culture hero eventually led him from prophet to political activist, permitting him radically to alter the consciousness of a people and to create a new community of trust which worked against self-destructive behavior and made concerted action possible. In Allah, Malcolm X had found a god with which to combat the Western one; this god, African in origin like himself, was the empowerer of ethnic pride and protector of the hopes of a heretofore unprotected people.

Once again myth is the necessary first step in the realignment of social order, so that what at first appears fantastic ends by altering the society, not as the myth foretold, but as only the myth, with its

30. *Ibid.*
31. *Ibid.*, p. 28.
32. Frantz Fanon, *Dying Colonialism*, trans. Haakon Chevalier (Harmondsworth, England: Penguin Books, 1970), p. 38.

enormous inflation of the collective identity, could have made possible. It works its effects by offsetting, in imagination, a realistic situation so overwhelming as to seem inalterable without the reassuring and enormous numinous companion projected by the imagination.

Furthermore, the rituals prescribed by myth provide a path of action, a symbolic action undoubtedly, but one that allows the paralysis of intolerable conflict to give way to active movement, actions which thus become ends in themselves in their ability to make a people feel that they are "doing something" about their plight, a feeling that may lead to real assertive action in regard to the real situation. In this connection might be mentioned the ability of Black Muslim ritual and ascetic prescriptions to "reform" the most intransigent prison inmates, and to return them to newly responsible roles in their communities on their release.

Often the myth seems to be outgrown, or at least to lose its ecstatic and millennial quality and to be institutionalized in sectarianism,[33] when the social reality of its believers has grown to a more humanly acceptable size and a more harmonious order instituted; though the myth, or one like it, may reappear in ecstatic form at a later historical moment when confidence is once again undermined by circumstance. In this context, as has often been noted, the apocalyptic elements in Christianity, which characterized its origins, are precisely those elements which were suppressed and postponed to the end of time by the established Church when it had reordered the Western world out of Rome's decay. But these elements remained underground, ready to erupt coincident with famine, plague, or overpopulation in the Middle Ages. In a similar way, it was precisely the idea of the Second Coming with its apocalypse, day of judgment, resurrection of the dead, and establishment of the kingdom of heaven on earth that captured the imagination of the New Guineans, Amerindians, and so many other oppressed peoples, often to the consternation of the missionaries who considered those prophecies to concern only spiritual promises for the faithful after death, or a distant prophecy of some unimaginably future event. Further, the syncretic nativistic innovator assimilated Christianity to his own myths of the ultimate return of the culture hero and the dead ancestors, and suddenly, mythological figures who heretofore had represented only the long hope began to appear just over the horizon in their native craft, in European steamers, in airplanes, or climbing down the trunk of the *axis mundi,* the sacred tree that connects heaven and earth, to regenerate and reverse the earthly scheme of things.

Where human order falters, the gods intervene. Shorn of its mysti-

33. For a lucid analysis and description of this process, see Wallace's "Revitalization Movements."

cal sense, this statement renders the psychological truth which seems undeniable, that the so-called religious emotion is produced by extreme states of consciousness, and that these extreme states are induced, among other ways, by excessive tension and the strains of seemingly insoluble conflict. Objects are intensified by their attachment to emotion; in the trance state dissociation from the conscious mind gives sensory distortion free play, so that time and space are distorted and perception altered in ways that correspond to inner feeling states. What is highly desired but absent in reality is magnified; the more extreme the deprivation in reality, the greater seems the tendency of images magnified to mythological proportions to appear. The ecstasy felt in the trance state, like the numinosity of its images, seems in direct proportion to the active misery of the waking state that produced the tension-induced trance.

The Vailala Madness in Papua (*ca.* 1919) derived its name from the ecstatic possession that swept through the populace. The Papuans described the phenomenon as "head-he-go-round" or "belly don't know." One informant described the second stage of possession as "belly he think,"[34] a very accurate description of a kind of gut knowledge breaking through to consciousness. Social deprivation, according to La Barre, is an instance of a larger category, sensory deprivation, which is common to the situations that produce trance: isolation, exhaustion, hunger, and the loss of order involved in the breakdown of personal and social certainties. Identity depends "on constant bounding by the cosmos";[35] thus the breakdown of a cosmic order implicit in social crisis is equally a crisis of personal identity and results in the sensory deprivation which precipitates trance and visionary distortions and compensations. This helps to explain why the prophetic vision often comes "in the wilderness," when the prophet, through removal from the presence of his fellows, suffers the particular form of sensory deprivation involved in social deprivation. And this is but reinforcement of a social deprivation implicit in cultural crisis where the old certainties have broken down and members of the society, even while at home, are "in the wilderness"—estranged from themselves and from each other.

Autism in the personality may form the pathological correlative of visionary response to the "wilderness" of social deprivation; the psychotic person in our society may find himself denied by forces not unlike those that alienate members of traditional societies who are disoriented by colonial rule. R. D. Laing, who understands so deeply

34. Worsley, *The Trumpet Shall Sound*, p. 75.
35. La Barre, *Ghost Dance*, p. 55.

the interpersonal origins of psychic disorders, treating these disorders as human responses to untenable social situations, describes the typical "schizogenetic" parent as one who rewards the child for what is basically unnatural behavior, and withholds approval from behavior which is physical, spontaneous, and instinctual. Thus the child is adjudged "good" for puppet-like behavior: for actions overly compliant and unimpassioned, for excessively polite and restrained deportment, for self-abasement and physical "absence." If he tries to be physically loving, self-assertive, or to express his appetites openly, he is rejected by the parent. Seemingly, the more he is absent, in every sense, the more he appears as a silent and obedient mask, the more acceptable he is to those on whom he must depend. Thus the social mask, or *persona,* does not result in instinctual gratification as it does in normal social-personal development, but rather in instinctual starvation, so that the increasingly dissociated self, denied and rejected, its *persona* threatening and unproductive of deep satisfaction, tends more and more to develop autistically in the direction of fantasy. Stated simply then, the person becomes split, his conscious life a false construction, his body felt as unreal; his real, feeling self is forced underground and is increasingly experienced as a phatasmagoric "other," an evil demon or a whole universe of appetites grown to mythological proportions through their frustration and inability to appear consciously and to seek satisfaction in the world. Eventually, the autistic side takes over, seeking, in often self-defeating ways, to force its will on a world that has denied its being.

Now, while admittedly his case is more isolated and extreme, the development of the psychotic personality can be seen as a paradigm for the colonial situation. Fanon, in describing the situation of the colonized Algerian, makes the parallel exact: "French colonialism has settled itself in the very centre of the Algerian individual and has undertaken a sustained work of clean-up, of expulsion of self, of rationally pursued mutilation."[36] The colonized "native" experiences a pattern similar to Laing's psychotic of false reinforcement from authority; he is expected to be subservient, to hold his tongue, to work in regimented ways at tasks that seem meaningless or stupid to him—in New Guinea for instance, to dig pit latrines for the community, when he understands that his feces must be hidden from sorcerers who may use them to work harmful magic on him. He is set at odds with what is most natural to him: he is reviled for his lack of cleanliness, his emotional outlet in dance and ritual is proscribed or suppressed, he is rewarded for a doglike obedience and for disloyalty to his own kind.

36. Fanon, *Dying Colonialism*, p. 50.

And he seems most valued when least visible. He feels increasingly like a divided person, speaking a *lingua franca*, bereft of the personal authority he took for granted, and despised for those things which are most precious to him. And then he is increasingly subject to the vagaries of a white market economy which he has no way of understanding; he is forced to become an adjunct to that economy by both physical co-ercion and his growing dependence on superior European goods. Thus his economic well-being becomes increasingly at odds with his self-esteem, and his family life is disrupted by the necessity to hire out as a laborer, his wife left to raise children and garden alone.

His attempts to make peace with this new authority meet with continued failure: he may work hard but get little for it, often losing what small earnings he makes to a head tax and to white storekeepers; he may convert to the Christian religion, hoping for the equality and material reward it seems to promise him, but end as poor and despised as ever—with a boring religion to boot; he may raise his hand against the new master, but find himself imprisoned or overpowered by superior weapons. Thus, like the schizophrenic, he finds his real, instinctual, and proud self reviled and refused, and a false, puppet-like personality approved by a powerful authority. Set in conflict with himself, he is increasingly tense, fragmented, and dissatisfied; increasingly, therefore, in the grip of the irrational—the ground has been seeded for a break into autism.

There is, of course, one primary factor which separates the suffering colonized person from the schizophrenic. The former has what the latter does not—a community of fellow sufferers with whom to make common cause. And it is out of the bonds of the collectivity that the source of new strength will be mobilized, passing through autism and regression to a new concept of selfhood which takes the changed situation into account and, imaginatively at least, masters it. And to take him through the terrors of transition there is the "mana-personality" with whom he can identify and from whose divine assurances he can draw strength.

The grandiosity of vision that appears is, as has been suggested, in direct proportion to the abasement of the society's situation and the extremity of its need. The four pictures on the following page, produced by a schizophrenic artist as his illness progressed, give concrete evidence not only of the loss of a sense of objective reality but also of a clear increase in imaginative power, an intense effort to construct a personal design out of fragmentation, and a movement, as the new design emerges, through trauma (2), from naturalistic (1) to mythological (4). In the series, breakdown and crystallization from fragments is made visible; in the last picture, a grandiose figure has emerged, both

1

2

3

4

From a brochure of the American Schizophrenia Association

human and animal, yet greater than both—luminous, crowned, and resplendent, and, in this case, malevolent.

The attempt to restructure the world in images of compensatory grandiosity and mythological numinosity is also common to the prophet's vision; it is not gratuitous delusion. That this vision has cultural precedents, like the Indian guardian animal spirit, a context which makes self-assertive forces appear genuinely protective, explains the benevolent transfiguration which the schizophrenic perceives as malevolent. "Laing contends . . . that patients might in many cases return normally from their psychotic or schizophrenic episodes if they were 'guided' through the experience rather than 'treated.'"[37]

There are individuals in every society and at all times who perceive their situation *in extremis* because of their peculiar experience and/or make-up, who experience disintegration as their daily bread. But again, when the visions of such individuals receive communal response, then the threat may be understood as general by being collectively affirmed; it may be taken not as the peculiar infernal sense of a special experience of the world, but as reflection of a general state so profoundly unsatisfying as to make reality legitimately demonic of the run of men. It is in this sense that the picture of the world projected in the new myth-dream can be taken as true, true to the experience of the people and true to their basic sense of their own health. Thus the findings of abnormal psychology are here immediately relevant, for in a truly abnormal situation one would expect the same aberrations and attempts at readjustment found among so-called abnormal people in more stable social settings, but which, for them, given their personal constellations of authorities, may be far from stable. And they may be, in addition, more sensitive to a disorder in society which is not yet generally acknowledged.

The myth-dreams which erupt are, first, as has been described above, cosmic in scope and overwhelming in the ferocity with which they seize the mind. The religions of stable societies are scarcely more than the pale ghosts of these intense visions of redemption which only deep disorder seems able to impel.

Second, they have the quality, described by Freud as common to hysterics, of great and unreasonable expectations. The expectations take two forms—one creative, the other destructive, answering to the contradiction of the moment. The latter is the sense of impending doom, of apocalypse, but it is a doom that is selective, that is gratefully expected as both a revenge and a liberation. The apocalypse, whether it be earthquake, tidal wave, fire, war, or volcanic eruption, will sweep away

37. Irving L. Givot, "Letter to the Editor," *New York Review of Books* (July 1, 1971), p. 39.

38 Gathering the Winds

the masters, the evil ones who destroy pride, as well as those among the tribe who refuse to believe in the prediction and to practice its ritual admonitions.

The vision of apocalypse has that condensed economy common to myth and dream—it serves to express, first of all, the enormous emotional psychic upheaval going on in the dreamer, embodying the breakdown and breakup of the old self, the overthrow of a tyrannical internal order, while at the same time it offers a symbolic outlet for the long frustrated desire for revenge, a wish-fulfillment for all the bottled up negative feelings against the oppressor. And it serves to empower the dreamer, to threaten his enemies within as well as without the tribe, to give him the enormous weapon of fear in instituting belief in the efficacy of his dream and its new mandatory prescriptions. And it satisfies the desire for purification, making way for renewal. It also serves, sometimes as substitute for, but also sometimes as motive power and paradigm for, active revolt in the real world, serving as the focal point for the organization of military and political movements designed to overthrow the existing power structure. Sometimes the myth-dream counsels pacifism and leaves apocalypse to divine agency, as in the case of the prophet Jesus, who probably saw the futility of the constant Zealot revolts and the terrible price which his people had to pay for their refusal to tolerate Roman rule. At other times the vision counsels warfare, making men the agents of the divinely ordained destruction, as in the case of Mohammed and the Amerindian Ghost Dance prophets, whose military revolts had such different outcomes— one consolidating a people and initiating an era of empire, the other finally destroying a nation and reducing a people to a pitiful remnant.

The second expectation, following the destruction of the demonic order of the world, is millennial—the expectation of a new world which embodies an inversion of the present situation: a world without masters, without illness, freed of work and obligation, often a world of eternal life, endless youth, of the return of the dead to life, and of the establishment of a perpetual reign of justice and good will. Blacks will rule whites, sometimes even their color will be reversed, and, in the cargo visions of New Guinea, European goods will be available in profusion to all. Even nature may be reversed—fruits growing in the earth, root plants from the trees. The vision of easy plenty, without work, a kind of eternal day off, is in direct proportion to the frustration of work at present and the sense of obligations which are without reward. Thus, the notion of obligation has itself been injured by being unrewarding; the compensatory vision may eliminate all obligations as a result.

Along with the apocalyptic and millennial content of the dream often comes a set of prescriptions for actions, these actions often being ritual ones, and usually social and ethical ones as well. In examining these prescriptions, which are believed by the cult adherents to be productive of the apocalyptic-millennial situation, two things are immediately apparent. One is that new actions, like the myth which prescribes them, are syncretic, that is, they combine elements of both nativistic and new, often expressing the ambivalence the cultist feels both to his own culture and to the alien culture which is intruding on his life space. There is a basic sense in which the new rites and rules make a kind of peace between conflicting orders in their institution of a new one.

The cult of Handsome Lake of the Seneca and Iroquois Indians in 1799 is a case in point. At the point of death from alcoholism, already being prepared for burial, Handsome Lake had his first of a series of visions in which the Good Spirit revealed to him a new way of life, which he, after a miraculous recovery, propagated in an austere code, one which not only warned the Seneca away from alcohol, witchcraft, and wife-beating (all negative symptoms of social strain) but also counseled literacy in English and the practicing of new agricultural methods, which for the first time made the male an active participant in farming. Deeply aware of the self-destructiveness of male warrior values in a dominant white world, Handsome Lake turned his men into farmers and rechanneled the hunting values of physical courage and prowess into more adaptive patterns, many of his descendants becoming the "high-steel" workers on American bridges and skyscrapers. Married to his new code were apocalyptic and millennial expectations resembling the Christian promises of heaven or hell, but this time heaven was to be reserved for good Seneca; no whites were to be admitted; "His doctrine was a mixture of the old and new, in part harking back to the good old days of the past, in part a practical and drastic accommodation to new times. . . . From being a frontier slum folk, the Iroquois became the best adapted and most populous Indian group in the East."[38]

The second characteristic of vision-prescribed actions is that they allow an expression of feeling, feelings for a long time either suppressed or forbidden, and it is partly the upsurge of these feelings which permits these rites to be seen as curative in and of themselves. This is to say that in some fundamental way it does not matter that the cargo never comes, the world never ends, or the buffalo never return. What matters is a rite and a vision which allows people to come into contact with feelings whose hurtfulness, both psychic and somatic, comes chiefly of being denied, that permits a transcendence of the "split"

38. La Barre, *Ghost Dance*, pp. 210-11.

state by putting individuals back into touch with the deeper levels of their own being and with each other. It is this, together with the fact that cult ritual is itself a restoration of the world of action, making men feel that they are the active agents of their own destiny, which constitute perhaps the major psychological gifts of the cult ritual.

The healing that is done, then, is that of a split self occasioned by a social malaise. The personalities being considered here are not secularized individuals whose sense of self can be separated from mythic symbols. The socially conditioned view of the self in the societies under study has traditionally been one defined by a relation to gods and/or ancestor spirits whose actions mirror interpersonal relations, and the ongoing assumption is that there is another realm running parallel to and determining much of what happens in the physical world. This point of view is not so much erroneous logic as simply taking seriously what goes on in the dream life of the imagination. The imagination is regarded as the place where the other world is joined; the visitations are as real to the dreamer as they seem. Seeming is simply not at issue. Thus, though the imagination works similarly in all men, based on structural principles whose source still largely eludes us, the interpretation of it is different according to their epistemological point of view. The role of the symbolic constitutents of personality change may be weighted differently according to what is conceived as real by the society; thus, within the context of a magico-religious view of reality, the cult is, quite simply, the cure that is possible. Further, as will be suggested in the following chapters, the sense of self can perhaps never be dissociated from mythic symbols; the search for wholeness seems never to succeed without their intervention, even if they are reinterpreted and recovered at a new level of consciousness.

What remains constant in all radical mental realignment is the return to origins, the awakening of primal and powerful emotions freed of the inhibitors of past social prohibition, and the resultant reempowering of a renewed self in some way quite different from the one that existed before the new dream and its accompanying rites seized it.

The foregoing observations reveal the artificiality of Ralph Linton's distinction between "magical" and "rational" nativism. It should be clear by now that all nativistic cult activity, to effectively produce changed consciousness, involves some magical, autistic behavior. Linton's classifications reveal more about his own bias in favor of conscious adaptation and his tendency to classify cult vision after the fact, by its consequences in the world of real political action. However, cults, it would seem, have components that are both irrational and rational; they adapt man to the world, and the world to man, and the degree of their eventual effectiveness is a function not only of the relative balance of these components in the cult but also of the resilience or recalcitrance of the external situation. At any rate, cult always depends on strong emotion to achieve its transformation; a purely or even predominantly rational nativism, like rational religion, is a contradiction in terms. The confusion engendered by Linton's kind of pigeonholing would seem to come from a basic misunderstanding of the processes at work, a lack of recognition that the function of imagination is precisely to join mind and body, and that to separate the two is an act of willful abstraction, symptomatic of a set of culturally learned defenses, the process of sublimation which has ended by obscuring the original identity of mind and body, conscious and unconscious, rational and irrational, in the work of visionary imagination, and in human life.

It seems the nature of cult material, originally generated by imaginative vision where symbol, flesh, and feeling meet in a kind of ecstatic totality, to grow cold as the new order which it has generated becomes an established and stable entity, until the order of things again appears as given, not subject to basic alteration. Reason, then, is put at the service of justifying the order that exists, and relatively unaware of the unconscious influence of instinct (which is now bound and served by that order), imagines itself free of instinctual domination while in fact the unconscious still impels the mind to an irrational quietism (which is considered highly "reasonable") about the order of things as they are. Thus the irrational is only perceived as it is disordered and unbound, but that the mind is permeated by the need to defend an order in which the organism feels at home is as evident in the conservative arguments for the holiness of the past and the *status quo* that keeps it alive as it is in the radical arguments for a totally regenerated and changed future, beginning now.

Only during the cultic moments, when the old constraints do not properly serve the instincts, when, as a result, new religions and new myths break through, does the deep irrationality of human motivation become visible, and it is these moments which are revelatory of much of what remains hidden—but nonetheless active—in times of relative stability. It is the nature of the chiliast to be living in the universe of his feelings quite directly, and it is this which accounts for his constant sense that the world is being transformed right now; his hopes for the future are not experienced as a distant ideal but as a live force at work in the world, of which he is an agent. He is thus impatient of methods and means; he is not so much building or conserving an order as experiencing an inner transformation; if he is questioned too closely about exactly how this new order is to function he becomes querulous. He feels new, and it is this sense of vitality to which he is subservient; he is emotionally charged and refueled, and it is this new sense of himself that he celebrates. The chiliast has shed apathy for excitement, and it is not evidence—but only exhaustion—which will reacquaint him with the mundane. Even then things are not as they were before; the sacred—the timeless world of imagination—had for a time invaded the profane, and despite eventual disillusionment, a new paradigm has left its shape in his mind and in his actions. He may recant, but the odds are he won't. If he does, his "conversion" may have been spurious; or he may once again be too afraid of the dominant order; the successful cult leaves its inheritance in a changed mentality—what Wallace calls a new "maze-way formation."

After the New Guinea episode of the Vailala madness had passed, and its excitement no longer gripped the people in their vitals, there remained, nonetheless, the memory in the society that there had indeed been a time of miracles when the gods had walked the earth. All institutionalized religions seem to bear this memory and to revere it; it is, most likely, the memory of that ecstatic time when visions seized the prophets (men often canonized in collective memory as culture heroes), spread through the populace, and the "gods," seen as this kind of imaginative phenomena of crisis, did indeed dwell among men. The Old Testament bears the traces of this origin of religion, and of changed social order; the God from the documents dated as earliest in the canon walked among the tents and spoke to Abraham; as time passes this God becomes more remote, appearing in dreams and visions only; finally, he becomes a kind of universal moral principle, an abstraction of a set of ethics firmly entrenched. Only among the prophets who arose in bad times, and in the eschatological dreams which grew in the Diaspora and reached their culmination in messianic cults, most notably that of the prophet Jesus, did the withdrawn God once again appear in the flesh, to which the New Testament, with its powerful apocalyptic vision and millennial morality is testimony. The proud code of the Old Testament, of a people who ruled their own kingdom and controlled their own wealth, is transformed in the New Testament into a code of meekness and acceptance, which saved pride ("the meek shall inherit the earth") while permitting survival in a new world of empire. The "last days' morality" ("give away all that you have and follow me") preached by Jesus was locked into place by the promise of imminent divine intervention in history ("on earth, as it is in heaven"); it was Paul who transformed the chiliastic expectation of the Second Coming into an other-worldly hope which made of Christianity a quietism and a faith for conservatives in a newly established order; it was not until the Medieval heretics, drawn from the lower classes, that the apocalyptic excitement was reborn, as it was again with Thomas Münzer's Anabaptists, who once more excited social turmoil by transforming social protest into a militant expectation of an immediate apocalyptic over-turning of the orders of the world.

It is precisely the compensatory elevation of a group or a society into an elect or chosen people whose actions are fated to change the very nature of man's being in the world, and the cultic excesses to which this view leads, that has made such visions appear madly ego-tistical and dangerously irrational to so many dispassionate observers. Yet it should be apparent by now how this collective inflation is a function of the extremity and hopelessness of the historical situation, and to wonder, therefore, not at the madness of cult vision but at a mechanism that restores hope and health and mediates change under such inimical conditions. Based on the evidence of how radical change in societies actually does occur, the observation is inescapable that it is in these recurrent chiliastic episodes that human beings remake their own image in creative adaptation to a changing world, even while the vision of what human order ought to be reappears and is renewed.

To keep this in mind is to take issue with descriptions like the psychoanalytical one of La Barre, who, in discussing visionary phenom-ena, says that our "sacred behavior" is, among other things, "con-trived . . . to hide recognition that a monstrous unsurrendered infantile omnipotence is the ultimate paradigm of God and the first of his many psychosexual metamorphoses."[39] This is indeed a monstrous concep-tion of the god-principle; in being a partial description of the visionary conception, it is, in fact, the "ultimate paradigm" for a false god, one who is transcended in authentic vision. Of course, regression to an infantile autism may be a necessary part of vision, but it is part of the process and not its end. As Jung has suggested, the symbolic paradigm for God is the mandala, the circle with a center, which he takes as the idealized image for unified selfhood, an internal unity which depends upon unity with the larger world. The African snake swallowing its own tail, the Eastern mandala, the Catholic rose window, the Chinese circle joining the Yin and the Yang, the Amerindian sun figure, the Roman dome and oculus, all of these redraw the same imaginative truth, joining time and eternity, life and death, matter and spirit, male and female, collective and singular. Religion, as Wallace defines it, is "the organiza-tion instinct." "This dialectic, the 'struggle' (to use an easy metaphor) between entropy and organization, is what religion is all about . . . But religion does not offer just any solution: characteristically, it offers a solution that assures the believer that life and organization will win, that death and disorganization will lose, in their struggle to become the characteristic condition of self and cosmos."[40]

39. *Ibid.*, p. 16.
40. Anthony F. C. Wallace, *Religion: An Anthropological View* (New York: Random House, 1966), p. 38.

All animals, it would appear, live social lives, and their social instincts seem as fundamental as their more purely individual ones. The bee hive is a carefully organized social group, as is the sheep herd, the fish school, or the wolf pack. Birds migrate in formation, and establish their respective pecking orders. Mating, territorial possession, food getting—all are more or less organized group activities. Animals, too, have their symbolic languages for communication: both auditory, like the song of birds, and bodily, like the language of bees. And they have their conflict-solving rituals, like the mating dance of geese, which ritualizes aggression and allows bonding to take place. Thus the division between nature and culture would seem, in part, artificial; though human society is intrinsically more adaptive and elaborated symbolically, it nevertheless would seem to rest on firm instinctual foundations. This is not to say that culture is identical with nature, but that a particular kind of social instinct is legitimately a part of that special form of nature that is human. If this seems dangerously close to reading human ideals backward into the design of nature, it is meant rather to suggest that the spontaneous eruption of cult vision under similar pressures argues that human nature, in unfolding itself, projects an ideal social vision which is somehow inherent in our particular structure as a species and natural, not to some universal design but to ourselves. And, as vision suggests, it is the endless adaptability of that ideal that makes it not a dead determinism but the very testament of human freedom.

The structure of the entire Western biblical canon, from Old through New Testament, may be seen as Northrop Frye, through his study of William Blake, came to see it, as the structure of one vast apocalyptic myth, beginning with creation and culminating in the millennium, the visionary record of one people drawing, from a long and various history, a timeless pattern that lives both within and outside that history. It was the English poet William Blake who saw, in the prophetic voice that bursts out at troubled intervals throughout biblical times and has its culmination in the prophet Jesus, the work of visionary imagination that renews and enlarges the spiritual order that must be constantly freed from the priestly tradition that stifles it and from the other worldly powers that pervert or oppose it. Direct descendant of the Renaissance humanists who sought the original and authentic Christian values beneath the worldly veil the Holy Roman Empire had cast over them, it was Blake who first made an explicit and total identity between prophecy and poetry, seeing them as a single archetypal stream fed from the same source of the visionary imagination.

By Blake's time, however, at the end of the eighteenth and beginning of the nineteenth centuries, the Renaissance synthesis which had renewed in new form the man-god, making the Word flesh again, presenting an order both mental and bodily, resonant with the well-being of a new-found confidence and integration—this synthesis had begun its mutation into another form entirely, as the huge forms of the Baroque began to speak of a world grown heavy with mass and matter, a world whose art mirrors the enormous dramatic energy, will to animation, and even violence necessary to raise an increasingly material world with its growing nations and appetites toward the ideal form with which it had seemed so naturally to dwell in the Renaissance. It was as if the very atmosphere had changed, giving to matter greater density, as if the discovery of the concept of gravity had, at first, increased its pull, and, straining against each other, great opposing forces were everywhere set into motion. By the late eighteenth century the synthesis had torn apart; the religious, mythic imagination could no longer contain the world of matter, and the rational voice, fleshless, with its cool geometry, all but banished imaginative vision, relegating it to the separate world of received, "irrational" religion, or to an artistically vitiated world of ghosts, pale fantasies, or "illusions"; while the forces which imagination had struggled to embody and so to master went underground, working their will, like the gods, in mysterious ways. It was the Lisbon earthquake that shook Voltaire from the complacency of Deism, that brought from him the cry that the worship of a rational and mechanical universe was "an insult to the sadness of human existence," that turned his wit against the articles of his own faith and left him, with his battered Candide, in the reduced state of an Adam who has fallen from the rationalist's garden of progress and is left to till with his own hands the remaining plot of his life. As the new century approached, the aftermath of the French Revolution raised widespread questions about the rational and libertarian millennium that was being ushered in. But the Industrial Revolution had claimed the day; it encapsulated its sensitive and creative minority in irrelevance or contempt, to keep from spreading the voice that would disturb the calm surface of its sensible utilitarian virtues. It was in this inimical climate that the imagination found its voice again, all unheeded, in the poetry and engravings of William Blake, whose vision, enlarged by the intellectual growth of the age of reason and brought to crisis by its contradictions, repaired the world in a single mind with a mighty apocalypse in which the beleaguered imagination presented to a deaf world its own most eloquent defense, a defense which, looked at from a later perspective, offers a paradigm of the unitary nature of religious and artistic vision, connecting the preliterate, prophetic myth-dream with the more sophisticated poetic imagination, identifying in them all a common source—what Blake called "Jesus," the "divine" human imagination.

2/THE UNCOMMON EYE
Vision in the Poetry of Blake, Beddoes, and Yeats

Of the things of the future, wise men perceive
approaching events. At times
during hours of serious meditations
their hearing is disturbed. The mysterious clamor
of approaching events reaches them.
And they listen with reverence. Although outside
on the street, the peoples hear nothing at all.

C. P. Cavafy, "But Wise Men Perceive Approaching Things"

The mantle of the prophet can only be conferred by the response of the community, a dislocated people who find, through the prophet's eye, a re-created center in a time of social storm. The mandala becomes existent; the prophet and his vision form a glowing center which gathers around it the individual members of the community in an unbroken circle of belief and restored confidence, an "eternal" design that makes past and future coexistent in a timeless, mythic present. Here the visionary imagination is received by a despairing people as revelation; the prophet, like the Pharoah in the Joseph story, dreams for the people.

But what is to be said of the visionary imagination that finds little or no communal resonance, the poet whose mighty apocalypse wins him not converts but the contempt of the community in which he writes, a community of whose revitalization, like communally received prophets, he also dreams? The imaginative patterns are much the same, but the society, insulated by its worldly success, complacent with the conventional mirror of virtue it held up to itself, avoiding psychological pain by the unexamined use of an idealistic language to shroud the realities of war, exploitation, and pursuit of empire, turned a deaf ear to the prophetic voice of William Blake, who offered the first full-scale critique of the industrial age just as it was gathering its strength. The crisis that produced his vision was not yet society's, but that of an uncommon soul who became aware of the contradictions in a system long before those contradictions, through their historical consequences, were to become apparent to the run of men. In his own sense, then, Blake was prophetic; for him, the prophet was simply an honest man who foresaw consequences:

> Thus: If you go on So, the result is So. He never says, such a thing shall happen let you do what you will. A Prophet is a Seer, not an Arbitrary Dictator.
> ("Annotations to Watson," p. 392)[1]

Thus Blake destroyed one world and built another in his rebellious imagination in a time when imagination itself was considered mere unreason and the poet, as Plato had dreamed, was all but banished from the State.

A society which has no use for its most imaginative members is already a sick society, limiting inner growth and committed to the repression of that sensitivity that finds mass slaughter and large-scale oppression unthinkable. It is no accident that the genius of Roman literature was for satire, and that its greatest epic, the *Aeneid*, begins in storm and ends in murder—the killing of an innocent youth by Aeneas— and that its central drama is the repression of passion in its hero. The scorn of Dido for Aeneas in the underworld and his own helpless tears at her disdain powerfully present the image of a Rome built on the grave of its own happiness. Roman mythology celebrates the triumph of the Father, the mythic form of the oppressive society which keeps its subjects dutiful children, which feeds its poorer sons and rebels to the lions and rewards its good children with the spectacle of the fate of the conquered or rebellious. The stable and relatively healthy society, on the other hand, brings the hero through separation to return and a reconciliation with the father, which allows him his full maturity. And where the society is oppressive and many of its members do not share in its power or rewards, the apocalyptic myth may capture the popular imagination, imaging the overthrow of a tyrannous father and the setting up in his stead of a permanent community of brothers, where father and son are again one.

The drama of apocalyptic or visionary imagination in the modern Western world finds perhaps its fullest statement in the art of William Blake. It is a story of the imagination in exile in its own society, of a poet dreaming for the common man in the language of an elite which will not listen, a man who has a vision whose time in his society has not

1. William Blake, *Blake: Complete Writings*, ed. Geoffrey Keynes (London: Oxford University Press, 1969). All subsequent references are to this edition and will be given in parentheses in the text.

yet come, stated in a language too arcane and intellectual to reach the poor for whom he speaks: "Were we not slaves till we rebell'd?" ("Tiriel," I, line 17, p. 99). Blake's imaginative certainty, the transformation enacted in him by the resolution of internal conflicts he never turned away from, made him proof against an age that destroyed so many lesser poets whose social irrelevance was more than their muse could sustain. When society sanctions the repressive and self-judgmental side of a man's mind, when he finds no allies for his creative forces, and if those forces are too strong to be repressed, his conflict may never be resolved and it may drive him into madness or the twilight realm of alcoholism, debauchery, inactivity, or suicidal despair. The fate of Cowper, Clare, and Smart, Blake's contemporaries, the brief candle of so many of the Romantics, and the tragic dissolution of the members of the Rhymers' Club in the time that followed attest to the fate of imaginative men who can find no social moorings for their vision.

The success of Blake's struggle, imaged in the struggle of Los with his Spectre of Urthona, was foreordained, for the mockery of his creativity by the Spectre, with its attachments to the world of everyday morality and necessity, never had, for Blake, the ethical sanction of the kind he most deeply recognized. Blake was, as Frye has commented, the healthiest of geniuses (Blake himself said he had only had one nightmare in his life); so healthy that he insisted that genius of his sort was the normal, despite his appearance as aberrant or mad to the world around him. He was never uncertain about which side life was on; he early championed the egalitarian ideals of both the American and French Revolutions, sided with the poor and enslaved, hated empire, profit seeking, and the selling of men in the market place, despised rationality abstracted from human life, and denounced equally the tyrants of Selfhood and puritanical moral constraints within and their political counterparts in the tyrants without. His insights into repression and the perversion of libidinal energy into violence were both Freudian and Jungian before their time; his fundamental opposition to capitalism, imperialism, and slavery conforms to the socialist doctrine which was not yet a gathering wind, as his progression through contraries agrees with later dialectical thought; his insistence that men are not the passive objects of their detached thought but the active creators of their own human reality parallels the later attempts of phenomenology, existentialism, and so much of contemporary thought to heal the bifurcated world of subject and object, to allow man to grasp his existence in its wholeness; his search for deep patterns in the prophets and poets of the past prefigures the mytho-poetic interest of art and comparative mythology of the later nineteenth and twentieth centuries; his inversion of Christian theology parallels the contemporary thinking of the death-of-god theologians of immanence, the re-sanctification of human life by the de-spiritualization of divinity; his understanding of how the cult of Virginal Woman dehumanized women and made them the enemies of men parallels much of modern feminist thought; his sense of man split off from his feminine component which thus possesses him from outside prefigures Jung's *anima* and *animus* as the constituents of every human's wholeness. He sympathized with all the underground forces, the Satanic demons of the conventional Christian mind, with the people and the passions that had been pushed under and turned ugly by their captivity; he championed an order which was not an accuser but an insurer of exuberant life.

Blake, of course, had no causal connection with the revolutionary thought of an age that would follow him; he accords so well with these modern modes of radical thinking, not because he was some sort of mystical clairvoyant, but because his imagination was prophetic in the true sense. Because he had seen so deeply into the nature of his own psychic crisis, perceived the laws of the imagination so clearly, he was able to see, from the position of his own integrated vision, the division in those about him, the deep ills of his society, the contradictions in the rationalization of the social apologists around him, the inevitable outcome of oppressive and righteous imperialism—all against a background of a millennial vision which made visible a society reordered in humane and life-serving forms. He knew too much to involve himself in the self-defeating errors of revolutionary thought which is too reactive, which loses its balance; he was opposed to neo-primitivism, that simplistic inversion of an over-mechanical system, for he knew that nature was not a garden but a vegetating jungle, and that the true garden was a humanized nature, a harmony between man and nature created by human culture; he opposed abstraction and cold rationalism, but was not anti-intellectual, was in fact the champion of intellect who saw the imagination as the highest intellectual act informed by the deepest experience and understanding of what is humanly valuable. His imagination penetrated deeper than the Romantics who followed him; their realm was for him Beulah, the refuge of the immature imagination in flight from experience, with its "moony night," its virginal or predacious females, and its fleeting, ephemeral joys. And he was not, finally, opposed to science, but to its dehumanization, to its reduction of human life to the mechanical laws it had discovered in matter, its subservience to its own system. In the final vision of Jerusalem, this is explicit:

> . . . & at the clangor of the Arrows of Intellect
> The innumerable Chariots of the Almighty appear'd in Heaven,
> And Bacon & Newton & Locke, & Milton & Shakespear & Chaucer.
> (*Jerusalem*, Pl. 98, lines 7–9, p. 945)

In the imagined land the contraries are preserved but enter into fruitful relationship of "intellectual war," science and art reconciled in a single human culture.

Perhaps the most revolutionary act of Blake's system is its explicit identification of God with the human imagination: "Imagination/ (Which is the Divine Body of the Lord Jesus, blessed for ever)" (*Jerusalem*, Pl. 5, lines 58–59, p. 624). The first chapter of this study attempted to show that the presence of the gods in human society was, in fact, the eruption of restorative imaginative vision in the midst of social disorder; that the seizing of men's minds by this vision was experienced by them as divine intervention in human affairs. Blake was the first visionary to make explicit the connection between religion and art, to see the imagination not as a "furor poeticus" through which the divine voice might speak, but the divinity itself. Jesus, the Word made flesh, energized order in human form, *is* imagination; the artist, or Los figure, is its active transmitter; Albion (or mankind) is its beneficiary; Jerusalem and Eden, Albion's city and garden, are its creations. There is no mystery in Blake, no inscrutable divinity lying behind the imagination; there is only the imagination itself, which is the redemptive power, and which, as the deepest source of man's vision, is sufficient unto itself. The consequences of this belief are as enormous as the giant forms they create; man is neither the absurd nor heroic victim of an overpowering God or nature forever beyond his comprehension, nor is he a half-way creature on a Great Chain of Being who must accept the often brutal orders of the world and nature because it is all part of a "good" plan beyond his limited ability to comprehend. The brutality of the non-human world is not to be acquiesced in; the imagination has the authority to hate what is destructive to human life, and to create in conformity with human need.

To consider that the mind is equal to the business of living, that it has within it the renewable vision of a harmonious and satisfying order, is to empower a confidence defeating the defensive and self-destructive tendencies born of fear. The imagination, as Blake's system makes clear, does not do away with the conflicts and contraries of human life, for "without contraries is no progression" (*The Marriage of Heaven and Hell*, Pl. 3, p. 149); quite the opposite, it does away with their negations, which make the conflicts insoluble. For example, reason, for Blake, attempts to negate passion; in so doing, it insures that passion will be rebellious and perverse, and war, heightened conflict and destruction, will be the result of over-rational order. Blake's faith is a denial only of the occult; there is nothing that is secret, there is only that which the mind has neglected or feared to regard. The belief that man is capable of coping with his contraries and of creating a culture which contains them harmoniously is simply the faith that man is capable of becoming everything that he potentially is, and that what he potentially is, is all he needs to be. The only thing debased in man, for Blake, then, is the denial of his own human nature, a nature which is neither corporeal nor disembodied spirit, but both—Jesus, as he would say, or the imagination. Disembodied religion, as Blake saw, produced natural religion; the worship of abstracted deity made man the enemy of his life; the reaction to such religion is the natural religion which worships nature and sacrifices life on the altar of an inhuman matter. "Thus men forgot that All deities reside in the human breast" (*The Marriage of Heaven and Hell*, Pl. 11, p. 153).

Blake's apocalyptic vision strives to do for humanity at large what the visions heretofore studied did for a tribe or a people. Jerusalem is a human city with many mansions, the coming together of all peoples in common human culture. Nevertheless, Blake's universality has a local base; he is aware of himself as an English prophet-poet in the line of Spenser and Milton; his Man is Albion, England's eponymous ancestor; London and the towns of England are the localities which his imagination rebuilds in Jerusalem. His villains are Newton and Locke's science, the Deist's natural religion, wars of empire, the slave trade, and other evils of his day. Thus, his own place becomes the microcosmos for his cosmic drama, which, like Dante's epic, transcends the topical even as it embodies it in parallel allegories. The ancestors he draws on are the Hebrew prophets of the Old Testament, and the culture hero he invokes is Jesus, the crucified human imagination which is liberated in the Second Coming of its final ascendance in the apocalypse and its aftermath. The apocalypse itself is the breaking through of the powers of imagination, and the heightening of the forces of error until their negative nature is fully revealed. These forces are brought out, as it were, into the light of day; the infant created by a perverse female will, woman objectified by man and thus his enslaving object of worship, is revealed as "a winding Worm"; similarly the hidden female, veiled in mystery and perceived by the deceived as beauty, is revealed as "Mystery, Babylon the Great, the Abomination of Desolation,/Religion hid in War, a Dragon red & hidden Harlot" (*Jerusalem,* Pl. 75, lines 18–19, p. 716), at the same time that "Jesus . . . Opens Eternity in Time & Space, triumphant in Mercy" (*Jerusalem,* Pl. 75, lines 21–22, p. 716). Thus truth and error are exposed together, for "Falsehood is prophetic" (*Jerusalem,* Pl. 82, line 20, p. 725); ugliness reveals its own nature, so all things conspire toward the vision that comes not so much after apocalypse as out of it. Here are the two faces of art: symptom and cure; Blake continually alternates the positive vision with the negative one, so that there is no danger of the ugliness of what he has to show leading the reader to despair: for, as he says repeatedly, "they became what they beheld."

Because it is vision which is triumphant, the millennium is viewed as an awakening: Old and New Testament prophecies and characters are invoked simultaneously with Blake's private characters and with his England, as eternity breaks through time in a single dream which binds the ages. At the nadir of Albion's deathlike sleep, England awakes, admits to having slain Albion in her sleep "With the knife of the Druid" (the Druids being for Blake the primal archetype for those who murder in the name of natural religion), and so awakens Albion.

> Her voice pierc'd Albion's clay cold ear; he moved upon the Rock.
> The Breath Divine went forth upon the morning hills. Albion mov'd
> Upon the Rock, he open'd his eyelids in pain, in pain he mov'd
> His stony members, he saw England. Ah! shall the Dead live again?
> (*Jerusalem,* Pl. 95, lines 1–4, p. 742)

Thus is created again the form of apocalyptic imagination that has been discerned in the cults of pre-industrial societies, but this time the universal human and personal psychological sense are present together with the myth-dream, explicit and not merely inferred. The apocalypse is the upsurge of the destructive and formative energies of the imagination; it brings into clear outline the enemies of humanity and destroys them in its fiery clarity. No longer is humanity confused into worshipping the power of its oppressors hidden in the outworn forms of hollow ideal images; the enemy is identified, overthrown, the archetypes are re-forged in vital, human forms and a restored humanity appears, its dead awakened, reconciled with its ancestors. Los, the prophet artist, is recognized as the friend of man by a newly born Albion who understands now that the good death is the loss of that fretful will that binds man to the false order and makes him isolated and afraid to love his brothers: "for Man is Love/As God is Love; every kindness to another is a little Death/In the Divine Image, nor can man exist but by Brotherhood" (*Jerusalem,* Pl. 95, lines 26–28, p. 743). The millennial state is man living in consonance with his imagination, his full sight restored; where body and spirit are one, male and female are contained within the one human form which is Albion, married to his own created order of civilization and cultivated nature in eternal amity—ethics and esthetics rejoined. The forms exist, for Blake, as they did at the beginning of time, and as they have always existed in the human imagination; thus the orders of the world are reversed, turned inside out: the "inner" world has become outer, the lower has been raised to the highest, the beginning has become the end, the world is as the imagination perceives it, perfectly structured by human intellect and desire—eternity given, quite literally, in human form.

Blake's attempt to separate authentic vision from what he considers to be the errors of legalistic and historical distortions of all "visible churches" makes him uniquely valuable as the self-conscious visionary whose subject contains its own exegesis—a vision which makes the process of vision itself visible, which sees with clarity not only the vision but the imaginative process that creates it.

Blake's vision prefigures Jung's view of the imagination as the key to "individuation," the integration of the human psyche which is its fullest potential, making clear the connection of the "individuation process" to that renewal of society which is the millénnial expectation—which is not the individuation process writ large, but the realization that the integration of any one soul *includes* a harmonious social vision since the psyche's internal form is interpersonal; thus to create the authentic man is simultaneously to create a human cosmos. "The poetic vision is therefore a vision of apocalypse, *total resolution*, the return of all things to unity."[2]

The larger image of unity, which is the product of apocalypse, comes also, Jung suggests, with the middle-life crisis, the crisis when a man realizes that he has become his father (Orc, as Blake would say, has become Urizen) and is the next to die. The apocalyptic vision leads, then, to the more mature vision, which comes of deep crisis, when the psyche, like the sick society, is faced, not with coming to manhood in the narrower sense of the adolescent taking his place in an ordained human world, but with its own death. Similarly, the death of order, which is involved in the awareness of how deadly and life denying that order has become, requires a larger imaginative effort, a return to what Blake calls Tharmas, the generative power of human life to create the human form which is appropriate to it, a power which is greater than the release of sexual energy that marks adolescence, a power which draws all forms together into the single form which says that life *is* order, that decay and rigidity are the temporary phases of the forming power whose victory is the basic assurance of life's primacy in what seems otherwise merely the depressing cycles of life and death. The "total resolution" of apocalypse is only, then, called up by the experience of the unbearable, an experience which comes to societies at large at the worst of times, to the uncommon soul merely by the refusal to look away from the death, perversion, and suffering which nothing less than apocalypse can resolve without relinquishing awareness. Thus it is Tharmas, through his agent and child, Los, the imaginative man, born out of the splitting of Tharmas from his "emanation," which signals disorder, who is the reigning power behind apocalypse, and it becomes clear why Blake sees in Tharmas a kind of radical innocence, the Lamb

2. Hazard Adams, *Blake and Yeats: The Contrary Vision* (Ithaca, N.Y.: Cornell University Press, 1955), p. 33.

of the New Testament prophecies, not the pastoral lamb of the tender imaginations who flee from experience into twilight Arcadias. Tharmas is the unifying urge, which, frustrated, produces despair, and then reawakens out of it; the instinctual energy that has as its drive both personal integrity and social integration, which empowers both sexual (Luvah) and intellectual (Urizen) powers toward the joining, which becomes for Blake, through vision, the single action and being of a complete Man (Albion). Thus while Blakean vision parallels the apocalyptic vision of the prophets who remake societies, he goes beyond them to illuminate the process which produces them all.

Blake's radical faith that the thread of linear time could be wound into a ball, that all men could share permanently the kind of vision he had himself (which is, in fact, the definition of millennium), is the brother spirit animating all the prophets of apocalypse. The difference lies partly in Blake's deeper awareness, his wider historical perspective, his sense of the cyclical nature of all the regenerative outbursts of human vision thus far, apocalyptic moments which cooled into constricting and oppressive forms once crisis was past and new powers established. The young Blake identified the apocalyptic tide with the American and French revolutions; with unclouded eye he watched these dreams darken into less than millennial realities, and saw illusion and tyranny begin again to obscure authentic vision. But the form of his own vision, after its self-questioning, retained its original shape, clarified and brightened by examining more deeply and with more complexity its original error. He did not give up on apocalypse, but only on its more local forms; retaining, even as he postponed the final moment, the sense that his age, with its heightened conflict and multiplying errors, was to be the last age crippled by the fall of vision into the snares of temporal power and corporeal ambition, the spectral side of all man's great eternal "Zoas," his life-binding and regenerative powers, perverted by the Satanic element he called "Selfhood."

Blake, too, looked "beyond the pleasure principle," but unlike Freud did not end in pessimism. Freud's genius was analytical, and it served life by tearing down what had been an almost opaque structure of defense, hiding man's instincts from his mind, even while they drove his body and disordered his imagination. But in focusing on the disordered imagination Freud missed something of its synthetic power: art, for him, was individual neurosis; religion, a collective one. Blake, too, saw the perverse and symptomatic art and religion in his age, but he saw the "golden string" running through, and had a unitive vision to hold against the perverted and fragmented ones he had inherited. Freud's "ego" was a kind of neutral arbitrator between warring sets of unreasonable demands, a kind of image of himself—a stoic and heroic

The Uncommon Eye 55

rationalist negotiating a middle road between the twin tyrannies of instinct and conscience. But Blake was a flaming partisan; no part of his mind was neutral. For Blake a totally dispassionate reason would have to end as Urizen exploring his dens, freezing into a cold tyranny and ending in a dark despair. Freud's thought develops from the notion that all destructive and self-defeating behavior is a perversion of a repressed and positive libido, to his late recognition of a negative instinct, the death wish, which for him is the desire to return to the original inorganic state, the hidden motive of the drive of self-preservation. Thanatos waxes as the generative tide of Eros, expressing the immortality of the germ plasm, wanes. But for Blake, Eros is not so limited a concept; it contains both Tharmas and Luvah; generation is superseded by regeneration; the living power of Tharmas is simultaneously a formal principle, wanting to unfold a human nature, a tongue that contains the Word, while Luvah is as much the fire in the loins as the love that seeks a harmony of parts. Thanatos remains for Blake a perversion of Selfhood, which, though it parallels Freud's notion of self-preservation, is not an instinct but an error that can be superseded, the negation of instincts which, for Blake, are essentially positive. Blake's Thanatos is the accuser who makes man see his nature as sinful and puts in him the fear of death, a detached and ironic intellect which mocks man with his fate. Blake's vision reverses Freud's at the last; the apocalypse finally is the assurance that life will triumph over death. For Freud, repression would always be necessary to civilization; for Blake, the highest civilization is the liberty of Jerusalem, which is not a chaotic anarchy of irrational impulse but the faith that man's deepest instincts are communal and integrative, and that therefore their fullest freedom would result in harmonious unity of each man and all men: "genuine religious experience . . . is a structural experience. Far from being an inchoate and vague expression of the emotions, it is an experience which is ordered."[3] How different this description is from Freud's sense of religious feeling as "oceanic," which he identified with unconscious memory of the womb.

The difference is one of temperament and vision. For Freud, structure was imposed over instinct; Blake's certainty about the positive structure of human consciousness coming from deep within has its source in his own inner sight. In their view of creativity, the two men are also distinct. For Freud the creative impulse always involved *disguise;* dreams and art spoke the language of repressed and infantile desires, forbidden wishes wearing shapes and costumes designed to satisfy both it and the censoring superego, like the covert and some-

3. Joachim Wach, *Sociology of Religion* (Chicago: University of Chicago Press, 1962), p. 30.

times perverse sexual life which was carried on behind the façade of
Victorian respectability. For Blake the creative impulse was the revelation of human form, the enemy of disguise, the lifter of the veil of
illusion, the veils of Vala, and the weaving of the fallen Enitharmon
who had enmeshed men in the false nets of bad art and perverted
"natural religion." All the negative images of Blake are concerned with
concealment; disguise is the work of a truncated, "fallen" imagination;
true imagination, for him, what he called vision, was precisely that: the
clear "lineaments" of intellect and desire. Mystery was Rahab, the
Whore of Babylon, "Religion hid in War," "hidden Harlot." And in the
fallen world, given here in iron images suggestive of the Industrial
Revolution, the daughters of Los are the weavers of merely comforting
illusion, veils whose price is the inner suffering involved for those whose
creation must be deception:

> Men understand not the distress & the labour & sorrow
> That in the Interior Worlds is carried on in fear & trembling
> Weaving the shudd'ring fears & loves of Albion's Families.
> Thunderous rage the Spindles of iron, & the iron Distaff
> Maddens in the fury of their hands, weaving in bitter tears
> The Veil of Goats-Hair & Purple & Scarlet & fine twined Linen.
> (*Jerusalem*, Pl. 59, lines 50–55, p. 692)

Again, Blake embodies his belief; perhaps nowhere is final vision
given a less mysterious and more human form. Freud sees healing power
in lifting a veil to reveal an infant lust ravening after a forbidden
mother; for both men this is the false mystery that keeps men children,
in bondage to a destructive virgin, but for Freud it is primal, for Blake,
primal error, born of a separation from the female which is not birth,
but death—the dissociation of man's reason from his emotions which
ends by the objectification of the tender, emotional side in an elusive
and never-to-be-possessed "emanation." There is much that is similar in
these two views of the necessity to break out of the magic circle of the
elusive love projected on an object, but for Freud there is a kind of
near-Romantic sadness, a sense that in the best and most mature love
there is a residue of dissatisfaction because the satisfactions of the adult
are always the less than perfect substitutes for the original loved
mother. For Blake, however, infant joys are recapturable, not by
thwarted infants, but by imaginative man who is married to his creation; there is no distance in Jerusalem between what is imagined and
what is; the latter is the former. When Jesus repudiated his earthly
mother, which Blake emphasizes in *The Everlasting Gospel,* he was
remaking himself as creative man, the imaginative individual who rebuilds his life according to the dictates of intellect and desire; he is
capable of constructing a relationship to the world *more* satisfying than

the one with the natural mother; humanity is his father ("I am doing my Father's business"); his female side is the creation of his love, no longer an object but a form allowing for the fullest and freest play of all his powers.

What is missing in Blake's final vision is any trace of the censor; Eternal Man is self-accepting man, the concept of sin as alien to him as the spectral mind which creates it by rejecting one part of itself in favor of another. The innocence which is ignorance may desire the fallen Beulah world of the mother; the innocence which is reborn on the far side of experience has the wisdom which makes the creations of the virginal mind appear not as lost joys but as false images of the soul in flight—what Freud would call defense mechanism, the work of the Urizenic mind cut off from its emanation, Ahania (wisdom), a mind capable only of those rationalizations and projections which shield the soul from familiarity with its own intuitive nature and protect it from the struggles out of which vision comes. Worship of a loved one is disguised self-denial and self-abasement; it is also the most indulgent self-aggrandizement, since it ennobles the passive into the ideal. So with all "abstract" love: "He who would do good to another must do it in Minute Particulars:/General Good is the plea of the scoundrel, hypocrite & flatterer" (*Jerusalem*, Pl. 55, lines 60–61, p. 687). The harder effort of the active form of love is what Blake would seem to mean by the joining of man with his emanations; it is the form of enactment, never the fantasy of mental object substituted for active risk. Thus Jerusalem is a special creation; it is the form of humane actions made manifest. No longer, after the apocalypse, is Jerusalem "clos'd in the Dungeons of Babylon/Her form . . . held by Beulah's Daughters" (*Jerusalem*, Pl. 60, lines 39–40, p. 693); no longer do men "nurse unacted desires" while committing horrible crimes, crimes motivated by the desire to kill all those things they most fervently desire but fear they cannot realize, "Destroying by selfish affections the things that they most admire" (*Jerusalem*, Pl. 41, line 28, p. 669): equivalence, compassion, exuberant life. It is not righteousness that makes these values realizable, but its absence. "We are Men of like passions with others & pretend not to be holier than others" (*Jerusalem*, Pl. 52, p. 682); the prophetic wrath is reserved only for those—or for that spectral part of themselves—who set themselves above the human condition as judge, who have the mistaken temerity to blaspheme their own life.

It is not necessary to believe, with Blake, that human evolution was already determined in the first seeds of life, as an oak is stored in an acorn, nor that full human consciousness is the mirror and destined end of the life process, in order to perceive the imaginative rightness of a system of thought that makes human life the source and end of all human institutions. The breaking through of imaginative power in man is his legitimate Genesis story; it is the humanization of nature, rather than the dehumanization of man by "natural religion." If man does not create a world in his own image then he remains a fear-ridden alien in an oceanic world of time and space designed merely to obliterate the traces of his footprints. The "new heaven, new earth" of Blake's vision is, in fact, the projection onto the cosmos itself of deep consciousness; the internal homeostatic rhythms of the body, the systole and diastole of its heart, the fires of its internal heat, the organs of its senses, the rivers of its blood, the luminosity of mind are directly perceived as unified form, perceived so powerfully that they are no longer felt as a self-enclosed organism but as the universe in which man lives:

> And Man walks forth from midst of the fires: the evil is all consum'd.
> His eyes behold the Angelic spheres arising night & day;
> The stars consum'd like a lamp blown out, & in their stead, behold
> The Expanding Eyes of Man behold the depths of wondrous worlds!
> One Earth, one sea beneath; nor Erring Globes wander, but Stars
> Of fire rise up nightly from the Ocean; & one Sun
> Each morning, like a New born Man, issues with songs & joy
> Calling the Plowman to his labour & the Shepherd to his rest.
> ("Fourth Zoa," IX, lines 827–34, p. 379)

It is the time again, as the black preachers say, when God walked the earth as a natural man. The corporeality of Blake's vision would seem to contradict his repudiation of nature, his insistence that the true eye is not of the mortal body and that man must escape a fallen nature to live most fully. But the contradiction disappears when it is seen that Blake understands that the external world of nature is inhuman, and that man's freedom from its indifferent laws comes precisely of the recognition that his internal climate is his true home, and that only the fullest imaginative perception of that internal landscape can transform the outer world into the forms of the harmony discerned within. Modern science suggests that this inversion of the way the world is usually perceived has, in fact, a solid evolutionary basis:

> Close to a hundred years ago the great French medical scientist Claude Bernard observed that the stability of the inside environment of complex organisms must be maintained before an outer freedom can be achieved from their immediate surroundings. What Bernard meant was profound but simple to illustrate.
> He meant that for life to obtain relative security from its fickle and dangerous outside surroundings the animal must be able to sustain stable, unchanging conditions within the body. Warm-blooded mammals and birds can continue to move about in winter; insects cannot. Warm-blooded animals such as man, with

his stable body temperature, can continue to think and reason in outside temperatures that would put a frog to sleep in a muddy pond or roll a snake into a ball in a crevice. In winter latitudes many of the lower creatures are forced to sleep part of their lives away.

Many millions of years of evolutionary effort were required before life was successful in defending its internal world from the intrusion of the heat or cold of the outside world of nature. . . . this hard-won victory is what creates the ever-active brain of the mammal as against the retarded sluggishness of the reptile.

A steady metabolism has enabled the mammals and also the birds to experience life more fully and rapidly than cold-blooded creatures. . . . Inside, we might say, has fought invading outside, and inside, since the beginning of life, by slow degrees has won the battle of life. If it had not, man, frail man with his even more fragile brain, would not exist.

Unless fever or some other disorder disrupts this internal island of safety, we rarely think of it. Body controls are normally automatic, but let them once go wrong and outside destroys inside. This is the simplest expression of the war of nature—the endless conflict that engages the microcosm against the macrocosm.

Since the first cell created a film about itself and elected to carry on the carefully insulated processes known as life, the creative spark has not been generalized. Whatever its principle may be it hides magically within individual skins. To the day of our deaths we exist in an inner solitude that is linked to the nature of life itself. Even as we project love and affection upon others we endure a loneliness which is the price of all individual consciousness—the price of living.

It is, though overlooked, the discontinunity beyond all others: the separation both of the living creature from the inanimate and of the individual from his kind. These are star distances. In man, moreover, consciousness looks out isolated from its own body. The body is the true cosmic prison, yet it contains, in the creative individual, a magnificent if sometimes helpless giant. John Donne, speaking for that giant in each of us, said: "Our creatures are our thoughts, creatures that are borne Gyants. . . . My thoughts reach all, comprehend all. Inexplicable mystery; I their Creator am in a close prison, in a sick bed, anywhere, and any one of my Creatures, my thoughts, is with the Sunne and beyond the Sunne, overtakes the Sunne, and overgoes the Sunne in one pace, one steppe, everywhere."

This thought, expressed so movingly by Donne, represents the final triumph of Claude Bernard's interior microcosm in its war with the macrocosm. Inside has conquered outside. The giant confined in the body's prison roams at will among the stars. More rarely and more beautifully, perhaps, the profound mind in the close prison projects infinite love in a finite room. This is a crossing beside which light-years are meaningless. It is the solitary key to the prison that is man.[4]

This passage has been quoted at length because it complements in so seminal a way the insights of Blake's vision, suggesting how man both protects and projects himself, asserting in cosmic terms his freedom from external nature through the adaptive processes of his own interior. The quote from Donne recalls Blake's "giant forms," the subterranean giants liberated by the imagination, giants whose function seems the preservation of the victory of inner over outer, both the guardians of the "minute particulars" where the fullest life is found and the expansion of those particulars into a transcendent macrocosm which defeats the isolating exteriority of a nature which has made separate cells the condition of life's survival. Only in the imaginative reconstitution of his world can man open the cells of his prison, while preserving their integrity and his own continuance. Expectedly enough, the giants reappear when the outer world impinges most directly on the inner, threatening, like a fever, to disrupt its harmony; and the giants of vision are Promethean; their genius is not the mere reinstatement of harmony as if the outer world did not exist, but a creative adaptation to that world which preserves equilibrium by reconstructing interior forms in an altered relationship to a changed environment which keeps man ascendant: "Inside has conquered outside." Man's consciousness makes him the least specialized of animals; the one least dependent on a relatively unchanged external world for the maintenance of his life; the one being, finally, least cyclical in nature. If Blake's imagination is able to escape the cycles which his earlier vision presented to him, it is because he works through to a new synthesis, which, while formally consistent with prophetic visions of the past, deals specifically with the rigidities of the orthodox Christianity of his day, a market economy and a growing materialistic view. Blake was able to separate the fossils of an earlier adaptation from the living matter of a new vision; in his imagery, a harrowing of a hardened earth of uninspired thought to permit a new and larger human growth. And Blake shares with other prophets the sense that his vision is the final one, because it is precisely the extent of the power of consciousness in his own mind, an enlargement past which the imagination in his own time could not go.

In earlier times, myths were articles of belief and myth-dreams

4. Loren Eiseley, *The Invisible Pyramid* (New York: Charles Scribner's Sons, 1970), pp. 47–49.

needed no defenders. In the eighteenth century, man was intoxicated with his rationality, and directed on his own creations the same cold and dissecting light which he turned on the natural world without. The imagination, in such straitened conditions, in order to satisfy a more developed intellect, had to bring its own processes to light, to argue for a new vision which was its own emancipation and, at the same time, defense. Imagination had to be shown to contain intellect in order to win the intellect to its side. The Promethean myth, and others resembling it, is possibly the ages deep memory, or at least retelling, of the original imaginative act which enabled man to survive on a crippled earth during and after the ice age; the stolen fire is literal, the new culture actual. For Blake the furnaces of Los are both actual and allegorical; the life energy of the imagination must be seen as the central need of man in the new ice age of Urizenic intellect; the combat of life against a world growing emotionally cold must be raised to a new, and more conscious, level. The two sets of complementary images which Blake gives negative weight are images of imagination grown sick, invaded, as it were, from outside. They are the two aspects of death, as Sylvia Plath imagined them: "the marmoreal coldness of Blake's death mask, say, hand in glove with the fearful softness of worms, water and other katabolists."[5] The Urizenic aspect of death-in-life is the world of abstraction, cold-bloodedness, stone, caves, ice, snow, desert, void, and frozen form. The empty reaches of mathematical space had somehow invaded man's interior, disturbed his equilibrium, left him locked in icy abstraction which had no use for his more sensitive side; at the same time, this detached order made his experience of the cosmos a kind of vertigo, a mind unmoored from its affective side and left to hurtle through the inhuman void of a mechanistic universe. The other side of man, cut off from intellect, is left to blindly vegetate; here are the fibrous images— the roots, the Polypus, the wormlike tendrils that call to mind the paintings of Hieronymus Bosch, and the snakelike and over-nervous vegetable arabesques of Art Nouveau. The two sides of exterior nature are here internalized: the green vegetable world and the gray inorganic one. The breakup of the prevalent world order, unholy to Blake, thus begins with the image of its own sickness: green snakes crawl out of a dead Pharoah's pyramid, signs of death and new signs, too, of an unearthly spring. The graphics of the modern M. C. Escher are the visual counterpart of this Blakean insight, a geometric world out of whose compulsively ordered designs crawl lizards and wormlike creatures on little wheels. More powerfully, the red Orc bursts up from below, in an

5. Sylvia Plath, quoted in "Sylvia Plath and Confessional Poetry," by M. L. Rosenthal, in *The Art of Sylvia Plath*, ed. Charles Newman (Bloomington: Indiana University Press, 1971), p. 70.

outpouring of libidinal energy, only to end nailed up in serpent form on the vegetative tree of good and evil, the generalizing principle turned against and deforming life's human form. The earlier poems of Blake, in which Urizen figures so largely and is so richly imagined, reflect his own internal struggles with a Urizenic intellect, a figure who fades in power by the time of the writing of *Jerusalem,* when he is known by his presence in the world and less and less by his presence in Blake's mind. Political tyrant, abstract reasoner, accusing conscience, hypocritical convention—all these detached tyrants fuse in the functional economy of mythic image. Against this figure are ranged the unifying powers of life, assisted by imagination as their central form, a form whose delineation grows in complexity and visualizing power, borrowing Urizen's intellectual power even as the earlier negative potency of the Urizenic forms decline.

It is interesting to note how the imaginative forms for the twin sickness of abstraction and naturalism can find no truer shapes than the ones suggested by Eiseley's comments quoted earlier, both regressive: the inorganic matter out of which life arose, a mental order divorced from human significance; and the reptilian forms of those halfway creatures less insulated from the outer world, as if human life, deserted by intellect and unprotected by the internal manifestation of full consciousness, were drawn back to an earlier evolutionary incarnation, imagining itself internally transformed into dragonlike creatures who are themselves little more than coldblooded thermometers planted in nature's side.

If Blake discovered, after his early championing of political revolution, that the evil ran deeper than that particular cure, he was able, simultaneously, to see this early error as a failure of imagination, a failure which is recorded in *The Book of Los,* a poem which stands as a compelling embodiment of the birth of imagination, making powerfully present the unifying process begun in Blake's mind, even while criticizing the limitations of an imaginative force too taken with its own new-found powers of vision. To follow Blake's canon chronologically is to watch the visible evolution of an enormous visionary imagination; *The Book of Los* is an invaluable document in that astonishing progression.

The birth and liberation of Los is, simultaneously, the genesis of life and light on earth, embodying Blake's belief that the ontogeny of the imagination recapitulates phylogeny, a phylogeny which is mythic as opposed to natural evolution, a return, through fall, to its own Edenic origins. Thus the imagination, which generates life out of its own higher consciousness, must fall with man into nature, error, and experience and move through them to the resurrection of its dismembered parts in the unity of its original state. Imaginative man wakes in bondage, breaks his chains, and mounts into the uncreated void, all rage and energy, so wild he frightens away the fires with which he would forge his materials into creative life, and so is left in darkness, imprisoned in impenetrable rock. The next movement of consciousness involves destruction of the solid state in which outer order has imprisoned its first rebellion, as each stage of growth finds new obstacles which must be overcome; thus Los splinters the "vast solid" and begins his long and vertiginous fall, through eons of time and space, raging and flailing like a newborn infant, until "wrath subsided,/And contemplative thoughts first arose" (*Book of Los*, Pl. 4, lines 39–40, p. 258). The fall is through "Error," the vacuity of the negation of true form, a form whose creation begins with dawning consciousness. Then the angle of fall becomes "oblique," as if the artist had discovered his necessary method, and the creation begins: "Branchy forms organizing the Human/Into finite flexible organs" (*Book of Los*, Pl. 4, lines 44–45, p. 258); man's body is to be the beginning and the end of creation, though the "Branchy forms" announce that this is fallen, vegetative image-making.

As the falling mind organizes itself, it begins to humanize its world; thus it creates an element in which it may move, and lungs begin to heave. But what the mind has not perceived pulls man, like a dead weight, back to the death of consciousness, of drowning, which may lead to a new awakening: "And the unformed part crav'd repose;/Sleep began; the Lungs heave on the wave:/Weary, overweigh'd, sinking beneath/In a stifling black fluid, he woke" (*Book of Los*, Pl. 4, lines 59–62, p. 258). Los, unlike weaker imaginations, will not drown; the immersion awakens him and he struggles to bring the rest of himself to form. Here Blake reveals again that this is to be the perverse genesis of a partial imagination, for the forms he creates are the "immense Fibrous Form" of vegetative, generative man, not the creation of a human form so much as a passive imitation of the natural growth of the outer nature. But this fallen form enrages Los with the beginning of prophetic wrath; his anger brings him up once again from the floods into which he had again sunk, and rage divides the dead matter from the living energy, which rises up in the fires that will permit Los to forge his vision: "Then Light first began" (*Book of Los*, Pl. 5, line 10, p. 259).

But the Being of Los is still dualistic, as the attempt to create by separation reveals; the moment light breaks, error is revealed; "Los beheld/Forthwith, writhing upon the dark void,/The back bone of Urizen appear" (*Book of Los*, Pl. 5, lines 12–14, p. 259). In a beautiful superimposition of imagery, Blake has Los see the backbone as serpent and iron chain, serpentine life force perverted into dead bone and the rigid structure that bound man "upright," frozen under the rule of the divided mind of "moral virtue" in its unforgiving tyranny, a tyranny which mirrors Los's error in separating energy from matter, rather than animating nature with human energy. Urizen here is dismembered, his structure separate from his body, a hybrid fragment of dehumanized, split form, which combines in a single image the twin forms of death mentioned earlier—the inorganic solid of cold abstraction and the flowing, vegetative, reptilian forms of half-formed, unintegrated feeling. Here too is the basic unity Blake had discovered in Orc and Urizen, the serpent Orc hardening through inevitable cycles into the chain of Urizenic bondage, as the rebellious son hardens into the tyrannous father, inspired revolution into tyrannous statehood.

Horrified by what his vision reveals, Los begins the construction of his furnaces, his anvil and hammer, the body heat and beating heart and "rage for order" which are the sources of artistic creation. His first act is the binding of Urizen; his second is to beat the down-flowing particles of light into the Orb of vision. This fiery Orb he heats in his Furnaces' "infinite wombs" through the ages, paralleling the slow, and as yet embryonic, maturing of vision. Los has created an image of the Sun, "self-balanc'd," and smiles with a joy which is soon to be revealed as too complacent, for the vision has as yet no true imaginative life; it is, rather, a "glowing illusion." The Orb is somehow generalized vision, an image of unity and light, but without "particularity," without the lineaments of the human form which must grow and fill the glowing orb; the orb is not yet transformed into the fulfilled human visionary eye. Thus, when Los binds the spine of Urizen onto the fiery orb, Urizen's split nature is demonically revitalized: "Till his Brain in a rock & his Heart/in a fleshy slough formed four rivers/Obscuring the immense Orb of fire/Flowing down into night" (Book of Los, Pl. 5, lines 52–55, p. 260).

Judging by the works which precede and follow The Book of Los, Blake here sits in judgment on his earlier vision and prepares for the fuller vision which will follow; he seems to be saying that a partial vision had seen the world flooded with apocalyptic light, had loaned its inspiration to revolution, thinking to bind tyranny to the fiery energy of its new image of unity, finding itself at last feeding a new tyranny in its fires, tainted within by its own righteous spectre, watching its millennium abort into "a Human Illusion/In darkness and deep clouds involv'd" (Book of Los, Pl. 5, lines 56–57, p. 260). The dual nature of man as Urizen-Orc, tyrant and victim, rock brain and fibrous heart, is reanimated in the four fallen "Zoas"; the apocalypse was yet to come. Blake continued his enquiry into the depths of the human psyche, carrying forward in imagination that deeper revolution which attacked

The Uncommon Eye   65

the *malaise* of the dualistic European soul, and left a document of the successful transformation of the soul in his "Bible of Hell," releasing the living powers from that hell to which Christian and Deist alike had condemned them; the growing tip of Western consciousness would be a century and more beginning to see the futurity Blake's imagination had opened up out of time.

What Blake provides, above all, is the missing link between religious vision and creative imagination, a link which had been lost when vision was split off from established religion and lost its integral connection with communal life. From the seventeenth century on, Western man, or at least the elite who created society's forms, demoted the dream life to the world of illusion and unreason, and with the growth of the bourgeois, captialistic world view, increasingly saw poetry and art in general as either a didactic and conscious instrument of their own narrow moral pieties, whose images were little more than analogies that easily came unglued from the generalities they represented, or as a mimetic mirror of their own social world. At worst, poetry was seen as the frivolous luxury of the effeminate dreamer, a kind of sickly, parasitic vine on the tougher fibres of the Darwinian evolutionary tree of those more fitted for survival. The creative energies of the society were given over to the Industrial Revolution, to the excitements of the new science, and to the sceptical and satirical dismemberment of the old gods who had kept men dreaming so long.

If Blake overstated the case for the imagination against the prevailing rational winds of his time, it is understandable; only from a later vantage point is it possible to see how much his imagination assimilated of Enlightenment thought, how much his ability to see so clearly the process going on in his own psyche was heightened by the analytic tools they gave him. Partly, the Enlightenment was self-justification and rationalization; partly it was authentic growth of knowledge and consciousness in a changing world, an outgrowing of old cultural clothes. Blake tended to overlook this second fact because of the first and because his ethical sense was so deep and so creative that he was able to do what the thinkers of his day could not—reconstruct and revalue the mythic forms which they had deconstructed and devalued. Yet it was their demolition of old forms that precipitated the crisis which empowered Blake's imagination; it is impossible to imagine Blake's "Bible of Hell" without the almost satanic glee with which a Voltaire pulled down the old Judeo-Christian firmament, stars, saints, and all, and the divine right kings with them. But, while Blake shared their hatred of false gods and tyranny, he did not share their optimism about the new mercantile order; it was the poor man, Blake said, who set Los singing: the slaves, the colonized, the exploited, and the suffering self within, all the victims of the new tyrannies; Blake's mind looked squarely at the evils that conventional morality hid from itself, offering the first major critique of a new age even as it was consolidating its strength. Blake's genius was too strong not to feel the weight of the new system on his mind; he lived through in full the crisis that would not come fully to society till our own time. Blake did not have to prophesy mass slaughter, exploitation, the selling of souls in the market place, men who divided themselves in order to conquer; this was already existent in the world about him. The contradictions Blake saw are now all too apparent; what his ability to feel the still hidden crisis provided was an apocalyptic defense of inner life, of imagination itself, a revelation of the restorative and transformational power of vision that joins the prophetic and poetic in one paradigm and offers an image of radiant health, fully envisioned, which helps to illuminate the despair of so many of the imaginative minds that followed him in time but could not follow him in vision. And his work helps equally to illuminate the mythic renaissance in art in our own century, and to suggest why it happens that the modern artist moves back into the cultural mainstream that increasingly looks to him for the prophetic voice that will illuminate and resolve its growing sense of crisis. From Freud on, the inner world that Blake explored becomes revalued, and after Blake, who brings so much to light, it seems hardly necessary to apologize for seeing in religious and artistic vision the same imaginative process at work. "It is merely an attempt to complete the humanist revolution," writes Northrop Frye,

> ... to point out that the conception of the Classical in art and the conception of the scriptural or canonical in religion have always tended to approximate one another; that the closer the approximation, the healthier it is for both religion and art; that on this approximation the authority of humane letters has always rested, and that the sooner they are identified with each other the better. Such a cultural revolution would absorb not only the Classical but all other cultures into a single visionary synthesis, deepen and broaden the public response to art, deliver the artist from the bondage of a dingy and nervous naturalism ...
> The great value of Blake is that he insists so urgently on this question of an imaginative icongraphy, and forces us to learn so much of its grammar in reading him.[6]

Blake, then, provides a visionary grammar, offering, like the myth-dreams of the prophets, both diagnosis and cure, and like them shed-

---

6. Northrop Frye, *Fearful Symmetry: A Study of William Blake* (Princeton, N. J.: Princeton University Press, 1969), pp. 420-21.

ding light on those powerful but darkened imaginations in whom growth has been turned, cancer-like, into destruction. It is this symptomatic art with which our own age is so familiar, of those artists who grappled with what Spengler has called our Faustian culture, and lost. Using Blake's iconography as our Virgil, we enter the modern hell first fully formed in English literature in the work of Thomas Lovell Beddoes, where another set of very different giant forms takes shape, and a negative apocalypse, almost a mirror image of Blakean restorative vision, erupts, in a world of monstrous egos, demonic wills, rejected tenderness, and living dead. Here will be explored an art of diagnosis rather than of cure, with an attempt to understand a suicidal imagination, and to sense how the imagination, of whose restorative powers so much has been made, can fail to cure.

If Blake's vision identifies him with the imaginative paradigm of prophetic vision in crisis-ridden societies, Beddoes' identifies him with a negative instance of crisis imagination, the epidemics of sorcery or "witch-hunting" which are symptomatic of social disorder. Belief in sorcery, or destructive magic, is a constant in most societies; its suspected outbreak in massive form is a sign of a deepening of social malaise which in more normal times is usually but a minor chord in the major movement of society. The fear of sorcery is the fear of negative impulses, of disorder, of entropy, of death, of all the fragmenting and divisive tendencies in mankind which are disproportionately large when the social structure itself is crumbling. Belief in sorcery both accedes to and attempts to control the demonic; the attempt to hunt down or mollify the sorcerer is society's attempt to extirpate or placate the powers of division and destruction. The sorcerer, unlike the shaman or the prophet, is the possessor of a destructive, rather than a curative, magic; he is thought to be the cause of disease, just as the other figures are its physicians. In the Christian West, these demonic men of the preliterate societies have their counterparts; Satan is the arch-sorcerer, and the demons who haunt the Christian imagination are his apprentices, while witches are the human agents of these negative forces. Connected with these figures, seemingly in all societies, are figures of the bestial and the grotesque, disfigured forms which offer miniature images of disorder, disharmony, the unnatural, the human invaded by the inhuman. The bat, uncanny hybrid of rodent and bird, bloodsucking, blind, and night-flying, is one such transformation of the vampire-like sorcerer; the familiars of witches, like black cats, crows, and owls, suggest the eerie prescience of dark spirits; in parts of Africa the sorcerer may transform himself into the jackal, the degraded beast who lives off carrion. Carrion eating is often associated with sorcery, as if to express intuitively that the sorcerer's power lives off death; in many of these societies, anyone seen near cemeteries at night is suspected of sorcery and may be thought to be involved, not only in eating the flesh of the dead, but in necrophilia, the copulation with the dead which again images the perversion of life energy into a love of death. The transformational magic of the sorcerer, whether it be his tendency to metamorphosis in his own body, or his ability to transform objects, is always in the direction of the grotesque, though, in a kind of unveiling of the process of ego defense mechanism, he may be capable of assuming beautiful shapes in order to lure his victim, until such time as he is willing to show his true monstrosity of form. When Moses turned his stick to a snake, he was warning the Pharaoh of his malign powers; in *Jerusalem*, Enitharmon flaunts her own perfect beauty and exposes to her horror, Hyle, the infant Love, as a hideous winding worm. The sorcerer's elixir, furthermore, is like an inversion of the alchemical process; it is a destructive potion or a poison distilled from an admixture of the ugliest ingredients: mandrake roots, toads, lizards, eye of newt. The very forms of the sorcerer's art betray their origins; the active imagination perceives as ugly that which is destructive of living order. What reveals decadence is precisely the beauty it finds in disease, the passive love it offers to its own sickness, like Huysmans playing the violin while staring with enchanted eyes at his beloved's disfiguring pock marks.

There is an ambivalence which surrounds the figure of the sorcerer in preliterate societies; he can be both hated and admired, destroyed or protected; in some societies, the suspicion of sorcery is tantamount to death or exile; in others, it draws a kind of magic circle around the man, making others willing to go a long way to appease him and to avoid his wrath. Then too, societies are of two minds about the practice of malign magic: if it is seen as justified, then the sorcerer is seen as the injured party and compensation will make him desist; on the other hand, the sorcerer may be regarded as wholly unnatural, an antisocial figure who will betray all human values and even turn his magic against his own kin. The first view of the sorcerer, as injured party, is an acceptance of guilt, presumably in matters where guilt can be admitted. But in matters of the deepest taboo, where the admission of guilt would involve more psychological pain than the mind can bear, the second kind of sorcerer comes to the fore; he becomes the lightning rod for the negative projections of his fellows—a symptom of displaced self-hatred, of repressed impulses involving the destruction of loved ones and kin, of unadmitted guilt for crimes covered over in the light of day, and of the ever-present fears of disease, dismemberment, or death. It is easy to see why witch-hunts crop up in societies threatened at large by plague, famine, or social dismemberment, when both fear and self-hatred are general, for it is both usual for men to assume guilt for their own misfortunes, and, when it becomes unbearable or seems unforgivable, to escape its pain by projecting it onto those figures who are alien or deformed enough to seem to embody malignity. Belief in sorcery of this sort is always a symptom and never a cure; it leaves, as has been suggested, the causes of social malaise untouched. It acts out negative impulses against the wrong objects; it is repetitive, like the internal violence that often characterizes colonized or ghettoized peoples, and is a symptom of fear and a disguised expression of violence toward the self. It is, finally, covert acquiescence in the master's or accuser's voice.

Apocalyptic vision has, of course, an opposite effect; it reinterprets humiliation and removes its sting, saves the soul from feeling guilt for its own oppression, which is the last nail in the coffin of despair. "The last shall be first" identifies the fallen with the chosen and begins the work of self and social repair. Sorcery epidemics, on the other hand, are a holding action, an active form of secret despair, and an inability to believe in or find a way to change. At root, society understands that a sorcerer is incapable of love because his self-love is injured—the dour, the bitter, the isolate, the ugly, the unloved, may be identified as the sorcerer; the desire to hunt him down is the desire to extirpate that threatening image of themselves *without actually changing*. The desire to kill the "Double," the "Shadow," the "Other," as this rejected part of the self has been variously called, leads always to brother murdering brother, to racism and genocide, and never to that wholeness where brothers unite to overthrow and form a new "Father."

A society's feeling that a sorcery epidemic is under way, that there is a "red conspiracy" or a league of demons preying on their tribe, is, above all, a way of containing and giving form to disorder, to relate it to a larger order of which it is but an "evil" part, and to provide an avenue of at least symbolic action against it. It is, again, a holding action of the old order, sensing its disintegration but trying to prevent the breaking through of the grotesque, the imaginative parallel to disorder, the abyss that opens under the feet when the solid ground of significance gives way. In a stable order the grotesque is no more than the occasional leering face of a gargoyle on a great cathedral; but when the parts of man, and the relationships of his world to each other and to himself, no longer cohere, then the grotesque, whose parts mock each other and annihilate coherence and harmony itself, may overwhelm the mind. The grotesque is radical satire, the vision of the estranged man in a permanently deranged world which belongs to death; in Bonaventura's *Night Watch*, the narrator tells us that satire is the next to last mask which removes all the other masks and covers "the last, permanent one which neither cries nor laughs—the skull without hair or tresses, with which the tragicomedian exits."[7] The skull is the last mask, and what it conceals is nothing.

In order to see how the sorcerer of preliterate societies with his malign magic shades imperceptibly into the satirist of literate societies, and how that figure may enlarge and take the center of the stage as the radical satirist, or nihilist, as order disintegrates, it is necessary to pause here and trace, following Robert Elliott in his book *The Power of Satire*, a venerable tradition from its roots in magic to its modern literary counterparts: the poet-satirist whose invective could kill, but who was also considered useful in driving out "evil influence through the magic potency of abuse."[8]

Greek comedy grew out of fertility rites, and its satirical side, according to Elliott who got it from Aristotle, grew out of the iambic verses incorporated in the earlier Phallic Songs, verses which interrupted these joyful hymns to life with abusive and often obscene attacks against malign influences in the community. Satire and invective, which are related generically to the sorcerer's curse, were barbs intended to kill, but to kill what threatened the community, and, often, those who had injured the satirist as well. The killing was symbolic; it was the destruction of a good name by a bad one, a psychological killing that, as in the legend of Archilochus, could drive its victims to actual death. Thus, "the iambic verses of a major poet, expressive of his hate, his will to destroy, his mockery, were believed to exert some kind of malefic power. The power seems to have resided, not in secret, esoteric spells or in the mechanics of sympathetic magic, but in the character of the poet himself—in his command over the word. The word could kill; and in popular belief it *did* kill."[9] Elliott traces the same institution of powerful satirical poets in Arabia and Ireland, pointing out that the invective of these bards was feared as had been the ancient curse; that they, protected by this fear, were often the scourge of men in high place, men ordinarily immune to criticism. It is easy to see in the figure of Jarwal ibn Aus, called the Dwarf, a seventh century A.D. poet who played this role, a parallel to the court jester, often deformed, whose mockery of princes helped purge the court of the otherwise inexpressible resentments against the ruler and the injustices of his rule. Whether satirist-poet or court fool, the bitter tongue was always in danger of stinging itself, for society set limits even to its institutionalized abusers: the poet who satirized unjustly was believed to have his curse turn on himself; the jester who abused his position was likely

7. Robert C. Elliott, *The Power of Satire: Magic, Ritual, Art* (Princeton, N.J.: Princeton University Press, 1970), p. 60.
8. *Ibid.*, p. 5.
9. *Ibid.*, pp. 14–15.

to fall from favor. Thus, within a relatively stable order, the satirist, like the sorcerer, had his uses in draining off malign energies, exposing evil to ridicule, acting finally as a safety valve that maintained the larger order, inhibiting actions which might result in ridicule, and perhaps bringing about some minor modifications in the internal balance of power and respect.

The malign magic of the sorcerer and the satirist are similar; the problem with both is separating the malignity of the man from the malign which he attacks; this, in fact, becomes the chief question which self-conscious satire asks itself: how far is the satirist implicated in that which he attacks? Undoubtedly something cold in the viciousness of satire's venom undercuts the humanity its barbs are designed to defend, which is why people tread lightly near the satirist, never counting on his good will. Yet it is precisely this coldness that makes the satirist such an expert and unrelenting dissector of the anatomy of human follies, even while the viciousness of his attacks testifies to some "infinitely suffering thing" within himself, some injury which can never heal over and which his own barbs seem continually to be lancing. But let someone else so much as touch this tender spot and he becomes pure venomous attack. He who attacks everyone can not himself be touched.

Thus, even in relatively normal times, the satirist is a special case, a man cut off somehow from full human love, partially excluded from community, intolerant of weakness in himself and unforgiving of it in others, secretly rejoicing in the sowing of discord because it makes him feel himself master of the discord in his own soul—as a divided state can only be held together by tyranny. He is like the Greek goddess Eris who is not invited to the wedding—for men wish to banish discord—and so throws in the golden apple "For the Fairest," which will set the gods themselves at war and end in the destruction of a civilization. Eris seems, in fact, the very muse of satire, for her disruptive act exposes the vanity and weakness which are as immortal as the gods.

Distrust, suspicion, competition, and vanity are normal parts of any society; the mythic and social structures tend to reduce these potentially divisive elements by stressing love, confidence, equivalence, and amity—the communal or bonding values which seem innate in the full range of human instincts. The balance is upset when the communal order becomes antisocial, that is, when it stresses the very same values which it is intended to counteract. The colonial order and the individualistic capitalist society share this same inherent reinforcement of divisiveness: the colonial order, superimposed on the tribal one, sows distrust among the members of the tribe, punishes one for the crimes of another, encourages loyalty to the master at the expense of loyalty to one's brothers. This larger order is itself perceived by the colonized person as arbitrary, unpredictable, and largely inscrutable. His existential situation, then, resembles closely the world described by the modern alienated absurdist. The experience of the latter grows in part out of a system which similarly reinforces distrust, suspicion, and competition, turning man against man with the social edict that working for one's private profit will somehow mysteriously result in the promotion of the public good. Thus interpersonal values are subverted and made subservient to selfish ones, so that there is no longer any constructive tension between preservation of self and of species which adaptive culture must always provide.

The death of god, then, is not only a metaphysical void but a concrete one—the disappearance of community and the sense of an order that assures it, and it is the genius of the apocalyptic imagination to re-imagine a world with these communal values restored. Since the social or loving instinct is part of man, as the anguish of alienation argues, the individual mind will suffer from internal division that mirrors that of his society, and insofar as he contains the corruption of order which marks his society, his art—while attacking it—will also mirror it. A man of powerful imagination cannot help hating the corrupt world he perceives, but insofar as he is hopelessly implicated in it, divided against himself, he can only fervently desire and imagine its destruction, and his with it. Whether the rotten world persists or is destroyed, he loses; the point is not to be passive—the last throes of the life force. Thus is loosed on the world the imagination of the grotesque with its doomsday vision.

In a world perceived as discordant by many, the satirist is no longer peripheral; in the twilight of the gods, when the world seems a cemetery or a madhouse, the prowler of cemeteries with the "Night Watch" vision becomes central, as he has in our own time. Thus the desire to rescue Beddoes from his undeserved obscurity and to explore his vision at length stems from his precocious modernity, his manifestly powerful poetic voice, and the way in which his despairing and demonic vision offers the negative image of a century whose contradictions he suffered and articulated at a time when they remained hidden to most men. Many of our own artists and thinkers share his sense that these contradictions are incurable, that they are in the nature of things and men. This view must be examined, as it stands in direct antithesis to the more optimistic vision which had its roots in the same historical time and place that brought Beddoes to despair, the vision of Karl Marx to which the last chapter will return. Beddoes came of age in England when the great Romantics had already done their work; when the positivistic spirit of Victorian England had won the day, the actual world had declared the futility of poetry and the "unacknowledged legislators of the world" were without a kingdom. Turning against his own early poetic bent, Beddoes left England after his undergraduate days to become a graduate student of anatomy in Germany. There .he became a doctor, though he remained secretly a poet, and became involved in the radical movement of the 1830's—the move for liberal and democratic reform in which so many young German intellectuals of the day were caught up. In the still feudal and absolutist Germany, the democratic ideals of liberty and rationality—for which Beddoes was a passionate partisan—were hopelessly distant from the actual world. Suppression of the reformers by the government led to Beddoes' exile to Zurich, and to the defection of many of his compatriots to the quietism of University chairs.

The triumph of German absolutism and the betrayal by so many reformers of the cause they had espoused were to feed Beddoes' despair of effective action in a world that seemed equally to mock poetic and political aspiration, a world which to him revealed the former as impotent, the latter as ultimately demonic. He had come to sense the absolutism with which the idealistic German protest against it was infected, an infection he shared; his moral revulsion, predicated on ideals whose attempted realization only seemed to reveal their source in an overweening ambition, found its embodiment in a poetic drama, written and rewritten during those years, the grotesque and spectral *Death's Jest Book* which was born, like its necromancer Ziba, from the loins of a dead mother, as the nihilist-satirist is always born from the corpse of his own ideals.

To his English friends and literary peers, Beddoes' work seemed merely "mad," the production of a failed artist with ghostly dreams. Their rejection of Beddoes, however, must be seen as their inability to absorb and their desire to repress what he revealed, so distant from their optimistic temper, so far beyond anything else in the English literature of the time in the modernity of its radical pessimism about the nature of man, the irrational animal mocked alike by his reason and his moral sense. Preserved only as a minor lyrical poet by a few non-representative but palatable pieces in Victorian anthologies, the real Beddoes was lost—the poet so astonishingly contemporary in his vision, with its completely atheistic world-view, its questioning of the signification of language, its dissolution of personality through loss of outside attachments, the destruction of logic by its own instruments, its mocking annihilation of artistic conventions, the surrealism of its primal images, and its creation of an essentially absurdist world—grotesque, self-parodying, nihilistic. For if his dreams were pale, his nightmares were far from insubstantial; they were powerfully realized in his poetry and gnawed on real flesh. The satirical poet resembles the sorcerer—he reveals to society its own sickness, attacking and gnawing the vitals of his own kind, no more the enemy of humanity than humanity appears to be the enemy of itself. Given the foregoing discussion, it is hardly surprising that the central character of *Death's Jest Book* should be a court fool, Isbrand, who combines the traditional satirist's role with that of what has been called the radical satirist, destroyer of order and creator of the grotesque; for Isbrand, like the Jacobean malcontent whom he echoes, is also an avenger, a great hater as well as a cold and mocking analyst, who plots to kill the tyrant Duke and usurp the crown of the master whom he so closely resembles. The choice of the Jacobean revenge hero, a kind of Hamlet without compunction, is not so much a question of influence as of similarity of mind and situation; the corruption and cynicism of the Jacobean world, against the background of an inflexible moral sense, is a world whose predicament mirrors Beddoes' own. For the world of Beddoes' poetic drama, despite its Elizabethan-Jacobean style, the ghost of English Romanticism that haunts it, and the strain of the English Gothic that runs through it, resembles most closely the new art of the grotesque which had taken shape in German Romanticism, in Jean Paul, E. T. A. Hoffman, Büchner, and others, so that both the study of anatomy and the country of exile which Beddoes had so consciously chosen seemed almost demonically suited to heighten the division he already carried within him, and to bring him at last to the suicide which was the final victory of the grotesque vision.

The division of Beddoes, as has been suggested, was peculiar to him, and yet it was only a slightly distorted mirror of the division inherent in his age. He combined in himself three major and conflicting tendencies which were also those of his time: the Romantic idealist, the Faustian power-seeker, and the rational scientist. Just as Romanticism had defined itself in opposition to the world of society and had remained cut off from real effect on or penetration into the powers of the world, so the sensitive, loving side of man was divorced from his intellectual powers and will, giving those powers, as Blake had understood, demonic and increasingly inhuman shapes. The sensitive suffering side of Beddoes was, from the time of his early work, in love with death, the escape of Romanticism into eternity carried, as Frye saw, to its natural conclusion; his will, unchecked by loving attachments in a life apparently celibate and certainly isolate, was left to rage for power in a joyless, soulless world it hated; his intellect to mock at the ghost of its own hope and the ultimate impotence of its own will. The insoluble nature of his conflict is already evident in *The Brides' Tragedy*, his first poetic drama, written at nineteen; the maturation of his intellect could only deepen the division in his later work, as it heightened his awareness, giving him a grim and hilarious objectivity on his own dilemma, leading his art from the pathetic to the grotesque. Thus, as the rift in Beddoes' divided self deepened, the satirist/sorcerer evolved out of the suffering, death-haunted young Romantic poet.

The Brides' Tragedy is based on a true story of a young man who murdered his low-born secret bride in order to get on in the world, a story that drew Beddoes for reasons which will become increasingly obvious. The play is a series of psychological seductions of three innocent women by a deceiving and self-deceived seducer, Hesperus— but the seductions are of a special sort—not sexual, but suicidal. First, his wife Floribel; then his new bride Olivia; and finally, Floribel's mother Lenora—three innocent, sugary, and relatively untroubled females, with the advent of Hesperus into their lives, turn their thoughts toward death, as Eros pales into Thanatos. Here, in extended dramatic form, is the central theme of Beddoes' peculiar brand of Romantic idealism, condensed in its archetypal form in the little "Tale of the Lover to His Mistress," in which Love comes one night to Psyche, but changed—more powerful, more sure with his arrows, more deadly. Here, turning the convention in his diabolic way, Beddoes has Love warn Psyche not to look at him:

> "Why should I not see then? art thou Love no more?"—"Aye, but not fleeting, earthly: eternal heavenly Love."—Just then the moon rose, and Psyche saw beside her a gaunt anatomy, through which the blue o' the sky shone and the stars twinkled, gold promises beaming through Death, armed with arrows, bearing an hour-glass. He stepped with her to the sea-side, and they sank where Venus rose.
> ("The Tale of the Lover to His Mistress," lines 16–22, p. 129) [10]

The reversal of convention is marvelous in its shock and consistent in its sense, and of a piece with *The Brides' Tragedy*. Fertility in life and eternity in death are perfectly confounded here: "they sank where Venus rose." Venus is the opposite of what is expected, for Venus, in the double sense Beddoes intends, is the evening star, herald of darkness and of the only consummation of love possible in Beddoes' world, the reunion of souls, and of man and nature, in the eternity beyond death, "the gold promises" of the stars. An alternate name for the star Venus is, of course, Hesperus, the portal star to night and death.

Psyche is the soul, and as Erich Neumann has suggested in his commentary on the myth of Amor and Psyche, the "eternal feminine,"

10. Thomas Lovell Beddoes, *The Works of Thomas Lovell Beddoes*, ed. H. W. Donner (London: Oxford University Press, 1935). All subsequent references are to this edition and will be given in parentheses in the text.

the guiding power not only of the maturing female personality, but the living ideal and loving guide of the creative personality in its quest for individuation. According to Neumann, the creative personality is guided by the "Lady"; it is her peculiar form of heroism, through love, that makes his quest to humanize the world successful. "In all these processes where 'Psyche leads' and the masculine follows her, the ego relinquishes its leading role and is guided by the totality. In psychic developments which prove to be centered round the nonego, the self, we have creative processes and processes of initiation in one."[11] It is revealing in Beddoes' version of the myth that Psyche sees Amor, not as the beautiful young man of the original myth but as a skeleton, and further, that she follows him without the separation and trials which lead to their final reunion; this male principle of ego-serving power and rationality dooms Beddoes' creative, loving side, condemning him to a life in which Amor will never be humanized by the power of Psyche. Nor will Venus, the mythic mother of Amor, subsumed in Beddoes' world to Hesperus, the female fecundating force transformed into the male evening star of evil omen.

Throughout Beddoes' canon, women serve as pale victims, mere phantoms really, of the power-maddened men who war with each other in their failed attempts to possess these powerless psyches. And the more primal female powers, the Mothers, are, in Beddoes, somehow dead to begin with: the primal memory, which haunts his work, is that of the infant in the horrifying arms of a dead nurse or mother—Leopold of the juvenile *Improvisatore,* Hesperus, Ziba of *Death's Jest Book*—all share this memory. The creative man, says Neumann, belongs to the Mothers, but the Mothers who cradle Beddoes are corpses, as are their daughters—like the dead wife of the Duke in *Death's Jest Book*, whom all the arts of necromancy cannot raise, or the fisherman's dead wife in that same play whose white face stares up at him, like a drowned moon, from the deep waters to which he had consigned her corpse. The creative or humanizing life force is thus equally dead, submerged and haunting—its ghost a reminder of what will *not* die, despite its exile from the living world.

The masculine ego is active in getting, in striving, but passive in love; while the psyche, passive in the power struggles of the world, is active in loving. Denying the psyche its active loving, Beddoes' ego is condemned to the permanent feeling of helplessness in love, and to the resistance against it which such vulnerability demands; and the ghost of that "womanish weakness" which Isbrand so abhores in his brother

11. Erich Neumann, *Amor and Psyche: The Psychic Development of the Feminine* (Princeton, N. J.: Princeton University Press, 1971), p. 151.

Wolfram in *Death's Jest Book* is the strength which can never chasten his ego and save him from himself. Thus the world that will emerge in Beddoes' poetry is one of monstrous, striving male egos, longing for love but bent on destruction, terrified of death precisely because, without the unifying, renewing power of Psyche, it has them in its thrall. The self-enclosure of Dante's *Inferno* is turned inside out in the salvation of the exteriorized consciousness of the *Paradiso* through the agency of Beatrice; the imprisonment of the sensitive and suffering nerves of the female epileptic in its forced attachment to a violent, monstrous ape-man in Eliot's "Sweeney Erect," finds liberation through the Lady of *Ash Wednesday*: "Blessèd sister, holy mother, spirit of the fountain, spirit of the garden."[12] Both are saved from the hells of egotism, guilt, punishment, and revenge by the same spirit of merciful forgiveness; Beddoes' characters remain in this hell, endlessly seeking revenge for a crime in which they themselves are hopelessly implicated.

In the fragment *Torrismond*, written after *The Bride's Tragedy*, a profligate son, Torrismond, finds himself unjustly accused of treason by an unforgiving father at the very moment he falls in love with the lady Veronica who seems divinely ordained to set him free from his empty sybaritic life:

> —O father, father!
> Must I give up the first word that my tongue,
> The only one my heart has ever spoken?
> Then take speech, thought, and knowledge quite away;
> Tear all my life out of the universe,
> Take off my youth, unwrap me of my years,
> And hunt me up the dark and broken past
> Into my mother's womb: there unbeget me;
> For 'till I'm in thy veins and unbegun,
> Or to the food returned which made the blood
> That did make me, no possible life can ever
> Unroot my feet of thee.
> (*Torrismond*, lines 181–92, p. 283)

The treachery belongs, in fact, not to Torrismond but to the courtier who accuses him to the king. But the accuser has his way; the father is implacable, and curses Torrismond, who resolves therefore both to die and to live as an avenging tyrant, two ways of saying the same thing. The speech is addressed, ironically and significantly, to Melchior, the false accuser, whom both father and son believe to be their friend:

> What shall we do?—why, all.

12. T. S. Eliot, *Ash Wednesday*, *VI*, in *Collected Poems 1909–1962* (New York: Harcourt, Brace & World, 1963), p. 95.

How many things, sir, do men live to do?
The mighty labour is to die: we'll do't,—
But we'll drive in a chariot to our graves,
Wheel'd with big thunder, o'er the heads of men.
(*Torrismond*, lines 213—17, p. 283)

The fragment ends here. The father's power over the son is unbroken; there is no room here for the heroic quest, made possible by the lady who believes in the son's innocence, a struggle against the accusing father that ends in the son's victory and his eventual reconciliation with the father. For here the son makes common cause with the false accuser, enters the unforgiving and endless circles of repetition of crime that ends, not in reconciliation, but in self-slaughter—the final identification with an inhuman nature which is the return to the dead womb, Blake's Ulro, or world of death.

Here, perhaps, is another clue to the primal scene of the infant in the arms of the dead mother, the archetypal memory which is oracular for Beddoes. What may have locked Beddoes into his circles of self-destructiveness was the death of his physician father when he was eight, a loss that A. Alvarez in his study of suicide has noted as a recurrent event in the early lives of literary figures whose careers ended in suicide. The struggle against the father, which is central to the maturation myth, and, in larger terms, to the apocalyptic myth which remakes not just a man but a world, may be subverted in the man whose parent dies too soon, a parent who is introjected to an extreme degree, and whose ghostly presence, as it absorbs the energies of the growing psyche, is locked into position by the irrational sense of guilt for that parent's death, a guilt which seems to arise naturally out of the hostility and aggressive feelings which are part of any child's feelings toward the father with whom he competes both for the mother and for his own manhood. The child, then, and later the man who carries the child in arrested form, becomes the captive and victim of the introjected, censorious father against whom he cannot fight with his one greatest weapon—a sense of his own innocence. Guilt locks the soul into Ulro, a guilt complicated by the pride that seizes on that guilt to implement its tyranny over a locked-in life. And if the sexual fantasies of the eight year old boy seem to result in his father's death, then love-death becomes an identity in which sexuality and creative force is seen inevitably as a drive producing death. Obviously the love-death theme of Tristan and Iseult is tied inextricably to the fact that Tristan has taken Iseult from her lawful husband, the King; it is this sense of sin which both heightens their desire and makes it a *liebestod*. One is reminded here of the young woman in *Steppenwolf* who comes, like the life spirit itself, to Harry, and says that when he loves her and will do anything she asks, she will ask him to kill her. Thus Beddoes' Germanic heroines seek lovers who will destroy them; the feminine principle cannot humanize the male will-to-power, but seeks only to give it dominion as if to placate its power, a power which is assured in the very attempt to satisfy its demands. This analysis is not, however, meant to reduce the sophisticated insights of Beddoes' drama to a demonically perpetuated Oedipal complex, but rather to suggest how a personal tragedy fed a cultural malaise in which men were bound by deep attachments to a past set of "ideal" imperatives whose demise left their "rational" world under its ghostly sway, disordered and seemingly without appeal.

The dead mother also has both this personal and transpersonal significance. It is possible to identify her with the horrible realization of the Oedipal wish to have the father dead, much as Oedipus' revelation of his crime resulted in the suicide of Jocasta. But the suicidal Jocasta, the death-seeking heroines of Beddoes, and the dead mother of his primal fantasy, also point to the archetypal level which the Jungians discern beneath the level of the personal unconscious—the death of the archetypal feminine in a society whose creative and connective principle is sacrificed to its monstrous egotism and lust for power. The wish for immortal life which is material, the obsession of Beddoes' life and art, is precisely the desire to be uncreated—"there unbeget me"—to be divested of the human life which must die, to return to the inorganic, to nature as the dead *mater* (or matter), the womb of stone which is equally the tomb. Beddoes' vision is the negative reversal of the resurrection myth, rolling the stone back onto the tomb, the culmination which comes at the end of *Death's Jest Book*. This is the meaning of Sartre's term *"en soi,"* the being that wants to be unchanging like a stone; and of Freud's "death wish," which is also, paradoxically, the instinct for self-preservation. But since life demands change, the existential result is that man becomes a permanent infant, helplessly insecure in the arms of a dead mother who not only cannot save him but who is, in a demonic way, the instrument of his own death-in-life, just as he is, somehow, mysteriously, the agent of her death. Thus the unmasking of satire reveals, not just the grinning skull beneath the flesh, but the death-in-life which is the result of repetitive and compulsive ego defense mechanism.

As evidence for this, consider the story that Hesperus tells the ill-fated Floribel of "the baby Perfume cradled in a violet," a baby smothered in a rose, whose murder both gives the rose its sweetness and stains it red with his heart's blood. Thus the very beauty of the rose, and of Romantic nature, is the emblem of a hidden murder, life arrested in its cradle, love smothered in its infancy, beauty and poetry born of its own destruction. And here again is the identity of womb and grave, of marriage and death, flowers and corpses, the fear of being smothered by women, a fear characteristic of the emotionally arrested— the horror of love, sexuality, and motherhood which marks Beddoes' work. Inevitably, in Beddoes' world, both woman and psyche must die; it is possible now to suspect that Veronica's attraction to Torrismond was inherently suicidal, the penchant of Beddoes' female characters to seek out the male who will destroy them. Veronica has had a dream about Torrismond which reveals his nature as a lover:

> and this imagined suitor,
> A glass-winged, tortoise-shell, heart-broken bee,
> Was—he you know of, heart.
> (*Torrismond*, lines 86—88, p. 274)

So fragile and artificial a lover can only splinter and lacerate the heart that tries to hold him. In identical fashion the women of *The Brides' Tragedy*, through the agency of Hesperus, are led to desire their own deaths, even as they passively cause his, and death comes to their minds soothingly, compounded of images of infancy, sexuality, and extinction. Thus Floribel, in the scene before Hesperus comes to murder her, lies dreaming of death, in images of infantile love: "thou sweet, thou gentle power," whom she once saw "beautiful as moonlight,/Upon a baby's lips, and thou didst kiss them,/Lingering and oft," and finally, "In thy fair arms, I'll lie, and taste thy cool delicious breath,/And sleep, and sleep, and sleep" (Act III, scene ii, p. 202).

Nothing, in Beddoes' world, is so fragile as life's soul, epitomized by the women and all the imagery which surrounds them; nothing is so active a force as death, a purely male force, with its peculiar set of double images, those of sexuality and of huge, elemental, and destructive natural forces—the forces of creation perverted and under the sway of those of destruction. Herein lies the key to the peculiar duality of Beddoes' style in *The Brides' Tragedy* and elsewhere: his precious, decorative sentimentality and his compressed, instinctive, and energetic voice. The images connected with this first style, which opens the play with the secret meeting between Hesperus and Floribel in the Beulah-like garden, are miniature in scale, fragile in weight, and illusory in nature—less a description of nature than a gauze of illusion stretched across the eyes; the colors are faded: "pale-petalled stars," "faded rainbows," "streaked with delicate pink"; the sounds faint, liquid, sibillant: "sighs and whispers," "a thousand tiny noises,/Like flower's voices," "soft rhymes"; the movements are quivering: "Like babies in their tremulous eyelid's sleep," "bees' wings," "Sweet soother of my senses, flutter near." Here is a world of little things, infinitely tender and terribly vulnerable: "flowers, and nightingales,/And small-lipped babes," tiny winged animals, insects, weak women, "cob-web limbed ephemerae," all delicate, and dear, and doomed: "the restless nightingale/Turns her sad heart to music, sweet it is" (Act I, scene i, p. 174). This Romantic music, an insubstantial and barely perceptible presence, is the faded echo of that Romantic ecstasy which was declining while Beddoes was maturing, till that great animating soul of Wordsworth and Shelley is little more than a dying ripple in a haunted gàrden. Beddoes here takes this strain of Romanticism to its ultimate conclusion: "The complete identity with nature, which is the fulfillment of life, is achieved visibly only by death."[13] Hesperus' friend Orlando gives the conventional Romantic sentiment: "The universe's soul, for that is Love./'Tis he that acts the nightingale, the thrush,/And all the living musics ... " (Act II, scene i, p. 185). But it is Hesperus who, in his strange wooing of Olivia, gives us Beddoes' version of the Romantic hope; his life with Olivia may be deceit, misery, and despair, but

> ... when our souls are born then will we wed;
> Our dust shall mix and grow into one stalk,
> Our breaths shall make one perfume in one bud,
> Our blushes meet each other in a rose,
> Our sweeter voices swell some sky-bird's throat
> With the same warbling, dwell in some soft pipe,
> Or bubble up along some sainted spring's
> Musical course, and in the mountain trees
> Slumber our deeper tones, by tempests waked:
> We will be music, spring and all fair things
> The while our spirits make a sweeter union
> Then melody and perfume in the air.
> (The Brides' Tragedy, Act II, scene iii, p. 193)

Thus is stated the theme that carries Romanticism's nature worship to its logical conclusion—a conclusion perverse in its promise, for it opens with equal logic into this world as a portent of doom. Here personal obsession and philosophic meaning meet—for all the beauties of life are but grave flowers, tokens of the soul liberated by death, so that the very animation of nature is, perversely, the sign of the dissolution of its body, a corpse "turning to daisies gently in the grave." Sibylla, in *Death's Jest Book*, will make the final, impassioned brief for this belief and the poetry which embodies it—but by that time, other voices will have gained ascendancy, and Sibylla will be but the last frail vessel for the ashes of a once great hope. That Beddoes has chosen from

13. Northrop Frye, *A Study of English Romanticism* (New York: Random House, 1968), p. 52.

the first to represent his "soul" in such fragile images already betokens the strength of the forces which are gathering against it.

This brings us to the other pole of Beddoes' style mentioned before, a voice less fanciful and more deeply imaginative, a voice as titanic, powerful, and instinctive as the other is tiny, muted, and artificial—a voice which will carry his poetry from the sentimental to the surreal. Even as the tiny figures of the first style have their artificial beauty and their perfect little proportions, "the enamelled flowers of song," the figures of the second are swollen, inflated, monstrous and *alive*. Where the first style twitters and jingles or gently flows, the second erupts, hammers, or pours out in sinuous lines, which revives the power of Elizabethan blank verse as it had not been written since Shakespeare. [14] As a matter of fact, it is this adoption of Elizabethan language and conventions by Beddoes that has cloaked for so many his modernity and led them to see him as archaic, simply because he had a vision for which a form did not yet exist. Beddoes, in trying to embody that vision, invented the expressionist drama in English through his manipulation of the Elizabethan conventions in such a way as to both mock the significance of the tradition which they embodied and overthrow the sense of reality of his own day. And although the Elizabethans had their dark forebodings and their ghosts, there is nothing in them like the enormous embodiments of the repressed instincts of Beddoes, which are not merely past but prehistoric, primal, subterranean, often submarine, grown ugly and destructive by their long confinement, awaking like Novalis' dead giant Atlas:

. . . with one general ague shake the earth,
The pillars of the sky dissolve and burst,
And let the ebon-tiled roof of night
Come tumbling in upon the doomed world . . .
(*The Brides' Tragedy*, Act I, scene iii, p. 183)

It is difficult not to see here the "return of the repressed," not only the repressed erotic life of Beddoes himself, but, conversely, the "evil" which both Romantics and Victorians repressed, the bloodiness in nature and in themselves which their conscious life sought to deny but which was increasingly making itself evident in historic action. Even as the Victorian mind lived in an ordered and respectable world, with only the ghost of evil to haunt it, so Beddoes, like a kind of reverse

14. In this style, thought and feeling are wed in that "unified sensibility" which T. S. Eliot attributes to the Elizabethan style, and which Heath-Stubbs, Lucas, and others have seen in Beddoes' poetry, which gives the lie to Symons and those others who saw in Beddoes nothing but the scholar-poet, and never believed in his passion.

image of the age, lived in a disordered and brutal world, with only the ghost of human decency, like Wolfram in *Death's Jest Book*, to haunt it. Like the sorcerer of preliterate societies, Beddoes carries the repressed tendencies of the community which shuns him, not only the parts of itself which it cannot look upon in the light, but also the growing disorder and disharmony which permeates it, the unintegrated materiality which had become, in secret, its ruling power.

Against the Romantics' unscientific worship of nature's animism, and the liberal positivists' vision of nature's laws as accessible to and therefore controllable by human reason, Beddoes uniquely set the poet's reaction to a scientist's knowledge of nature's enormity and inhuman force and scale, reinforced by a social world ruled by the twin inhuman powers of industrialism and autocracy.

The materiality of worldly power without human limits, with its ethical vertigo, was thus equated in his mind with the new descriptions of matter and the universe by science—a matter in ceaseless motion and a universe too vast to compass: "This desart of vacuity" ("Fragments," p. 249). Where was human significance to be found in "this boundless emptiness"? "Find thee, thou atom, in this wilderness!" ("Fragments," p. 249). In this perpetual wilderness, the human voice goes on crying, a mere figment of a mad cosmic mind:

Why what's the world and time? a fleeting thought
In the great meditating universe,
A brief parenthesis in chaos.
("Fragments," p. 248)

The Word, instead of gathering the spheres to its command, is but a tiny aggregate of harmonious sounds in the cacophony of chaos which the universe has become; connections become absurd in a cosmos of stellar distances, where light is not the illumination of vision but the tardy messenger of events centuries past that puts in the shade all of human history and its hopes:

. . . This was one who would be in friendship constant, and the pole wanders: one who would be immortal, and the light that shines upon his pale forehead now, through yonder gewgaw window, undulated from its star hundreds of years ago. That is constancy, that is life. O moral nature!
(Death's Jest Book, Act II, scene ii, p. 401)

The terrible consequences of human love and hope are, in Beddoes, somehow identified with the vast annihilation which comes from knowledge of an enormous and inhuman nature. Imaging this, his character Valeria in a fragmentary play, *The Second Brother,* answers her attendant who speaks to her of a dawning love by comparing the girl to a daisy who feels but the first drop of what is to become a flood that will swallow all of life:

> How thou art like the daisy in Noah's meadow,
> On which the foremost drop of rain fell warm
> And soft at evening: so the little flower
> Wrapped up its leaves, and shut the treacherous water
> Close to the golden welcome of its breast,
> Delighting in the touch of that which led
> The shower of oceans, in whose billowy drops
> Tritons and lions of the sea were warring,
> And sometimes ships on fire sunk in the blood
> Of their own inmates; others were of ice,
> And some had islands rooted in their waves,
> Beasts on their rocks, and forest-powdering winds,
> And showers tumbling on their tumbling self,
> And every sea of every ruined star
> Was but a drop in the world-melting flood.
> (*The Second Brother*, Act II, scene i, p. 302)

Here Beddoes' two styles meet in all their inequality—the daisy and the cosmic flood—the tiny meadow star of Romantic love confronts the elemental forces that melt worlds, the brute forces in men identified with the ruined reaches of interstellar space and the oceanic powers of a subterranean earth. What opens in these spatial images is equally the immensity and nonhuman extension of time; the death of a humanly ordered world and the discoveries of Darwinian evolution come together for Beddoes in this poetic image of discovery of a lost city and a prehistoric and monstrous life beneath the stratum of the present:

> I followed once a fleet and mighty serpent
> Into a cavern in a mountain's side;
> And, wading many lakes, descending gulphs,
> At last I reached the ruins of a city,
> Built not like ours but of another world,
> As if the aged earth had loved in youth
> The mightiest city of a perished planet,
> And kept the image of it in her heart,
> So dreamlike, shadowy, and spectral was it.
> Nought seemed alive there, and the very dead
> Were of another world the skeletons.
> The mammoth, ribbed like to an arched cathedral,
> Lay there, and ruins of great creatures else
> More like a shipwrecked fleet, too great they seemed
> For all the life that is to animate:

And vegetable rocks, tall sculptured palms,
Pines grown, not hewn, in stone; and giant ferns,
Whose earthquake shaken leaves bore graves for nests.
(*Death's Jest Book*, Act III, scene i, p. 421, variant)

A ruined, subterranean, alien world, organic and inorganic compounded, titanic in proportion, "too great . . . for all the life that is to
animate"; such is the natural history revealed by evolution, its unnatural growth reaching up and holding the graves of men in its
branches. What lies below the familiar earth, and seemingly within the
mind's depths, is a natural power so vast and brute that it appears in a
form that can only swallow human life and hope in the alien enormity of
its evolutionary destruction.

What becomes clear here in the negative power of the giant
underground forces of Beddoes' world where scientific knowledge and
psychic horror meet is the difference between prophecy and sorcery,
between apocalypse and doomsday. When, years after *The Brides'
Tragedy* first announced it, Beddoes' conflict had reached crisis proportions, the graves began, as they did for Blake, to thunder under his feet:

An earthquake of the buried shake the domes
Of arched cathedrals, and o'erturn the forests,
Until the grassy mounds and sculptured floors,
The monumental statues, hollow rocks,
The paved churchyard, and the flowery mead,
And ocean's billowy sarcophagi,
Pass from the bosom's of the rising people
Like clouds! Enough of stars and suns immortal
Have risen in heaven: today in earth and sea
Riseth mankind.
("Doomsday," lines 10–19, p. 106)

But whereas in Blake the mighty rising of the dead, the breaking of the
stone of the sepulchre, is an image for the victory of life over death, for
Beddoes it is the opposite, for the mighty living energy of the imagination which tears the oppressive old world apart has been put in the
service of death: "the fiery child of the Vesuvian womb" ("Doomsday," line 40, p. 107) who announces the event is not a prophet come
to restore humanity but a ghost, embittered and alone, who returns to
make his own loss universal, and so be reconciled:

None has wept upon its stone,
And ne'er a flower has grown
Out of its broken heart to prove
How in life it abounded with longings of sweet love.
("Doomsday," lines 65–68, p. 108)

86 Gathering the Winds

The rising of the dead is not the resurrection of life but the final triumph of dead matter and death, whose victory requires the final separation and extinction of the stubborn human spirit: "World, wilt thou yield thy spirits up and be convulsed and die?" The human part of Beddoes feels dead, but like a ghost, refuses to leave him in peace:

> How he groaned in the moonlight's glory
> In yearnings of desperate agony:
> For he could not wring from his eyes in the sea
> One little tear to shed
> In love above the dead,
> But sighing sunk in the waves away
> And lies beside the budding sun of blessed doomsday.
> ("Doomsday," lines 81–87, p. 108)

What is past tense here are the Romantic agonies associated with the moon, doubly past since the last agony is that of the dry soul that can no longer care; the present tense of "lies" refers to his passive waiting for the solar powers, the male archetype separated from the feminine lunar one, which comes only to destroy. Unlike the apocalyptic vision which rejoins a split world, the doomsday vision is the chilling celebration of a permanent and final separation—the final triumph of one side of being over the other, a death which will end the desire for unity that is the ghostly soul's perpetual agony, precisely because of its powerlessness ever to achieve wholeness.

As early as *The Brides' Tragedy*, Beddoes had embodied the murder which was to twist his vision and embitter his life. The clue to the real meaning of Hesperus' murder of Floribel comes with the following passage, where the two voices of Beddoes and the two sides of Hesperus meet:

> (Blindfold moth)
> Thou shalt not burn thy life; there, I have saved thee,
> If thou art grateful, mingle with the air
> That feeds the lips of her I thought of once,
> Choak her, moth, choak her.
> (*The Brides' Tragedy*, Act V, scene iv, p. 235)

This astonishing little passage is always commented on in the same way, as revealing the contradiction of Hesperus' nature: the way he acts with such tenderness in saving a moth from death, and then turns, at once, to thoughts of murder. But this literal reading wants a deeper one, as in it lies not just the revelation of Hesperus' contrary nature, but the key to it, and a compressed image of Beddoes' dilemma. Metaphorically, the moth is one of those small winged creatures, so ephemeral, which mark

Beddoes' images of the soul; further, the moth and the flame is a conventional image for obsessive desire; the union of Psyche and Amor is, for Beddoes, the triumph of death. Thus, what Hesperus reveals here is that he does not want to die, he who seduces the others to death; it is the repression of love and tenderness, and not the expression of it, that is here performed, and with an incredibly deep psychological insight, Beddoes makes the moth the instrument of Floribel's death, and thus of its own, for in repressing love one turns that powerful force against oneself: "Just now a beam of joy hung on his eye-lash;/But as I looked, it sunk into his eye,/Like a bruised worm writhing its form rings/Into a darkening hole ("Fragments," p. 241). The metamorphosis of the soul, and of the emblematic moth, is here unnaturally reversed; the concealed and refused joy turned in loses its wings and becomes the worm which gnaws at the heart, until, grown ravenous within, it returns with all the revenging hate of a bruised life force, ". . . like a giantous anatomy/Of that dead antemundane serpent, whose mouth/Is monumental hell" ("Fragments," p. 240).

In the play there are too many motives given for Hesperus' crime, which cancel each other out. First, the play tells us that Hesperus must kill to save his father, then that he does it out of jealousy, then that he has a recurrent madness because his nurse was killed while he was an infant in her arms. All of these point back to childhood traumas of the young Beddoes; what they add up to is that the crime is a compulsion, and like all compulsions it is symbolic. The killing of Floribel is the killing of tenderness in himself, the loving and creative side of himself which he seems to equate with a passive and helpless femininity. The weak, i.e., the loving, are the victims; to survive, one must be cold, alone, invulnerable.

This seems to be what Hesperus' murder of Floribel is really about; despite his repentance, which was conventional with Romantic villains and which the young Beddoes must have believed morally a requisite, the last lines of the play reveal Hesperus' real project in the murder, that by becoming the cold-hearted killer of love, he would be proof against weakness and death:

> Come hither, Murder;
> Why dost thou growl at me? Ungrateful hound!
> Know not thy master? Tear him off! Help! Mercy!
> Down with your fiery fangs!—I'm not dead yet.
> (*The Brides' Tragedy,* Act V, scene iv, p. 235)

Hesperus dies, not repentant but defiant; his dramatic descendant, more mature, more intellectual, and a purer spirit of revenge will be Isbrand— the cold, isolated, mocking hater of *Death's Jest Book.* "Art thou alone? Why, so should be/Creators and destroyers" (*Death's Jest Book*, Act I, scene i, p. 342). "But the heart I have/Is a strange little snake. He drinks not wine/When he'd be drunk, but poison; he doth fatten/On bitter hate, not love" (*Death's Jest Book*, Act II, scene iv). And from the other side of Hesperus, his softer side, that loved Floribel and dreamed of reunion of souls in eternal life, comes Isbrand's brother, Wolfram, who says of himself: "O bless the womanish weakness of my soul,/Which came to slay, and leads me now to save" (*Death's Jest Book*, Act I, scene i, p. 338). Wolfram is the first victim of the play, the dupe of his own good will, who is for Isbrand not virtuous but merely cowardly, weak, and foolish. But it is the soft-hearted Wolfram who comes back from the grave, as tender-hearted a ghost as he ever was a man, as the sensitive side of Beddoes comes back ever to haunt him.

This double Beddoes is projected first in the contrary Hesperus, then in the two warring brothers of the unfinished tragedy, *The Second Brother*, and finally in the two pairs of opposing brothers of *Death's Jest Book*, which suggests, not a healing, but a widening of the split, and a growing fragmentation of his inner life. Perhaps there is here, as some critics have suggested, a repressed homosexuality, but to say this is really to explain nothing. For to invoke homosexuality is only to invite deeper questions about its source; what can be said is that Beddoes had, in extreme form, a cultural division which is not yet cured. The equation of the intuitive feeling self with the feminine, and the aggressive rational self with the masculine is a division whose cultural counterpart was the rationalist's idea of a mechanical, self-adjusting nature which knowledge could master, opposed to the Romantic's worship of an elusive, feminine Nature, his art an urn inscribed with the image of a man forever pursuing a woman he would never be one with. Containing these contradictory attitudes in himself, Beddoes creates an art that embodies not the beauty but the terror of this Romantic pursuit in life; his art is "the present of a dream-figured bowl/For the black poison" ("Fragments," p. 243), the image of "bitter past" and "untasted future" in one poisonous draught, the distillation of his own experience, where every image of unity contains destruction. For Beddoes, the integration of Jung's *anima* and *animus*, of his own being, could only take place in a sublimated and idealized realm—the lovers' reunion after death, a love and a selfhood never to be consummated in life. But this was an equivocal eternity in which, as materialist and scientist, he could not really believe.

As this idealist hope faded, another, informed by materialism, egotism, and instinct was to take its place under the guise of science; unsatisfied with the unprovable immortality of moth-like souls in some questionable hereafter, refusing the natural immortality of love and the germ plasm,[15] and despairing of his chances at the other immortality of fame and artisitic permanence, Beddoes, as if already dead, turned to the skeleton, seeking there the cabalistic bone "Luz," the seed from which could grow a resurrected body—the quest of the Duke Melveric in *Death's Jest Book*. It was the failure of this last hope which brought Beddoes into a full awareness of his own folly, and that produced the third voice, mentioned earlier, out of a deep awareness of the insolubility of his conflict—the sardonic and yet exuberant voice of the absurdist—the lyrical grotesque. Realizing the futility of his quest for the material conquest of death, Beddoes' wounded ego sought the last refuge from despair, that of scorn—the scorn of the man who sits atop the heap of bones of his own murdered hopes and "laughs right merrily."

The Brides' Tragedy ended with the words: "not dead yet"; *Death's Jest Book* with the word: "dead." The play is one great will-to-negation, an artistic tour de force of splenetic and negative energy; for all the power of the play, its enormous life is the exuberance of despair and goes into its destruction. As in "Doomsday", graves open up the abyss, disorder the world, until finally all meanings dissolve and nothing is left solid or standing. The characters are all fragments of Beddoes himself and play out all the sides of him, each to the detriment of another. In the same way the play turns conventions so as to mock and destroy them, and brings to ruin by showing their irreconcilability all the great cultural props of his age: scientific progress, revolutionary chiliasm, Romantic idealism, Gothic revivalism, conventional morality; and, finally, it calls into question the very survival of "the bloody, soul-possessed weed called man" (*Death's Jest Book*, Act III, scene iii, p. 436). The doomsday prediction of the play is made explicit in this stunning passage, a description of a passing parade of knights, like Time itself, the past flowing into the future it will destroy:

> . . . 'twas a human river,
> Brimful and beating as if the great god,
> Who lay beneath it, would arise. So swings
> Time's sea, which Age snows into and increases,
> When from the rocky side of the dim future,
> Leaps into it a mighty destiny,
> Whose being to endow great souls have been

15. Freud's description of Eros as the force insuring the perpetuation of the species through the germ plasm seems, as it appears in *Beyond the Pleasure Principle*, reductive. This genetic immortality of the species takes on deeper psychic significance in the classical myth of Psyche and Eros, which ends with Eros' maturity and freedom from the matriarchal force of Aphrodite, Psyche's elevation to immortality, and the birth of a daughter, the infant who is, simultaneously, earthly pleasure and divine joy, reminiscent of Blake's "infant joy."

Centuries hoarded, and the world meanwhile
Sate like a beggar upon Heaven's threshold,
Muttering its wrongs.
(*Death's Jest Book*, Act II, scene iii, p. 403)

Life slowly drowns in time, until that mighty destiny, a kind of
cosmic suicide, leaps into it, and the dead, "great souls . . . centuries
hoarded," have their day, saved, as they were, to fuel the world's
death. As in the Doomsday poem, concealed and unsatisfied emotion
turns vengeful in its tomb, and the world itself is wished to extinction.
But in this wish for the world's death there is not merely wounded
narcissism but the most profound moral outrage:

Nature's polluted,
There's man in every secret corner of her,
Doing damned wicked deeds. Thou art old, world,
A hoary atheistic murderous star;
I wish that thou would'st die, or could'st be slain.
(*Death's Jest Book,* Act II, scene iii, p. 413, variant)

The play, then, as in the satirist's ancient curse, both seeks the poet's
revenge and attacks the corrupt—to kill with the word. But here the
corruption is so total that it is the world the satirist wishes to kill, and
so uses language against language itself, as if to destroy the significant
signs which are the foundations of a shared sense of order. Thus
Beddoes' play is built of mocking contrasts, in character, scene, content, conventions, diction, and tone, presided over by the jester Isbrand, and even he will turn out to be no proof against the contradictions, for Beddoes' indictment of society is also self-indictment.

Briefly, the plot of *Death's Jest Book* is composed of a series of
plots that turns man against man in a chain of destructive acts that end
in the annihilation of all the major characters. The sons of the deposed
Duke of Münsterberg, Isbrand and Wolfram, sworn to revenge their
father, take service with his usurper, the Duke Melveric—Isbrand as
court fool, Wolfram as his knight. To the unrelenting Isbrand's disgust,
Wolfram becomes attached to the Duke and goes to save him from
captivity in Egypt. The Duke, discovering that the woman he loves,
Sibylla, loves Wolfram, rewards his saviour by murdering him, and
returns in disguise to Germany where he discovers a plot by his two
sons, Athulf and Adalmar, urged on by Isbrand, to overthrow him.
These two sons, a dreamy and hedonistic poet and a warlike knight,
both love Amala; Athulf, to prevent her marriage to Adalmar, kills his
brother after a failed and humiliating suicide attempt. In the meantime,
Isbrand has replaced the body of the Duke's dead wife with Wolfram's,
and when the Duke, through the agency of his necromancer Ziba,
attempts to raise her from the dead, it is the murdered Wolfram who

materializes to haunt the Duke. Isbrand's revolt seems at first to succeed, but when he shows himself to be as great a tyrant as the Duke whose power he usurps, his followers turn on him and murder him; Athulf, at his father's urging, takes his own life as recompense for his brother's murder; Sibylla and Amala both resolve to die in the hope of reunion after death with their lost lovers. The Duke, understandably weary with life and power, resigns his dukedom and follows Wolfram into the family crypt. Running parallel to the main plot is a comic subplot involving the clownish servant Mandrake, a man who like Isbrand and the Duke is out to cheat death, and whose main function is to refract the action through another distorting and self-mocking mirror.

The scene of this action is set in two places, whose conventional associations get inverted, with large consequences for the sense of reality of the waking mind. The main action is set in medieval Germany, a choice congenial with Beddoes' Gothic sympathies, a past indistinct enough to offer his age a haunted image of what it has lost. But behind this past is another, more ancient one; even as he revivifies the medieval past, Beddoes undercuts it by the eruption of a deeper past, a grave within a grave. The more ancient past is the "mummy country," Egypt, the world of mystery, of the dead; this is made clear by the name of the ship, Baris—Charon's boat—which takes the Christian knights there and brings them back. But it is this world which has immediacy—the natural setting and solitude of the Romantic vision; it is this world to which the servant Mandrake accompanies Wolfram in order to learn the secrets of raising the dead to life, secrets to which Ziba, the dark magician, himself born from a dead woman in a tomb, is privy. And when the ship returns, this Egypt, the pregnant mummy, bears its fruit; and in Germany, which had seemed the land of the living, the scenes are predominantly set by "The ruins of a spacious Gothic Cathedral and churchyard. On the cloister wall the Dance of Death is painted. The sepulchre of the Dukes with massy carved folding doors, etc., by moonlight" (*Death's Jest Book*, Act III, scene iii, p. 423), or in the sepulchre itself. Here Wolfram rises from the dead, and lest that be taken too seriously, so does the comic Mandrake, whose wisdom agrees with Isbrand's but undercuts his spleen, whose clownish magic corresponds to Ziba's but makes the sinister seem foolish, and whose resurrection resembles Wolfram's but casts a comic light on it. At any rate, Mandrake is the game within the game, the overall effect of which is to destroy all sense: to ask, with Wolfram, "But dead and living, which are which?" and answer, with him, "A question/Not easy to be solved" (Act V, scene iv, p. 482). "Perhaps," Wolfram goes on, "you are the dead yourselves: And these ridiculous figures on the wall/Laugh, in their safe existence, at the prejudice,/That you are anything like living beings." And that "perhaps," like Floribel's earlier "never," pays all. If Wolfram, the ghost, isn't sure, then the game's a cheat. There is yet another level to the irony here, the more purely Romantic irony which Beddoes may have learned from Tieck and the Schlegels: "those ridiculous figures on the wall" who come down to dance and sing, are, after all, *painted* figures, so that we are consciously aware of their imaginative and artistic origin, and yet their dancing puts them in an uncertain relation to reality, calling attention to the creator, to the drama itself as artifice, and yet still embodying the Romantic possibility that the created image may be somehow more real than the matter-of-fact world, something "noumenal" and essential, which, as Kant was at pains to show, is not accessible to reason.

That Beddoes was consciously contrasting opposing views and tones to undermine convention, and just about everything else, seems largely proven by the revised version of Act I, in which he not only improves the poetry but also enlarges the play, always in the interest of heightening the mockery. For example, in the first version, Wolfram, having just been mortally wounded by the friend he saved, says: "O Melveric, why didst thou so to me?" But in the second version, Wolfram says: "O Melveric, wherefore didst thou me abandon?" The obvious echo of Christ here is studied travesty, and if it doesn't do a thing for Wolfram, who is already cynically cast as an honorable fool, it goes a long way in the reduction of the Christian myth and also prepares the way for Wolfram's resurrection—by necromancy and not God, who is notably, and expectedly, absent in this precociously modern world of Beddoes. In the enlarged Act I, as Wolfram, the Christian knight, sets out on his mission, his brother Isbrand again mockingly picks up the parallel: "Now then he plunges right into the waters,/Like a possessed pig of Gallilee" (Act I, scene i, p. 341). (If memory serves, the second half of this line was expunged in the first printed edition of *Death's Jest Book* in 1850, but was later restored, when times were riper.) After this speech, Beddoes adds a conventional song from the ship—a sea chanty, which allows him to indulge his considerable lyric talent, and then to follow it with a speech by Isbrand which tears up all this exuberant and conventional nonsense:

> The idiot merriment of thoughtless men!
> How the fish laugh at them, that swim and toy
> About the ruined ship, wrecked deep below,
> Whose pilot's skeleton, all full of sea weeds,
> Leans on his anchor, grinning like their Hope.
> (*Death's Jest Book*, Act I, scene ii, p. 343)

Thus the grotesque deforms the happy lyric, grinning up at it from below, the bony remains of the "order figure" or pilot whose death coincides with the plunging of man's ship and its safety into the chaotic sea of unconsciousness, and yet whose ghostly existence—the refusal of the old order to fully die or to be absorbed in the new—mocks and disfigures the daylight world.

In the same way that the various dictions of the play turn on each other, so do the characters: the Duke on Wolfram, his "foster-brother"; Athulf on his brother Adalmar; Isbrand on everyone. Men turn on their lords: the Duke's sons on their father; Isbrand on his master; Isbrand's confidante Siegfried plots his murder, and his follower Mario turns on him at the last and kills him; only Thorwald remains faithful to his original master, the Duke, but whether from loyalty or lack of opportunity because he is locked in the dungeon is hard to say. At any rate, he inherits the dukedom, though, on account of the recent carnage, more or less by default.

The characters are unpredictable, changeable, and unstable:[16] Sibylla dearly loves Melveric until she sees Wolfram again, and her reversion to the latter is instantaneous; Amala resolves to marry Adalmar, but turns to Athulf when she sees that he has poisoned himself out of love for her; Melveric kills to keep Sibylla, but as soon as he gets home his love reverts to his dead wife; Wolfram changes his mind several times in as many minutes about whether to save Melveric from the Moors; Athulf resolves to kill himself, then, after taking the poison, changes his mind; Mandrake disappears altogether. Only Isbrand remains relatively fixed in his course, but he, unlike the others, is unattached to other humans and so not subject to the same vagaries of emotion, and the goal he pursues is his own godhead—a fixed and inhuman star. It seems fair to assume that these sudden and constant shifts were not Beddoes' failure in plotting, as his contemporaries thought, but his intentional portrayal of human weakness, lack of center, and of man's passivity before his own inexplicable passions and the shifting of contingent circumstance. Isbrand's and Mandrake's cynical comments on the unreliability and duplicity of humans support this contention, as does the Duke's speech:

> But never hope to learn the alphabet,
> In which the hieroglyphic human soul
> More changeably is painted than the rainbow
> Upon the cloudy pages of a shower,
> Whose thunderous hinges a wild wind doth turn.
> Know all of each! when each doth shift his thought

16. For this observation, I am indebted to Donald William Good, "Thomas Lovell Beddoes: A Critical Study of His Major Works" (Ph.D. diss. Ohio State University, 1968).

More often in a minute, than the air
Dust on a summer path.
(*Death's Jest Book,* Act III, scene iii, pp. 425–26)

Another characteristic, typically Beddoesian, which the characters share, is their lack of conventional moral response to the consequences of their actions; in this, Beddoes departs from the prevailing mind of his time, striking deep into human psychology in an unflinching way which is uncharacteristic of both the Romantics who precede him and the Victorians of his day. Early Romanticism stirred with millennial hopes and visions fed by the French Revolution, later recoiling from the bloody excesses of the revolution and the tyrant Napoleon; something had gone wrong, and Romantic drama chewed over this indigestible aberration of the humanist dream, trying to hold to some kind of moral center in the face of an evil which they were at pains to subdue somehow to their sense of goodness in the natural order of things. All of them were fascinated by the tyrant-villain, who replaces the hero as the center of interest in poetic drama, but all, Byron excepted, were concerned that "the unbridled, unprincipled tyrant . . . must be won back within the fold of common humanity through the awakening of his conscience to the pangs of remorse."[17] This was the theme of two poetic dramas, Wordsworth's *The Borderers* and Coleridge's *Remorse.* The Victorians moved further under the sway of a growing liberal blindness, domesticated their vision until the bloodier side of human nature had become a housecat with its claws pulled, or, as Heath-Stubbs points out, an unintegrated force that erupts as the dissociated fantasy of the ghost story. Only Beddoes seems to have had the deep moral sense and the moral courage (and perhaps the masochism) to see how the nature of things mocked morality; to see violence, passion, and the abuse of power not as an aberration of human life, but as somehow endemic to it. And he had the imagination and insight to perceive that villains do not repent, that conscience makes them not docile but more monstrous, that their self-hate bodies them forth to their own imaginations as something inhuman and ugly, and that this ugliness becomes the law of their beings: "Who should be merrier than a secret villain?" (*Death's Jest Book*, Act III, scene i, p. 422). The weaker of them may be driven mad; the stronger of them have the courage to identify with this monstrousness, and their regret comes not in moral guilt but simply in the wild despair that they have not ultimately succeeded, that they too must die or be abused in their turn. Isbrand, in the Elizabethan convention of the revealing signature speech at death, is, first of all, like

17. R. Fletcher, *English Romantic Drama, 1795–1843: A Critical History* (New York: Exposition Press, 1966), p. 106.

Hesperus, defiant, and in the same way reveals his project to master death, which fed his power-lust:

> But think you I will die? Can I, that stand
> So strong and powerful here, even if I would,
> Fall into dust and wind? No: should I groan,
> And close my eyes, be fearful of me still.
> (*Death's Jest Book,* Act V, scene iv, pp. 483–84)

But then, unlike Hesperus, because he is so much more clear-eyed, rational, and aware, Isbrand realizes that he, who would play the fool to make fools of others, is now indeed the fool in turn, the satirist satirized:

> I jest and sing, and yet alas! am he,
> Who in a wicked masque would play the Devil;
> But jealous Lucifer himself appeared,
> And bore him—whither? I shall know tomorrow,
> For now Death makes indeed a fool of me.
> (*Death's Jest Book*, Act V, scene iv, pp. 484–85)

Here is the cruel Beddoes from whom his contemporaries recoiled, but if it is the cruelty of a loveless vision, it is also implacably honest; it is not so much evil that men fear, he says, as it is to be made fools of, to be shown their littleness, and by the same token there is nothing they more delight in than to make fools of others. "Behind the feeling of shame stands not the fear of hatred, but the fear of contempt which, on an even deeper level of the unconscious, spells fear of abandonment, the death by emotional starvation."[18] The prevalence of this fear of contempt, then, is itself a symptom of the utter insecurity of a vulnerable infant life in the arms of a dead mother, Beddoes' primal emotional event. Love is the only extenuating circumstance and love, in Beddoes' world of extinct mothers, is ephemeral and doomed; Thanatos and its accomplice, the will-to-power, which arise out of this premature experience of total insecurity, rule the earth. This is Darwin's bloody competition for the survival of the fittest, an amoral nature, not the natural philosophy of German idealism with man's consciousness the great unfolding of a dialectical progression that is the revelation of nature's reason and unity. The will that the German Romantics worshiped, from Fichte through Novalis, in a great but failed attempt to unite reason, natural science, morality, and desire—a voice which Beddoes' echoes demonically in Ziba (the Novalis-like "magic idealism" speech, "I looked abroad upon the wide old world" [*Death's Jest Book*, Act I, scene ii, p. 346]), and Isbrand ("I have a bit of FIAT in my

18. Gerhard Piers, quoted in Elliott, *The Power of Satire*, p. 86.

soul" [*Death's Jest Book*, Act V, scene i, p. 472]), as Harrex[19] has shown, is a will which Beddoes unmasks as the will-to-power, a conclusion in which history seems to have concurred. The "wicked masque" is human life; as the painted Deaths again come down from the wall to dance, Wolfram, Beddoes' soul of irrelevant honor who lived buried in him to the last, sums up the play's strategy and its purpose—to unmask the wicked masque: "*The antimasque,/I think they call it; 'tis satirical*" (*Death's Jest Book*, Act V, scene iv, p. 485). Here is Bonaventura's definition of satire as the last mask that unmasks the others—and leaves us, finally, with the skull of Yorick. And here is the cold eye of Beddoes, the anatomist, turned on living matter. As Wyndham Lewis has said: "That objective, non-emotional truth of the scientific intelligence sometimes takes on the exuberant sensuous quality of creative art: then it is very apt to be called 'Satire,' for it has been bent not so much upon pleasing as upon being true."[20] The question of whether the anatomist's eye is equal to the task of human truth, or is itself a terrible distortion, is answered by Blake this way:

Then spoke Jerusalem: "O Albion! my Father Albion!
Why wilt thou number every little fibre of my Soul,
Spreading them out before the Sun like stalks of flax to dry?
The Infant Joy is beautiful, but its anatomy
Horrible, ghast & deadly! Nought shalt thou find in it
But dark despair & everlasting brooding melancholy!"
(*Jerusalem*, Pl. 22, lines 19—24, p. 645)

And Albion, refusing Jerusalem's counsel, answers in a voice and with an act that are startlingly like Beddoes' own:

Hide thou, Jerusalem, in impalpable voidness, not to be
Touch'd by the hand nor seen with the eye. O Jerusalem,
Would thou wert not & that thy place might never be found!
But come, O Vala, with knife & cup, drain my blood
To the last drop, then hide me in thy Scarlet Tabernacle;
For I see Luvah whom I slew, I behold him in my Spectre
As I behold Jerusalem in thee, O Vala, dark and cold.
(*Jerusalem*, Pl. 22, lines 26—32, p. 645)

For Beddoes, the pursuit of an ideal Jerusalem, given the nature of man, which for him is incurably perverse, is but another form of monstrosity. Athulf's murder of his brother Adalmar over Amala, whose very name is love (with "alma," soul, concealed in it, as it is in Adalmar), is a case in point, as is Isbrand's revolution, and the Duke's

19. Anne Harrex, " 'Death's Jest Book' and the German Contribution," *Studia Neophilologica* 39 (1967): 15—37.
20. Quoted in Elliott, *The Power of Satire*, p. 226.

attempt to raise his wife from the grave. The fratricides in Beddoes are images of the soul at war with itself; the murder of Adalmar by Athulf is a mirror image of the murder of Wolfram by his "foster-brother" the Duke. In the latter, the aggressive ruler kills the sensitive, chivalric partner; in the former, Athulf, like Beddoes, the "Good friend of Bacchus and the rose," "Peace's lap-dog," kills Adalmar, "Battle's shaggy whelp," "Whose sword's his pleasure." Clearly the Duke is more fitted for murder than Athulf, for while the Duke kills with impunity, Athulf suffers the horror of the imaginative man who sees what he has become. While Isbrand is a heroic Beddoes, Athulf is closer to his reality, ending, like his creator, in suicide—not so strangely, at his father's request. The amazing passage where Athulf sees himself horribly transformed by his violence to his brother is a revision of an earlier fragment called "Leonigild's Apprehension," apparently written by Beddoes shortly after his mother's death, when he made the decision to transform himself from the Romantic poet of his youth to the disciple of anatomy, doing violence to one part of himself for another. And perhaps, at the same time, attempting yet another hopeless atonement with his dead father by becoming, like him, a doctor and scientist.

> . . . Oh! I am changing, changing,
> Dreadfully changing! Even here and now
> A transformation will eclipse me. Heark!
> It is God's sentence muttered over me.
> The spell of my creation is read backwards.
> Humanity is taken from my form,
> And my soul's immortality's annulled.
> I am unsouled, dishumanized, uncreated;
> My passions swell and grow like brutes conceived;
> My feet are fixing roots, and every limb
> Is billowy and gigantic, till I seem
> A wild old wicked mountain in the sea:
> And the abhorred conscience of this murder,
> Shall be created and become a Lion
> All alone in the darkness of my spirit,
> And lair him in my caves,
> And when I lie tremendous in the billows,
> Murderers, and men half ghosts, stricken with madness,
> Will come to live upon my rugged sides,
> Die, and be buried in me. Now it is;
> I break, and magnify, and lose my form.
> (*Death's Jest Book*, Act IV, scene iii, p. 464)

Here is deep imaginative power (and the only reference to God) whose insight agrees exactly with Blake's vision of evil: "Humanity is taken from my form." Beddoes' imagination knows its powers are being reversed: "The spell of my creation is read backwards"—rather than the poet humanizing nature, nature dehumanizes him. It is the loss of the human shape which is central to Beddoes' world, that very shape that Los labored to restore, and here again is that double transformation to the rooted vegetative form and huge rocky shape of Blake's fallen man: dehumanized man becomes his own inhuman world given over to death in its two forms. Man, swelling to become greater than he is becomes less, a mountainous landscape of rock and roots, prowled by a lion, bestial but lordly embodiment of the male solar power, an unforgiving father, or conscience, who has captured all that remains of the energy of the natural body:

> A murderer of its own Body, but also a murderer
> Of every Divine Member: it is the Reasoning Power,
> An Abstract objecting power that Negatives every thing.
> This is the Spectre of Man, the Holy Reasoning Power,
> And in its Holiness is closed the Abomination of Desolation.
> (*Jerusalem*, Pl. 9, lines 12–16, p. 629)

The abstract puts the ideal outside man while simultaneously bringing exterior, inhuman nature within; rather than look within to find the human shape that unifies and makes the world Jerusalem, a human habitation of humane deeds, Beddoes' characters pursue a self-aggrand-izing ego ideal that poses as perfection; its true nature is revealed by the imaginative distortion that reveals the loss of all proportion: "I break, and magnify, and lose my form." The love that men seek to possess in the idealized woman is in reality not love at all but self-idealization, the magnification of Blake's Selfhood, the spectral will that makes men monsters. If reason could free men, as many in Beddoes' age believed, then Isbrand would be free—but he too aspires to godhead, to create an idealized projection of his power in the material world, in his perverse creation of a bridal city which is not Jerusalem but Babylon:

> . . . Well done, Prometheus!
> . . . The tools I've used
> To chisel an old heap of stony laws,
> The abandoned sepulchre of a dead dukedom,
> Into the form my spirit loved and longed for;
> Now that I've perfected her beauteous shape,
> And animated it with half my ghost;
> Now that I lead her to our bridal bed,
> Dare the mean instruments to lay their plea,
> Or their demand forsooth, between us?
> (*Death's Jest Book*, Act V, scene i, p. 471)

In the very moment that this politicized Pygmalion has created this "beauteous shape," he himself becomes divided, a tyrant; he who dreamed of revolt and revenge to free a kingdom from a tyrant now wants to make puppets of those who were, but a moment before, his compatriots, and so his beautiful creation is revealed for what it most purely is—his inner tyranny given outward form. Isbrand, in the scene before the speech quoted above, had lamented the loss of Adam's unfallen state, for

> Now we're common.
> And man is tired of being no more than human;
> And I'll be something better:—not by tearing
> This chrysalis of psyche ere its hour,
> Will I break through Elysium. There are sometimes,
> Even here, the means of being more than men:
> And I by wine, and women, and the sceptre,
> Will be, my own way, heavenly in my clay.
> O you small star-mob, had I been one of you,
> I would have seized the sky some moonless night,
> And made myself the sun; whose morrow rising
> Shall see me new-created by myself.
> (*Death's Jest Book*, Act IV, scene iv, p. 470)

The imagery is consistent; it is by tyrannous male power, imaged again in the sun, and not by the metamorphosis achieved through the psyche, that Isbrand will achieve his inhuman transformation, creating himself by his own will, ridding himself of "This old plebeian creature that I am" (*Death's Jest Book*, Act IV, scene iv, p. 470), seizing dominion over his own mind on an appropriately "moonless night."

The grotesque is born out of this awareness of the monstrous project of self-idealization; if men become monsters out of the creation of ideal beauty, then perhaps they can become more sane by creating hideous images out of a deeper perception of what that perverse ideal really is. The creation of the grotesque, then, is the shield that mirrors the Medusa, and saves the man, an attempt to image and somehow contain the powers of disorder. It might work, of course, provided that man could get beyond his "tedious self," live without his egotistical ideals, but Beddoes could not and believed that men could not. As a matter of fact, he scorned those who could, calling them dead in life, soulless. So it seems that we are back to the mark of Cain (Isbrand), the second original sin, brother murder or self-division, without grace (or only the faded hope of it). The soul must be preserved, the moth saved from the flame, but to save it is to kill it; to pursue the ideal is death, to give it up is death: we end with pure negation. An "ecstatic animal," Jung writes, "is a monstrosity"; and that, Beddoes' art says everywhere, is man.

Thus some of the turns of plot are explained: Duke Melveric kills Wolfram over Sibylla, but strangely, it is not Sibylla he wants but, put rather bluntly, his own way. When Wolfram opposes his will, he kills him; once Wolfram is gone, Sibylla becomes unimportant; it is then his dead wife he wants, because her absence is a painful reminder of his own limitations, of the impotence of his own will. At first he loves Sibylla because she is, in a way, his own creation; he has brought her out of an Egyptian dungeon, created her, given her a kind of birth. He becomes avid for this creation when it seems to get out of his control. But Sibylla loses herself in mourning for Wolfram; the widow of one's victim is, after all, an object of pity or of irritation, not of love. The Duke then seeks another creation, this time, through the agency of Ziba, his servant, to raise his wife, body and soul, from the dead. Here is Melveric bent on the project of Beddoes' own early student days in Germany; to find in the occult the key to the literal resurrection of the flesh, to make the mind the master over matter.

The relationship of Ziba to the Duke and to the action is revealing; the Egyptian Ziba is the archetypal dark "other," a magician who has the key to unlock the deeper realms of being, its subterranean side. It is this shadow-self, and not reason, who fathoms the secret springs of life and death, and is born where they meet. Unlike Shakespeare's dark "other," Caliban, whose nature is sexual, Ziba's is asexual, ascetic even; where Caliban is lust, Ziba is the will-to-power, the dominant "dark" instinct in Beddoes' world. Ziba is almost androgynous: female in name, masculine in nature; master of the forces of life and death and yet submissive to Melveric's will—a projection, in fact, of that will. European mythology has always tended to project forbidden impulses onto a lower class and an alien culture; Melveric is the idealist, the lover; Ziba the necromancer, the poisoner, the instrument of his master's hidden will. Ziba is born like the demonic will-to-power, out of a dead mother: "in the world of death, or Satan, which Blake calls Ulro, the human body is completely absorbed in the body of nature—a 'dark Hermaphrodite,' " as Blake says in "The Gates of Paradise."[21]

Ziba, who is privy to the secrets of the "Luz," which Beddoes was finally to call "that great joke," raises the dead, but it is first Mandrake who embodies the joke, and then Wolfram, the dead soul, who appears. Melveric's creation of Wolfram is emblematic of a Beddoesian truth: what we create, when we create truly, is not what we want, but what we are. Melveric has not created the ideal but has murdered his better part, and knowing himself as he does, he is not only resigned to having the ghost he created around, but finally resigns his joyless kingdom and follows Wolfram into the grave.

Thus, to make the mind the master over matter is Beddoes' project

21. Northrop Frye, *The Stubborn Structure: Essays on Criticism and Society* (Ithaca, N.Y.: Cornell University Press, 1970), p. 191.

in *Death's Jest Book* itself; yet, both Isbrand's fall and the form of the grotesque which takes shape from that work, is the evidence that the cold, objective, and moralizing eye produces in imagination its opposite, a vision that is surreal, illogical, and finally one that defeats reason altogether. The logical eye is the unattached, unloving eye; it must, therefore, see as deformed that strange collection of desires and organs that is human life: "Looked at from the height of reason," wrote Goethe, "life as a whole seems like a grave disease, and the world like a madhouse."[22]

The nihilist, who is only the extreme logical extension of the rationalist and moralist, reveals the limits of his imagination; unable to conceive of any order other than that which he has inherited, he falls with the order he clings to, judging the world in its light, rather than reexamining the adequacy of his sense of order in the light of what is. The disordering of faculties which is inherent in the art of the grotesque reveals, then, a deep conservatism, the covert clinging to an artificial order which is no longer viable. Thus the nihilist, despite his claims to having annihilated an order, is really its last adherent; Beddoes' attachment to an unforgiving father is the personal corollary of his attachment to a life-denying sense of order. It is Beddoes' imagination which throws up to him images of the grotesque and monstrous, which are, in fact, the evaluation of his own values, and not a description, as he thought, of "man's all."

What the absurdist finally celebrates, in spite of himself, is the creative principle, which is never neutral. Its images are not so much disguises as the only way in which experience can be revealed and perceived, as it is lived, and thereby, judged, not by some objective standard, but by the response of the whole man. When Beddoes describes the "pale soul . . . fluttering in rocky hell" ("Fragments," p. 238), he is describing his own existential situation, generalized to man's, which, reflecting as it does a duality inherent in his time, does have some general application. To understand his image, which is not a symbol so much as an existence made palpable and evaluated simultaneously, it is necessary to enter imaginatively into it: to feel the frustration and horror of something infinitely delicate and threatened, something unmoored, desirous of freedom, yet impossibly confined in the lightless and impenetrable cave of a monstrous materiality—a spiritual ideal imprisoned and rendered helpless by the very act of elevation above actuality. Trapped, desperate, the living thing fragile, the confinement monumental; that *is* his condition, and the entrance into his

22. Quoted in Wolfgang Kayser, *The Grotesque in Art and Literature*, trans. Ulrich Weisstein (Bloomington: Indiana University Press, 1963), p. 60.

imaginative world gives the nature and lineaments of his imprisonment. The imagination, whether he intended it or not, is full of admonitions. The man who is possessed by horror is not so much the prey of his unconscious as he is of his attitude to certain impulses which he feels with enormous weight and presence; transforming night images into those of light really involves changing one's attitude toward them; then, experienced differently, they alter in form: "For the eye altering alters all."[23]

> I'll be a new bird with the head of an ass,
> Two pigs' feet, two men's feet, and two of a hen;
> Devil-winged; dragon-bellied; grave-jawed because grass
> Is a beard that's soon shaved, and grows seldom again
> Before it is summer; so cow all the rest;
> The new Dodo is finished. O! come to my nest.
> (*Death's Jest Book,* Act III, scene iii, p. 433)

Strangely enough, despite its grotesque inversion of human order into an inhuman disorder, its creator imaged in this dodo-like, grave-jawed muse of Isbrand's song, an extinct and unnaturally constructed hybrid which is mired in and half transformed into the earth that is materiality divested of spirit, seductively inviting us to the grave— *Death's Jest Book* does create an image of the unkillable human form. It is the ghost of Wolfram, whose name betrays the natural, instinctual life he carries, who haunts the play, and in the end rules the Duke himself, who had ruled the kingdom. And Wolfram is a peculiarly revealing multiple image. He is emblematic of the "knot" that ties Beddoes' best conception of the human to an archaic embodiment of it, the "ghost" of an earlier conception of the human hero. Wolfram is the ghost of the proud Elizabethan conception of man which haunts Beddoes' verse and makes the Elizabethan style so appropriately his own. Beddoes' play, for all its destructiveness, is not depressing, because man's fate *matters* so much; the play refuses to reduce what it destroys—in fact, in part does destroy in a frenzied attempt not to reduce.

Isbrand, despite his leadership of a revolution, is no egalitarian, but an avenger who would replace his master. The choice of a medieval setting is no accident, for Beddoes is not only a materialist who is, like his society, a dualist, but an aristocratic, hierarchical man who wished to place reason and will (Isbrand) in the lordly position of ruler, as did his age—with similar results. But it is Wolfram who is revealed as the true aristocrat, defender of the weak, and yet he is tied to the past,

---

23. William Blake, "The Mental Traveller," *Poems of William Blake*, ed. W. B. Yeats (London: George Routledge and Sons, Ltd., n.d.), p. 127.

even as Isbrand makes common cause with a demonic present. Wolfram is the broken heart of a dead ideal, for whom Beddoes can find no living form and so gives us a medieval knight to haunt a modern hell, powerless to set it right, yet weirdly indestructible. Human nobility, whose form Wolfram mirrors like a negative afterimage of a once bright ideal, requires a new embodiment, and not that of the mad "superman" of Germanic Romanticism, whose fate Beddoes properly foresees.

In the same way, the pastoral meadow scene in the last act of *Death's Jest Book* articulates exactly the project of poetry and of the mythopoeic imagination, as Sibylla says:

> Thus it is with man;
> He looks on nature as his supplement,
> And still will find out likenesses and tokens
> Of consanguinity, in the world's graces,
> To his own being.
> (*Death's Jest Book*, Act V, scene iii, p. 475)

To which the innocent young Lady adds:

> And therefore earth and all its ornaments,
> Which are the symbols of humanity
> In forms refined, and efforts uncompleted,
> All innocent and graceful, temper the heart,
> Of him who muses and compares them skilfully,
> To glad belief and tearful gratitude.
> This is the sacred source of poesy.
> (*Death's Jest Book*, Act V, scene III, p. 475)

Thus poetry intends to humanize the natural world, but Sibylla, another of Beddoes' doomed psyche figures, is dying—a death, moreover, which she (like the Sibyl of old) welcomes, because to her, idealist to the end, the human soul errs when it finds these human forms in the living world; the soul which has known experience sees "few features of mankind in outward nature;/But rather signs inviting us to heaven" (*Death's Jest Book*, Act V, scene iii, p. 475). Flowers, for Sibylla, are "fit emblems" only for "a bridal with the grave"; the immortal power that the Romantic relocated below or within nature, but which remains largely an animating force which has not yet found the precise and human "lineaments" which it had in the lost past, is here identified by Sibylla with death, the "grim anatomy" whose chalky finger points the soul to a unified state only on the far side of life. The creative soul lacks a metaphor for a living unity; thus, poetry, to be true to its own nature, must live in a "ghost's abode," its language here as archaic as its form for a human ideal.

In Cervantes' novel, when Don Quixote dies, it is not only the delusion of Romance that dies with him, but the spirit of human nobility whose vehicle had become as bony as Quixote's nag Rocinante. The soul remains a medieval aristocrat, thus becoming irrelevant; the cult of "art for the sake of art" is but the decadent extension and dead end of the lonely Romantic artist-hero who defines himself as apart from and against society. He was not wrong in detecting his irrelevance; it was only Blake who had the creative power to re-imagine a society in which creative imagination had regained its centrality. In doing this, he got beyond the artist as aristocrat; his hero Los is an artisan at work at his furnaces; in Blake there is no impossible tension between an aristocratic aesthetic and a social democracy. What is uncommon, for Blake, is what is most common; the true apocalyptic vision is of a man and a world without masters. This is perhaps the central despair of Beddoes' last work—that such a world is possible only among the dead. Thus his play ends with the suicidal reconciliation at last of a divided self, for the tyrannical Melveric and the humane Wolfram go together to the tomb, into the arms of "Death, the leveler."

Beddoes' lopsided development—his arrested emotional development and his enormous intellectual growth—paradigmatic in an extreme way of his society, expire together in his masterwork, along with that aristocratic, hierarchic conception of social order, whose forms had become irrelevant, as had the equally hierarchic and fading notion of soul as separate from the human body and its actions in the world. The rejoining of souls in death no longer had the force to compel the modern materialist imagination; the creative principle had gone out of the old forms; revivifying them could only keep them haunting the world with the sense of their loss. In Blake's *Jerusalem* the voices "who disregard all mortal things" (Pl. 55, line 1, p. 686) ask: "What have we to do with the Dead?" (Pl. 55, line 6, p. 686), the question of the active imagination when confronted with forms that must be destroyed by the spirit which originally bodied them forth; in that sense, an order of perception that is inadequate is mortal, that is, clearly tied to a past historical moment. Order once again appears as immortal, or timeless, when it finds a new form adequate to man's present situation in a way that seems, for the moment, to deliver him from time, from the history which, in fact, produces the vision itself.

But the doomed psyche in Beddoes is still elevated, its pale sublimation being the sign of his distance from the inner reality the image no longer has the energy to represent; thus the "lower world" contains the power cut off from the forms that could humanize it, the ghostly forms which it swallows back and which are forced to serve it, like the "snowy trochilus . . . tearing the hairy leeches" from the throat of the "river-dragon" (Fragments," pp. 237–38), the only task left to the soul in a world where creature lives on creature and the soul may prevent a small predation only to serve a larger one. So Wolfram saves the Duke from the Moors, serving thereby a tyrant who rewards him with death; the spectral human forms that haunt Beddoes' inhuman, spiritually starved world only help to increase its appetite, serving the destructive powers which entrap but cannot utterly extinguish them. So Beddoes set out to destroy what he could not revivify, the ghost of human nobility, along with the conventions of British poetic drama which had, for him, become, like human hope, "a haunted ruin."

It was for a later poet, William Butler Yeats, to begin the revivification anew, to attempt, against the modern world which he too despaired of, to refind and reanimate, not only poetry and poetic drama, but the aristocratic dualism of an older Western world in a form material enough to satisfy the materialism which he shared with his age. He attempted this through the construction of a cyclical system which imagined the actual rebirth in the flesh of an ancient Irish feudal world in which the "noble and the beggarman" shared a common dream, and in which the body and the soul were held together in a hierarchical synthesis once again viable in the world. Yeats's imagination is less "modern" than Blake's; it is dualistic in the old sense, but insofar as it is materialistic like its age, it can only imagine a resurrection in the material world, but of an old, not a new, order. In this sense Yeats is an apocalyptic, not a doomsday, poet, seeing a world rebuilt on the far side of apocalyptic destruction, the "darkness of the moon," a world closer to that of "intellect and desire" in himself. But there is something peculiar in his vision, something which makes it different from the apocalyptic myth-dreams thus far considered, a crucial difference which must be accounted for. In Yeats, the rebirth of the ideal aristocratic-folk society is not to be the culmination of history, a new unity imaginatively found and thus transcending time in the permanence of its sense of synthesis, but rather it is to be but a recurrence of a cyclical pattern, and will fall again even as it was recreated. The endless cycles of the moon's phases, by which Yeats, in A Vision, imaged history, thus projects his own uncertainty about the power of his imaginative synthesis, for it is locked within a sense of tragedy, "all things fall and are built again," and of a stoic tragic gaiety, "and those who build them again are gay."

It is illuminating here to consider Frye's comment that "The fatalism of A Vision is in part a reflection of the passivity of mind in which Yeats received it, but even so it is important to realize that A Vision is Yeat's Inferno, his demonic or Thanatos vision."[24] It is, however, also important to remember that Yeats believed that the

24. Frye, Stubborn Structure, p. 272.

voices who dictated *A Vision* came to bring him metaphors for poetry, and that, if Frye's insight is correct, then the force of Thanatos was also a dominant one in his poetry, in which the union of sun and moon, of *animus* and *anima*, of body and soul is, as will be shown, only realized outside of life—in art or, as becomes clear at the end of his life, in death. Yeats fights this tendency in his own vision, but in a way which is undermined by the power his heroic images, the "mask" of his art, contain because of the dualistic aristocratic preconceptions that give them both their shape and, ultimately, their sanction.

Thus Yeats believes that his ideal, aristocratic world will return, which helps him bear the growing disorder and cheapening of life in his own day; but he suspects the finality of his own reassuring vision by seeing it in the larger context of another decline and destruction. What this reveals is something fundamental about the structure of Yeats's mind, something essentially different from either the restorative apocalyptic or the nihilistic doomsday vision; that the unity of his mind, which attempted to create a harmony between the materialistic and the spiritualistic affections of his own being, was a unity "hammered" into shape by the power of his will toward "Unity of Being," but which was constantly being undermined by the mind which made it, so that it had ever and again, to be created anew. Thus the parallel structures of cosmology-history-psychology which are the ingenious creation of *A Vision* are a revelation of his own habit of mind; the cycles of history, made of warring opposites that slowly replace each other in dominance, creating a synthesis and then losing it again, are precisely the existential data of his own mind, which, like the cosmos it imagined, was a hard-won unity of opposites that was, in some fundamental sense, an artifice, and so was always in danger of splitting apart, of breaking down, and was constantly in need of being rebuilt. Yeat's mind thus resembles the people of his poem "Lapis Lazuli," who must be forever building again that which is destined to fall.

In that poem two Chinamen and a serving man (already a hierarchical grouping) climb to "the little half-way house." "There, on the mountain and the sky,/On all the tragic scene they stare"; this vantage sets the perspective of Yeats's art: a half-way house, a cliff-hanging compromise, caught between rather than unifying extremes. This is like his "Fifteenth phase," half-way on the cycle between utter subjectivity and blank objectivity—body and soul, subject and object unified *only* outside of life: "body and soul cast out and cast away/Beyond the visible world."[25] Outside and above, from there comes Yeats's artistic

25. "The Phases of the Moon," p. 74. This and all subsequent references to Yeats's work are from *Selected Poems and Two Plays of William Butler Yeats*, ed. M. L. Rosenthal (New York: Collier Books, 1966), and will be found in parentheses after the quotations.

incarnation; the swan that fathers history on Leda comes from above—
"the brute blood of the air ("Leda and the Swan," p. 115); the moon
(which in its dominance of his astrology already upsets the union of
contraries his system claims to contain) in its heavenly course images
and directs all the phases of life on earth; the swans rise "and scatter
wheeling in great broken rings" ("The Wild Swans at Coole," p. 51);
Juno's peacock screams from on high; the "yellow-eyed hawk" ("The
Hawk," p. 63) images the mind; "the wind-blown clamour of barnacle
geese" ("Beggar to Beggar Cried," p. 44) call the beggar to eternity just
when he chooses an earthly life; a tower, with a winding stair, stands
above the "filthy modern tide." The direction of ruin is a fall into
equality: "Till that be tumbled that was lifted high/And discord follow
upon unison,/And all things at one common level lie" ("These are the
Clouds," p. 36).

Cold often accompanies these images of height and power, an
image of a peculiarly Yeatsian form of desire: the host of the Sidhe, who
"ride the North when the ger-Eagle flies, with heavy whitening wings,
and a heart fallen cold" ("The Unappeasable Host," p. 20): "the cold
and rook-delighting heaven" ("The Cold Heaven," p. 49); the soul
emblem swans paddle in "the cold/Companionable streams or climb the
air" ("The Wild Swans at Coole," p. 51); "we dreamed that a great
painter had been born/To cold Clare rock" ("In Memory of Major
Robert Gregory," IX, p. 54); "Before I am old/I shall have written him
one/Poem maybe as cold/And passionate as the dawn" ("The Fisherman," p. 62). The heights of art and the passion it embodies are cold,
that is to say, lonely: "A lonely impulse of delight," "the lonely height
where all are in God's eye." Union comes always momentarily and from
above, as if from the imposition of the mind, whose ultimately lonely
power is taken as a sign of grace: "And I, that after me/My bodily heirs
may find,/To exalt a lonely mind" ("Meditations in Time of Civil War,"
II, p. 104). Images of high and solitary things—moon, stars, birds,
towers, and other lofty organizing forces—which draw circles from their
ruling vantage begin to cluster into meaning: "The Primum Mobile that
fashioned us/Has made the very owls in circles move" ("Meditations,"
IV, p. 106). And so do a complementary set of images which suggest a
kind of ground of materiality, quite literally a ground or floor; what is
missing in Yeats's imagery is, characteristically, an underground. "The
uncontrollable mystery" is "on the bestial floor" ("The Magi," p. 49);
there is the Druid's "dance upon the level shore," "the white breast of
the dim sea," the "blood-saturated ground," and, perhaps what is most
clearly emblematic for the solid stopping place of Yeats's poetry:
"Marbles of the dancing floor . . . those images that beget,/That
dolphin-torn, that gong-tormented sea" ("Byzantium," p. 133). Here

the sea itself, while it floods this image of art with its life, is at the same time only the hard surface of artistic design—a marble dancing floor, which, though it is animated, "dancing," remains an ornamental floor.

Finally, there is that extraordinary apotheosis of apocalypse that ends "The Second Coming": "twenty centuries of stony sleep/Were vexed to nightmare by a rocking cradle,/And what rough beast, its hour come round at last,/Slouches toward Bethlehem to be born?" (p. 91). The cradle is, of course, in Yeats's symbolism, the new crescent of the moon, the beginning of a new "antithetical" age with a "primary" creature, so that the high imagery again dominates as originating force. But what is most peculiar is that the beast is already slouching toward Bethlehem *before* it is born. The energy that spawns the image comes from above; its natural birth from inside or below is in some basic sense unimaginable. Somehow, born before its birth, the creature seems an act of poetic will, the artistically necessary "rough beast," an act of mind contemplating an increasingly disordered and unruly earth. It is, like the dragon kites of Chinese children, a sublimated image dragged down to earth, not some primal force pushing up from below like the giants of Blake or of Beddoes, forces of repressed power liberated by their own enormous materiality and energy. Somehow it is mental will and not instinctual force that presents the problematic beast before it can be born, as if to head off its dangerous force by formulating it in advance of its real appearance. This perhaps is the difference between sublimation and deep imaginative transformation; the former keeps experience at a remove, while the latter is simultaneously formed and immediately experienced, unifying conscious and unconscious. At any rate, the beast is given us as perhaps too explicitly archetypal, "a vast image out of Spiritus Mundi," the great animating world mind that seems so like Yeats's own.

For Blake the sculptures in the halls of Los, great works of imaginative art, are the way by which "every Age renews its powers" (*Jerusalem*, Pl. 16, line 62, p. 638), and among them are not just the works conventionally thought of as literature or art, but the "Divine Law of Horeb & Sinai,/And . . . the Holy Gospel of Mount Olivet & Calvary," art and prophecy united as works of prophetic imagination. And for Blake the construction of Golgonooza, a city of art, by Los, is the work of imagination which allows man understanding of his own depths, human inner life exteriorized because fully realized, through which all may be enlightened, so that Jerusalem may appear on earth, the eternal vision of Golgonooza, which all men build through creative action when humanity at large shares in the deep knowledge of itself which will free it to create a truly just society. Thus Golgonooza is the work of prophets and poets through the ages, constantly rebuilding an eternal image with ever-increasing illumination, building toward the culmination of apocalypse.

For Yeats the city of art, "the holy city of Byzantium," is .the aesthete's paradise, the world of art where material substance and ideal form are united in the creation which joins body and soul, just as the hierarchical society of Byzantium united in a shared vision the higher and lower orders of mankind, man's knowledge united with his power. That these categories were impossibly split for Yeats and could be healed only in the "artifice of eternity" which he was forced to make over and again in his vision is imaged most directly in the Byzantium he dreamed of, and recreated—his Fifteenth-phase society, a past society resembling in its hierarchical structure and shared dream the imagined heroic past of Ireland, which his system of thought sought to reanimate. The Byzantine art which corresponds to his sense of the ideal is a hieratic and frozen unity, intense with blue and stiff with gold; its heavenly king and queen and their ceremonial attendant figures, rigid around them, stare with eyes of fixed intensity that do not answer the viewer's gaze, but like the eyes of the paranoid seek to hypnotize by looking *through* the other's gaze, as if they seek to make his will their own. The will to unity is everywhere in Yeats's poetry; but the duality of art and life, spirit and body, subject and object, remain in the very hierarchy of his ideal fusion in art, and in the basically tragic view that overshadows it. Precisely because there is something forced about the unity, Yeats's deep imaginative awareness knows that such a unity is always threatened.

Yeats's imagination knows more than his theory, no matter how greatly that theory helped structure and empower it, for his imagination undermines by its choice of images the very perfection that Byzantium represents for him in his theory:

> Byzantium . . . substituted for formal Roman magnificence, with its glorification of physical power, an architecture that suggests the Sacred City in the Apocalypse of St. John. I think if I could be given a month of Antiquity and leave to spend it where I chose, I would spend it in Byzantium a little before Justinian opened St. Sophia and closed the Academy of Plato. I think that in early Byzantium, maybe never before or since in recorded history, religious, aesthetic and practical life were one, that architect and artificers—though not, it may be, poets, for language had been the instrument of controversy and must have grown abstract—spoke to the multitude and the few alike. The painter, the mosaic worker, the worker in gold and silver, the illuminator of sacred books, were almost impersonal, almost perhaps without the consciousness of individual design, absorbed in their subject mat-

ter and that the vision of a whole people . . . an incredible splendour like that which we see pass under our closed eyelids as we lie
between sleep and waking, no representation of a living world but
the dream of a somnambulist. Even the drilled pupil of the eye,
when the drill is in the hand of some Byzantine worker in ivory,
undergoes a somnambulistic change, for its deep shadow among
the faint lines of the tablet, its mechanical circle, where all else is
rhythmical and flowing, give to Saint or Angel a look of some
great bird staring at miracle . . . assent to a full Divinity made
possible this sinking-in upon a supernatural splendour, these walls
with their little glimmering cubes of blue and green and gold."[26]

Here, as in the poem "Sailing to Byzantium," the imagery belies the
message. The miracle at which the Byzantine saint stares is imaged in
the "mechanical circle" of the eye, set off against the natural "rhythmical and flowing." It is difficult not to see this as microcosm of
Yeats's great moon cycles, those geometric diagrams of order which
organize a flowing reality into mechanical and determined movements,
where history is but the working out of a pattern set high above in the
"Anima Mundi," though available to the inner eye, reducing life,
somehow, to a dead determinism through what is, essentially, an
individualized astrology.

And it is curious how "sinking-in upon a supernatural splendour"
merges into "these walls . . . with their glimmering cubes of blue and
green and gold." The imagination is stopped by the wall, which is
reminiscent of the "sages" of "Sailing to Byzantium," "standing in God's
holy fire/As in the gold mosaic of a wall" (p. 95). There is evidence
everywhere in Yeats of an enormous construction of an art of defense
against disorder, rather than the kind of integral ordering force found in
apocalyptic vision that tears down the world's walls from below and
reorders life from within. The walls, with their cubes, so like that
organizing geometry of particulars into interchangeable bricks that
Blake decried, bring to mind another revealing line from "The Double
Vision of Michael Robartes": "the particular is pounded until it is
man" (p. 79), the hammering of some insistent force from outside on
the original stuff of life until the material is forced and formed. The
images of floor, wall, and tower, to which the concept of mask must be
added, all point to the same constructed defensive system, the artifice
of unity that is Yeats's artistic emblem for eternity. This building of an
impenetrable but glowing face to present to the world, this mask which
was for Yeats the construction of his art, reveals, by its two-

26. William Butler Yeats, *A Vision* (New York: Collier Books, 1966), pp.
279-81.

dimensionality, his self-dramatization and enclosure, the very alienation it denies. His whole system is somehow a heroic attempt to heal man's rift from the "cold and rook-delighting heaven" of his mind, and simultaneously to find symbols that would reunite the artist with his community, and the imagination with the world of seemingly indifferent matter.

> With the help of his myth he could look on humanity and the universe in his own exalted image; and then he could control and reshape what he saw because he had made it. *A Vision* helped him to set in order and to interpret everything he knew. And it gave traditional sanctity and justification to whatever he believed, to his troubled personality, and even to himself.[27]

But the myth is all of a piece in what it reveals of Yeats's peculiar unity, the imposition of order from outside and above: just as the artist sets up his tower of tradition in a time "half-dead at the top," the society he imagines is an aristocratic one, an order ruled by autocrats who move the public body by their will, and his cosmology is in the same pattern—a lunar cycle whose invariable patterns of change and return through opposition pulls the whole of human history in its wake.

Those dolphins in the marble floor of Byzantium restate Yeats's own admiration for an art which contained some enormous force just under the surface; the restrained passion he so admired can also be seen as the will's refusal to admit into full freedom those sublimated underground forces whose disordering powers Yeats had reason to fear; it seems nevertheless the risk which must be taken to achieve that fully integrated and clarified unity of being which Blake's work bespeaks. This is related, too, to Yeats's fascination with the occult, the "mysteries" that Blake rejected. The society of the Golden Dawn, in which Yeats spent so many years as an adept, and whose symbols fed and enriched his poetic imagination, seems symptomatic of a certain sort of self-rejection, mixed with the authentic search for integrating symbols. When one sees pictures of members of this society in their regalia, the immediate effect is more than slightly ludicrous because the costumes are so studiedly mysterious, so Arabian, exotic, so like the clothes of Shriners and stage magicians, and the people in them appear such self-conscious *poseurs*. Of course, these adepts may be sincere according to their lights, but self-deceived nonetheless, for surely spiritual forms live in our own experience and our own dress, or they remain, in some sense, spurious.

27. Morton I. Seiden, *William Butler Yeats: The Poet as a Mythmaker* (East Lansing: Michigan State University Press, 1962), p. 135.

This attraction to the occult and the exotic alien, the sign of a split self seeking integrative power from something outside itself, is parallel to Yeats's artistic integration achieved by imposition: "the grand intention," as Donoghue says, "to make himself over again." Donoghue refers to the tendency, current among Yeats's contemporaries, to recoil "against the current of liberal democracy as if it were what Pound called it in the ABC of Economics, 'a mess of mush.' Their preferred values were formal, precise, hierarchical, often authoritarian; it is a painful story, and we do not understand it in full. Yeats is an extreme example. . . . In the Diary of 1930 he said: 'We wait till the world changes and its reflection changes in our mirror and an hieratical society returns, power descending from the few to the many, from the subtle to the gross, not because some man's policy has decreed it but because what is so overwhelming cannot be restrained.' He had lost confidence in the discovery of order among natural materials; order must be imposed if it is to prevail."[28] Donoghue relates the elitist and authoritarian political dreams of Yeats (and of Pound and Eliot) to the improper analogy drawn between the aesthetic and the active real, making "imagination . . . the sole law."[29] Yet, while admitting this, it is possible to question the aesthetic itself, and to ask whether Yeats's imagination, at its greatest strength, did not undermine the aesthetic to which his art and his theory seemed to bow. The question being raised is whether imagination itself was not imposed upon by an act of prideful will, and whether the heroic "mask" of the poetry of Yeats, like that of Robert Frost, does not contain its own unmasking. Frost created in his poetry the mask of the wise and kind old country man; a deeper reading, like that offered by Paul Carroll[30] of "The Mending Wall," unmasks him, for true imagination is somehow transparent in revealing devious motives, in whose service it is put. In that poem, as Carroll points out, it is the same kindly persona who mocks the neighbor who "moves in darkness," mouthing his father's saying: "Good fences make good neighbors," who has called his neighbor out to mend the wall in the first place. Thus the irony turns on itself; if good fences make "good" neighbors, Frost is in fact saying, then let us be that kind of neighbors. But he manages to have it both ways in the poem—both mending the wall (hiding himself), and seeming to favor that living "something" that "doesn't love a wall." In the same way

28. Denis Donoghue, *William Butler Yeats* (New York: Viking Press, 1971), p. 128.
29. *Ibid.*, p. 24.
30. Paul Carroll, *The Poem in Its Skin* (Chicago: Follett Publishing Company, 1968), pp. 59–60.

Yeats manages to have it both ways at once—he would "hold in a single thought reality and justice,"[31] the dream of the noble and the beggar-man. But what have beggars to do with justice? What kind of unity·of culture is it where men must beg their bread of others, or unity of being where the body must beg the soul's permission? And where the beggar, or the body, finally, is enabled to bear his life because he, like Sancho Panza, is allowed to share vicariously in the exalted dream of the nobleman, in which the noble, unfit for life, plays the hero's role? Yeats's tower seems like Frost's wall, a privileged sense of self, missing, through arrogance and self-enclosure, the true unity where all men are seen as sharing a common condition, a human condition which transcends the hierarchical notions of class and race. In this condition Arabs are no more mysterious than Anglo-Saxons; if all know themselves, then no one comes under the sway of another's mystery.

The end of "Sailing to Byzantium," as many have commented, contains the image which unmasks; the imagination, taken out of nature, becomes a gold enamelled bird singing on a bough "Of what is past, or passing, or to come" (p. 96). The artist has been transformed into a mechanical singer, whose living subject, for all its transitoriness, animates the artificial singer, the poet on "the golden bough," the hero's quest for society turned into a frozen art by a mechanical ordering of that central myth. Here the imagination rebels against and subverts the autocracy of sublimating intellect and will which have forced Los, like the "Grecian goldsmiths," to hammer nature and their edicts into a forced unity. "The Tower," also written in 1927, reveals a similar insight into the dualism that marks Yeats's view, that allowed him to feel superior to the condition in which he was very much involved; a view that is so different from Blake's belief that:

> Man has no Body distinct from his Soul; for that called Body is a portion of Soul discern'd by the five senses.
> (*Marriage of Heaven and Hell*, Pl. 4, p. 149)

High on the battlements the poet paces, sending out his imagination to question his relation to the scene around him, and to its images and memories. The first thing imagination brings him is the story of Mrs. French, the lady in the great house, whose servant "could divine/ That most respected lady's every wish," and brought her "an insolent farmer's ears . . . in a little covered dish" (p. 97). This story was supposed to have really happened in Yeats's neighborhood, when a servant took too literally the violent wish expressed by his mistress to have the ears of an upstart farmer. She was, of course, properly

31. Yeats, *A Vision*, p. 25.

horrified when he turned her own wish into action. This little anecdote carries thought at a number of levels: it has much to say about the relation between the ideal and the real, about the distance between poetic justice and political action, and it reminds the reader of the horror experienced by Yeats when the most noble of his patriotic ideals for Irish liberty and an Irish Renaissance eventuated in the violent destruction of the Civil War recorded in "Nineteen Hundred and Nineteen." And there is revealed in this story the baser motives which ideal conceptions often mask from themselves, just as the noble aristocratic poet wished to maintain his high position and purity and yet wished to catch the ears of the upstart and philistine public he despised, partly as a way of doing violence to them, for his power in some way depended on them, and on the recognition of his imperious position in respect to them. The mocking tone of the verse about Mrs. French suggests the way Yeats saw through the pretention in a position so like his own.

Yeats was always aware that the wisdom of imagination seemed inimical to the desire for power in the world; he wanted both. The noble combines the two in his imagined realm, as does the poet. Yeats yearned for the kind of society where art is more integrated into life, where the "other world" of the spirits is open to men again, as it was to the Irish peasantry, where the poet could once again be the "magus," his words making him the awesome figure that the Irish bard had been in times past. In the first story in his youthful *The Secret Rose*, the poet's severed head sings to the lady after its death, and the bushes wither for miles around; here is the first attempt by Yeats for the orphic poet to find renewed power after his own dismemberment, and to recreate a time when such power was actual in the world.

Despite his desire for a spiritual power that had actual authority, Yeats had the sense that there is, after all, something bestial in this force which combines knowlege and power but is separate from, above, and preys on the human. In "Leda and the Swan," god and mortal couple as beast and human; Blake's "eternity in love with the works of time" becomes a rape; the consummation is brief and the opposites of love and war are born as its consequence. Again a momentary unity imposed from above (in the sublimated sexuality that is so peculiarly Yeatsian, since the sublimation is incomplete and reveals openly its sexual source) is followed by the rebirth of division and opposition, Yeats's own condition seen as the microcosm of history itself.

The emotional force of attachment to the human condition that has the wisdom regarded by the worldly as foolishness, that integrative force which heals division, is somehow doomed in its unifying power in Yeats by its low status. The Irish peasantry, who embody this force, are both loved and looked down upon by Yeats who uses them in his poetry as the other pole from that created world of Byzantium. They are as lusty and as full of life as his golden bird is mechanical, and they draw him like "the warm hillside/Or the kettle on the hob" and "the brown mice . . . [who] bob/Round and Round the oatmeal-chest" ("The Stolen Child," p. 4). When Yeats was seriously ill, Crazy Jane spoke the life fighting in him; when he recovered, she fell, a "raving slut" who had become a nuisance. He went to her as an aristocrat slums in the people's quarters, wearing their dress and speaking their tongue, seeking their wisdom and their warmth, but returning by dawn to his castle, secure in his superiority and safe from the poverty and squalor of their lives.

In "The Three Bushes" Yeats combines the elements of his being, which are assigned characteristic roles, yet the parts remain decidedly distinct. A lady platonically in love with a lord sends her chambermaid to take her place at night in the bed. When the lord is thrown from his horse and dies, the lady, in true Romantic fashion, expires with her ideal; the chambermaid survives to live a long and presumably happy life. She tends their graves, planting a rose bush on each, whose branches intertwine. When she is old and dying, she confesses to an understanding priest, who buried her

> Beside her lady's man,
> And set a rose-tree on her grave,
> And now none living can,
> When they have plucked a rose there,
> Know where its roots began. (p. 163)

The rose is One, but its trinity of origin tells all: the bodily desires and the life force are associated with the chambermaid, the ideal soul qualities with the lady, while the man is planted between them, having enjoyed them both separately. The poem, of course, mocks the lady and the deceived lord with Yeats's characteristic imaginative honesty, but it draws the parallels of upper class with soul, lower class with body, transcending and preserving the parallels at the same time. Yeats is far from the young man who inscribed *The Secret Rose* with the epigram from Villiers de L'lsle Adam: "As for living, our servants will do that for us." But the mature rose reveals its roots; Yeats's dream of a reborn Ireland, a single culture, like the rose, formed of aristocrat and folk sharing a common vision, is but a more serious framing of the same hierarchical unity. The union of roses is in the light an apparent image of unity, while the roots, though they grow from a common Irish ground, reveal, hidden in the dark, the secret fact of their separation, and that what feeds them is dead and gone.

It is fascinating how Yeats's vision avoids the examination of that underground darkness which would reveal division, and keeps the eye always focused on the upper world with its appearance of unity. Perhaps the greatest of Yeats's unmasking poems, "The Circus Animals' Desertion," is a descent from the sublimated construction of a "painted stage" to the naked heart, but the heart itself is a "shop," an above-ground construction of a materialist's world; the floor remains the fixed bottom of the Yeatsian vision. "Players and painted stage took all my love,/And not those things that they were emblems of" (p. 185). But then "those things" are seen as debased, precisely in the light of the heroic idealizations, the masks which Yeats here sees as play-acting. But the heroic stage creates, despite the poem's statement that the creation is the other way around, the conception of their actual counterpart as nothing but a heap of objects, old and broken fragments of junk from which his vision was hammered into unity: "A mound of refuse or the sweepings of a street,/Old kettles, old bottles, and a broken can./Old iron, old bones, old rags, that raving slut/Who keeps the till" (p. 185). She, who always counts the cost, like the Philistines Yeats attacked in "September 1913," is the world's actual ruler and not those who never count the cost, who are only "allegorical dreams," "Themes of the embittered heart." "I must lie down where all the ladders start,/In the foul rag-and-bone shop of the heart," is a descent, like that of civilization in "Meru," "Into the desolation of reality," a desolation accomplished by thought which destroys the ordered "semblance of peace" brought about by "manifold illusion" (p. 157). Again, this describes the progression in the mind of Yeats, who at the end can imagine nothing better than to begin the rebuilding of that "manifold illusion" once again:

> "I would but find what's there to find,
> Love or deceit."
> "It was the mask engaged your mind,
> And after set your heart to beat,
> Not what's behind."
>
> "But lest you are my enemy,
> I must enquire."
> "O no, my dear, let all that be;
> What matter, so there is but fire
> In you, in me?"
> ("The Mask," p. 35)

Here is the rhythmic tension of Yeats's poetry, vacillating between the construction of a mask and the images which unmask the player, as if the imagination were always pushing the man to the recognition of the artificiality of his vision. "To be great," Yeats said, "we must seem so.

Seeming that goes on for a lifetime is no different from reality."[32] But seeming, by its nature, requires towering defenses even while it creates its own reality: it ends in the artistic demagoguery of "Under Ben Bulben," while its counterforce ends, like "The Circus Animals' Desertion," in the powerful poetry of an authentic despair.

"A complete despair about the meaning of life," writes Binswanger, "has the same significance as man's losing himself in pure subjectivity: indeed, the one is the reverse side of the other, for the meaning of life is ever something trans-subjective. . . ." He continues: "A man must decide whether to cling to his 'private theater' in pride and defiance or to seek a mediator between the private and the communal world, between deception and truth. . . ."[33]

A private theater too long lived in, as Yeats's imagination knew, leaves reality a desolation; the mask, too long worn, turns to stone. In his *Last Poems*, "The Gyres" (p. 158) presents the image of "Old Rocky Face," who, lamenting the coarsening of life and "A greater, more gracious time" that "has gone," looks on with tragic joy, expecting the return of that time again. But the sounds and images of the poem work against the sense of joy. The stone of the sepulchre will be broken, but the impermanent resurrection reveals a peculiar hollowness at the center of the vision and an equivocal message in its pattern. "Those that Rocky Face holds dear,/Lovers of horses and of women," shall appear "from marble of a broken sepulchre," almost as if they were themselves chiseled and artificial figures; or, the poem continues, they shall appear from "dark betwixt the polecat and the owl, or any rich, dark nothing disinter. . . ." Here is darkness at the center of vision, a "nothing" between the two poles of power and knowlege, earthbound polecat and the sky denizen owl, worldly power and dreaming wisdom, primary and antithetical, carrying in their very names the sound of a divided and disfigured soul. The word "disinter" takes the ear from the idea of rebirth to the sense of "disintegrate," as the last two lines leave us not with the sense of a reborn wholeness but of an endless circularity: "The workman, noble and saint, and all things run/On that unfashionable gyre again." The repetition of the "n" sounds—an, ain, in, un, on, un, ion, ain—leave the poem with the futile sound of spinning wheels; the cracking of the stone of the sepulchre is never sounded in the language at all, but only named; the endlessly turning cycles remain the imaginative fact. Finally, there is nothing between the "arrested posture" of Old Rocky Face and the eternally spinning gyres of predetermined change.

32. Quoted in Seiden, *William Butler Yeats*, p. 61.
33. Ludwig Binswanger, *Being-in-the-World: Selected Papers of Ludwig Binswanger*, trans. Jacob Needleman (New York: Basic Books, 1963), p. 234.

The tragic myth is part of a larger apocalyptic vision which ends with the hero's recognition of the limits of individualism and his accession to the larger communal vision, so that the tragic fate of the individual brings a new awareness which points toward the vision of Comedy and of commonality, the triumph of life. But for Yeats, for whom "cold and passionate" go together as do "perfect" and "lonely," the passion does not end in the *anagnorisis* of, say, Gail Hightower in Faulkner's *Light in August*, whose delivery of Lena's baby tears him from his obsession with the past and brings him to the circular vision of all the human faces he has known in a single form, the vision which ends his isolation. For Yeats, the vision of the past retains its hold, as does the ego it enhances; Cuhulain will return; his fight with the unconquerable sea of time will be victorious at last; the skein of time will be rewound, and like a magic tape play him again. But if the play will be the same, if the Second Coming will end in a repetition of the crucifixion, then the final shape of Yeats's vision is not tragedy but irony, where the two-edged sword of his antithetical vision cuts its moorings in both directions, and unity spins off into the empty void, leaving its impossibility behind. This is the art of social dislocation, when old meaning has been lost and new not yet found. The attempt to bring back the past in a kind of right-wing millennium reveals itself as order imposed by fiat; it is not the opening up to the energies which can forge a future, but a flight into the imagined past posing as a prophecy of an assured future. Yeats's imagination, however, has provided its own corrective, by the subversive unmasking of his poems through their own images, by revealing in such lines as "the dolphin-torn, the gong-tormented sea" the powerful tension between his art and the real life which it represses but which is still pressing it. And most powerfully, Yeats has provided, in a play called *Purgatory*, written in the last year of his life, the last and most powerful unmasking of his canon, a truly tragic vision which points beyond itself and calls out with its last lines on some larger unity that will save the soul from going endlessly in its own obsessive circles:

> O God,
> Release my mother's soul from its dream!
> Mankind can do no more. Appease
> The misery of the living and the remorse of the dead.(p. 209)

Here is the retelling of the central drama of the Cuhulain myth which haunted Yeats all his life, the killing of a son by a father, who, crazed after discovering the identity of his victim, went out to do battle with the sea, another image perhaps of the self-destructive futility of trying to turn back the tides of generation. In *Purgatory* Yeats retells this story, but stripped this time of its heroic mask. Now there is no hero, but an old man standing before a ruined house, the great tradition that is represented throughout Yeats's work as a great and lighted house, like Coole Park Manor of Lady Gregory. The tree before it is bare, stripped by a thunderbolt, and the house is open to the sky, its roof burned out, its window lit only by the haunted repetition of a sexual act with bloody consequences. The old man, while the boy with him stands by seeing nothing but his father's lunacy, watches the replaying of the night he was conceived, when his high-born mother waits with desire for her new husband, a base-born stable groom, who comes home to her drunk from the public house. Before reliving the scene of his conception, the old man tells the boy all that followed it: his mother's death in giving him birth, his father's wasting of the family patrimony:

> They had loved the trees that he cut down
> To pay what he had lost at cards
> Or spent on horses, drink and women;
> Had loved the house, had loved all
> The intricate passages of the house,
> But he killed the house; to kill a house
> Where great men grew up, married, died,
> I here declare a capital offence.(p. 204)

The son of this coarse killer of tradition was educated by those who "half-loved me for my half of her." When he was sixteen years old, his drunken father burned down the great house, "Books, library, all"; that night, the son murdered him in the burning house, then ran away to become "a pedlar on the roads,/No good trade, but good enough/ Because I am my father's son,/Because of what I did or may do" (p. 205).

Then the wedding night is replayed in the lighted window; it is revealing that the sexual encounter is seen above and at a distance—an explicit unmasking perhaps, of the sublimation of sexuality in Yeats, one which, as was said before, is clearly sexual in content but still at a remove. The mother's ghost is condemned by remorse to repeat the act endlessly, begetting again the life that will end hers and murder her husband, even as he will destroy her inheritance. And the old man realizes that in repeating the act she repeats its pleasure, and so endlessly renews her remorse. It is then, as the light in the window fades, that the boy tries to steal his father's bag of money, this "bastard that a pedlar got/Upon a tinker's daughter in a ditch" (p. 205), that "foul ditch" that runs through Yeats's poems:

> I am content to live it all again
> And yet again, if it be life to pitch

Into the frog-spawn of a blind man's ditch,
A blind man battering blind men;
Or into that most fecund ditch of all,
The folly that man does
Or must suffer, if he woos
A proud woman not kindred of his soul.
("A Dialogue of Self & Soul," p. 125)

The foul ditch is simultaneously a female sexual image, physical life in the world, and what it psychologically seems to be to the proud idealist, the humiliation of the world's, or the wordly woman's, power over him. In the poem just quoted, Yeats ends by "cast[ing] out remorse," but in *Purgatory*, remorse becomes remorseless.

The boy insists that he is no thief but is only taking what is his, since his father has never given him his "right share," and he and the old man struggle over the money, which scatters, as the window in the house lights up again and a man is seen pouring whiskey. The old man sees him with his mother's eyes, handsome, "and yet/She should have known he was not her kind" (p. 208).[34] Meanwhile, the boy, who is sixteen, just the age when the old man killed his father, threatens to kill his father in turn, but is stopped by the sight of the apparition whom he now also sees. The old man, thinking of his mother, dead and so "alone in her remorse" (p. 208), turns on his son: "My father and my son on the same jack-knife," and so murders him. Maddened, he sings a mock-heroic lullaby:

"Hush-a-bye baby, thy father's a knight,
Thy mother a lady, lovely and bright."
No, that is something that I read in a book,
And if I sing it must be to my mother,
And I lack rhyme.(p. 208)

The heroic song has become an empty parody, something not living but out of a book; and so the poetry stops. The stage is dark, only the bare tree stands in a white light:

Study that tree.
It stands there like a purified soul,

34. This seems to be a reference to Yeats's pursuit of Maude Gonne, that "sweet extremity of pride/That's called Platonic love" ("All Soul's Night," *A Vision*, p. 303). Later Yeats was to view her as "a woman not kindred to his soul." a pursuit of that other, primary pole opposite to his antithetical soul. In Yeats, the creative personality who belongs to the moon, or female archetype, the pursuit of the female (or "other") becomes the pursuit of the solar archetype, or animus, reversing the usual male heroic quest. Yeats's difficulty here is immediately apparent to the woman reader whose problem is "becoming the man she wanted to marry," just as Yeats, through the construction of his opposite mask, tried to become the assertive woman he originally wanted to marry.

All cold, sweet, glistening light.
Dear mother, the window is dark again,
But you are in the light because
I finished all that consequence. (pp. 208–9)

The old man sees himself as a purifier who has killed his son to free his mother's soul and to keep the son from passing "pollution on." He will stick his knife in the sod, bring it up cleaned of stain, and take to the road again, "and there/Tell my old jokes among new men" (p. 209). But the consequences are not finished, for now the old man hears the sound of hoofbeats and knows that the scene he has murdered to end is about to be repeated once again: "Twice a murderer and all for nothing./And she must animate the dead night/Not once but many times!" (p. 209). And so the play ends with the call to God to put an end to the incessant circles of human crime, which, in trying to end, he has only perpetuated.

Here, to stand beside "The Death of Cuhulain," is the unmasking of the myth, for in resurrecting Cuhulain Yeats has resurrected his crime, the murder of a son he fails to recognize as his own. The play is a deep self-condemnation, for it spells out the criminal futility of man's refusal to accept the law of generation because it seems caught in a downward, primary cycle, because the old traditions have been defiled, the great house burned; the spirit of Ireland, his "mother," lusting after an ignoble and base object, is destroyed in the impossible attempt to mix that blood with hers. The old man is the living embodiment of that unholy mixture, of materialism and spiritualism, commerce and poetry, pedlar and scholar. His desire to end the crime and free the Irish spirit is from his mother's side, his spirit; his actions are formed by his father's side, and so further the crimes he sought to end. Like Yeats, he would turn back the clock to a greater, more heroic age, undo the consequences of modernity; like Cuhulain, he would fight and turn back the "filthy moderntide" and rescue the Irish soul from the recurring nightmare of her pleasure in possession by a low born opportunism and her spawning of the base men who ride that filthy tide. Here is sounded the false note of his aristocratic trumpet:

Irish poets, learn your trade,
Scorn the sort now growing up.
Base-born products of base beds.
Sing the peasantry, and then
Hard-riding country gentlemen . . .
("Under Ben Bulben," p. 192)

But Yeats himself is a divided man, the hero infected by the very things he abhores, and his attempt to restore Ireland has murdered, symbolically, a father and a son, the generation which spawned him and bastardized Ireland, and the future to whose bastardization he himself, by his double attachment to the world and its powers and to an aristocratic dream of the past, has contributed. He sees himself as the most unnatural of men, his hand turned against both past and future, the primal crimes of Laius and Oedipus compounded in a single man. In his rejection of the world around him, in his inability to find reconciliation with father or with son, his actions are perverted into the crimes of misguided idealism, the lofty mind that makes of the world a foul ditch. And he is left with nothing but an empty nursery rhyme of a knight and a lady to sing his murdered modern son to sleep.

The great dream of a resurrected Ireland becomes the nightmare vision of a haunted ruin in which Yeats's Romantic imagination had remained locked so long. Seldom has a writer offered such a dark and revealing counterpoint to his own work, or had the courage, at almost the last hour, to tear down the defenses he had been a lifetime building. Yet in the same year that he wrote *Purgatory* he could also write "The Black Tower" and "Under Ben Bulben," the last constructions of his defensive, heroic mask, with the corpses of "The Black Tower," another mask that unmasks itself, propped upright in the tomb in the traditional Irish military manner, still "oath-bound" and awaiting the sound of "the king's great horn" (p. 190). Even dead, the rigid defenses stand their equivocal guard, revealing that peculiar ability of the contradictory mind to see through and to maintain its illusions at the same time.

The word "mask" in Yeats is itself an unmasking image, suggesting the attempt to make a unity by creating an external face for the world, to cover and complete a being whose inner face is turned away from that world. Yeats's aesthetic of detachment points both to the stoic art with which he wished to confront life and master it and to the basically introverted nature of his feeling life: "Amid a place of stone,/Be secret and exult,/Because of all things known/That is most difficult" ("To a Friend Whose Work Has Come to Nothing," p. 40). The Yeats who more and more successfully wore the golden mask could find his place in the primary sun; the sensitive Yeats found refuge in the moonlit imagination of "Beulah," its "proper dark": more and more, toward the end, he began to look toward death, where the Janus-face might be reversed and brought together, where, as he said of Florence Farr, he saw her "Moon as plunging, at her death, into the Sun, and she, free at last, 'sunk in her own delight.' "[35] For Yeats, as for Beddoes, true

35. Quoted in Virginia Moore, *The Unicorn: William Butler Yeats' Search for Reality* (New York: The Macmillan Company, 1954), p. 442.

wholeness finally could be imagined only beyond life, in art or in death; except this Romantic faith seemed as strong in Yeats as it was faded in Beddoes. He wanted nothing less than to artificially construct the nest in which the egg of futurity would hatch, to construct the archetypal paradigm of wholeness in which the past could be reborn, in a full materiality that united matter and dream. Man may be grotesque, a hunchback or a lunatic as civilization moves toward the darkness of the moon, but the moon will wax again, and the particular be pounded back into the old, noble human shape.

At the end of *A Vision* Yeats relinquishes his role as master director of cosmic and human destinies, throws up his metaphysical hands, and writes a last word which somehow undoes the whole system he has constructed. What undermines his system is another apocalypse, one which transvalues the traditional aristocratic values on which his system rests, one which sees the democratic tides of the century not as filthy but as a rising tide which will cleanse the world of autocracy and of the commercialism which Yeats so categorically connects to the democratic. This difference has everything to do with the organization of parts—the external reflecting the internal order and valuation man gives to parts of his being. Clearly the Christian Medieval hierarchy of fallen body and immortal soul, the one clearly below the other in order of value, was a metaphysical paradigm for the feudal world of lords and serfs, and the emotional depth of that view of the world outlived the society that created it, for reasons of psychology related to laws of inertia—connected, as Freud saw, to the power drive, or instinct for self-preservation. As both modern science and a new sense of social contract entered the Western world, they were often perverted by this old division, so that scientific knowledge and progress, despite their increasing hegemony, seemed to many an inevitable spiritual loss, and the feeling side of man was more and more turned away from the new world he was creating. It seemed that the more man proved his power in the physical world, the more it reduced him in his own eyes, since he had already tied his hopes to a single anchor, and that not of the world as it was becoming. The inability to humanize the technological world he was creating, or to find in his new knowledge anything but the destruction of his fondest hopes, comes partly out of the imperious hold the old values and forms still had on his new mind, as well as out of the dominant role of industrial capitalists in the first wave of modern democratic revolutions. In many ways the Romantics, and most certainly Yeats, were symptomatic of this imaginative lag. Yet even while this inertia infected the Romantic mind and made it both nostalgic and antithetical to the world, Blake's apocalyptic vision had already suggested another valuation of man's parts, a more energetic imagination that was increasingly in the nineteenth and twentieth centuries—not through his influence but out of a similar understanding—to offer the old myth of fall and redemption in a new form. The "nausea" of the West when it first fully noticed the indifference of objects which the old symbol system could no longer vivify or humanize, and its vertigo at the cold expanses of universal space, began to give way to the sense that man could humanize the object world by finding a new relation to it, humanize his instincts by making them his partners and not his prisoners or his slaves, and humanize his space by living in it directly, by ending the long star-gazing that had, for so long, kept the serf harnessed to the endless round of his plow. The socialistic and communistic prophecies, the product of the Western imagination, found no contradiction in a vision that was both humanistic and materialistic, and that began to imagine a world that was materialistic *and* communal, rather than assuming that material belonged to the capitalists or that the world belonged to the devil.

This new imaginative conception robbed the old gods of their powers, argued for the equivalence of human beings, not for the leveling of the difference in their abilities: "from each according to his ability, to each according to his needs" suggested that though abilities varied the needs of humans were relatively equivalent. The new vision had to fight not just the old Christian conception but the inertia which held it in place, the inertia that makes men seek to be the masters of others and simultaneously to wish to lay the burden of their life at another's feet: "I have spread my dreams under your feet;/Tread softly because you tread on my dreams" ("He Wishes for the Cloths of Heaven," p. 27)—the common dream of the noble and the beggarman. At the end of *A Vision* Yeats writes:

> . . . I have felt the convictions of a lifetime melt though at an age when the mind should be rigid, and others take their place, and these in turn give way to others. How far can I accept socialistic or communistic prophecies? I remember the decadence Balzac foretold to the Duchess de Castries. I remember debates in the little coachhouse at Hammersmith or at Morris' supper-table afterwards. I remember the Apocalyptic dreams of the Japanese Saint and labour leader Kagawa, whose books were lent me by a Galway clergyman. I remember a Communist described by Captain White in his memoirs ploughing on the Cotswold Hills, nothing on his great hairy body but sandals and a pair of drawers, nothing in his head but Hegel's *Logic*. Then I draw myself up into the symbol and it seems as if I should know all if I could but banish such memories and find everything in the symbol. But nothing comes —though this moment was to reward me for all my toil. Perhaps I am too old . . .

Then I understand. I have already said all that can be said. The particulars are the work of the *thirteenth sphere* or cycle which is in every man and called by every man his freedom. Doubtless, for it can do all things and knows all things, it knows what it will do with its own freedom but it has kept the secret.[36]

But the thirteenth sphere, like the thirteenth floor in many buildings, has been left unmarked. The center of the vision of a possible future remains dark, for Yeats has never confronted openly his own freedom; he has the courage and imaginative power to see the artificiality of his own constructions, expressed in the tension of his poetry, but he always returns to them, for he cannot relinquish his love for those old forms and free his imagination for a new and more genuine synthesis. The old hierarchical synthesis will not fit, as his poetry's vacillation shows, the new materialist he has become.

Blake's *Jerusalem*, as a true millennial vision, does what Yeats cannot; it gives man the form of his freedom, for Jerusalem is synonymous with liberty:

SUCH VISIONS HAVE APPEARED TO ME
AS I MY ORDER'D RACE HAVE RUN.
JERUSALEM IS NAMED LIBERTY
AMONG THE SONS OF ALBION.
(*Jerusalem*, Pl. 26, p. 649)

Since Jerusalem is the emanation or creation of Albion, it is clear that man's freedom is identical with the fullest realization of his creative life, what Blake calls the "Divine Vision" in every individual, the Holy City of Peace, the perfect society. Thus the old dichotomy between individual freedom and social order disappears; the deepest and freest vision of the individual is also the social vision.

Here ends the examination of three crisis visions, representing three archetypal responses to a crisis of order, Blake imagining a new order; Yeats attempting to materially reconstruct an old idealistic one; Beddoes attempting to destroy order altogether; the first is curative; the second, defensive; the third, suicidal. The visions of each have their imaginative counterpart, respectively, in the prophet, the shaman, and the sorcerer of preliterate societies; in literary generic terms they correspond to the apocalyptic, the tragic-ironic, and the grotesque. Their value systems are, roughly, humanistic faith, heroic fatalism and scepticism, and defiant nihilism. The nihilistic vision embodies the isolated individualism of the unforgiving, which the visionary faith of Blake overcomes. It is not, as Yeats said, that Blake made "a religion of art"; it seems from the preceding that religion and art speak the same

36. Yeats, *A Vision*, pp. 301-2.

language: the tongue which Blake associates with Tharmas, the "Angel of the Tongue," the "parent sense," assimilates the world and returns it transfigured through speech, which is associated with the water of life, and contains the Word, the source and renewer of human order. "Energy is the only life, and is from the Body," reason is the "outward circumference of energy," and since the "Body is a portion of Soul discern'd by the five Senses" ("Marriage of Heaven and Hell," Pl. 4, p. 149), Tharmas combines the intellect's symbol and the body's sense, and so is the ordering organ of energy or life; further, it is the primal organ of the infant's gratifying connection with food and mother, and the sophisticated organ for human connection in speech. Thus there is no distance between the tongue as speech and the tongue as flesh organ. The disordering of Tharmas, by the splitting off of his Emanation Enion, is the entrance of chaos; the fallen Tharmas is the spectral side of life's order, "Eternal Death," which is brought into the world by the warfare of Luvah and Urizen, the destruction of unified significant language by the division of intellect from loving attachment. Eternal Death, then, in human consciousness, is "the False Tongue," "the Vegetated Tongue," which devours life and meaning with its false doctrines, its inner and outer censors. Then words become disconnected from things, as the loving connection that animates the world disappears, destroying the sense that the symbol and the state of being are the same. There are only words on man's tongue, and outside them, hopelessly detached, the obdurate and meaningless objects of the world, the void opening between. As the Duke says in *Death's Jest Book:*

Aye, Aye, *the name—*
Methinks there's nothing in the world but names:
Things are dead.
(Act II, scene iii, p. 412).

Thus, the "earth is the grave's sky"; the ground of being opens up beneath the feet; concrete images themselves give way, and, with formative energy disconnected from the world and submerged, man becomes divided, haunted by his own unkillable partner: "My wife died on such a night, we had no money to have her buried, and she was sunk into the sea. When the moon looks up at me from the water, I always think of her last look" (*Death's Jest Book*, Act I, scene iv, p. 385). The attempt of Beddoes to animate the dead, his own search for the bone "Luz" which would regrow the body from its bony seed, is the materialistically perverted search for the light of vision which, in Blake, renews the creation of human form and that significant language or image system which *is* the human form of creation, man's real life.

Yeats stands half-way between these two "tongues," for his is a language of power and ideal which seeks by its energies to bind opposing forces, which are neither integrated nor unrelated, but endlessly desire each other, their union *only* in the symbol, an emblem only possible in the imagination, which is itself at war with the life it loves.

> For wisdom is the property of the dead,
> A something incompatible with life; and power,
> Like everything that has the stain of blood,
> A property of the living . . .
> ("Blood and the Moon," p. 127)

Wisdom, eternal forms, exist Platonically, above and beyond life; life, however, has the energy, the power, and also the base stain of blood. But the forms of eternity no longer seem to exist in the world of society and materiality, even in the imperfect form in which they did for Plato; ideal and material meet only in the imaginative emblem, a correspondence between the two realms which has the form of the higher world and the energy and power of the lower. Thus the symbol is the union of the two, but it is somehow outside of life—in art, a world of "time overthrown, . . . dead yet flesh and bone" ("The Double Vision of Michael Robartes," p. 81). This is the world of Yeats's fifteenth phase: "All thought becomes an image and the soul/Becomes a body: that body and that soul/Too perfect at the full to lie in a cradle,/Too lonely for the traffic of the world: Body and soul cast out and cast away/Beyond the visible world" ("The Phases of the Moon," p. 74). Art gives this duality form, as in Beulah "Contrarieties are equally true" (*Milton,* Book the Second, 30, line 1, p. 518); it is missing in life, except in that imitation of art which is heroism, man's action transformed into passionate ideal for a dramatic moment—until the inevitable defeat. Poetic language is for Yeats emblematic of the meeting of ideal and real; it is the privileged tongue which is the password between the worlds that desire news of each other; it speaks to eternity of man, and to man of eternity. Like the tower, it connects heaven and earth; it is constructed in the earth and views it from the high place where the moon is visible in the window to shed its light below. But the image is not, as it is in Blake, the state of being itself; it is for Yeats ennobling, precisely because it is *not* what being is, but only what it always strives impossibly to be. Both Blake and Yeats believe in correspondence, but though each looks within to discover the microcosm, their inner worlds are so differently constructed in terms of the weighting of the significance of their parts that the very doctrine of correspondence itself shifts its meaning. Blake's correspondence is discovered through penetration of the mystery of inner being by descent into his interior, an exploration of center that is marked by struggle against those autonomous systems, like Urizenic conscience, which attempt to devalue or inappropriately weight the parts of the being's structure and therefore pervert the pattern of innate structure according to *preconceptions* which interpret, rather than find the form by imaginative *perception* unclouded by prior judgment. Yeats begins with traditional preconceptions, and his struggle is not against the judgment that sets the parts at war, but works *within* the acceptance of that war as the inevitable consequence, not of his view, but of what he takes to be man's split being. The end result of this essential difference is that Blake ends with a vision of a *humanized* world that gives everything the forms of the human body, while Yeats ends with an *idealized* world and a debased reality, debased by the ideal of intellectual mastery with which he begins, an essentially inhuman and abstract lunar cycle that draws the world in its own image. Correspondence, for Yeats, is *not* equivalence; life may have the energy and power, but it is the pattern outside life, the abstraction that reveals and determines the interaction of contraries, that binds the energies of the world within his system, like the emblems of art, to charge the ideal patterns with the energy of an idealistically unsatisfactory life. Thus *A Vision* is the anatomy of an art work, the structure abstracted from the poetic expressions where their concrete form gives them a tense and viable power that *A Vision* lacks—as it reveals the mind that turns the wheel on which the world is stretched and bent.

No literary judgment is being made here, for both poets have a supreme power to make visible their own internal life, and artistic judgment does not quarrel with what that internal life is so long as it is transparent in the forms of the art. What is significant for this study is, however, what the differences in these internal lives signify in relation to the larger question of public and private order, and their relative wholeness in providing a harmonious setting for human life. To see Yeats as symptomatic and defensive, and Blake as curative, is to begin to sense the reason for the negative and positive valences associated with certain artistic images, and to begin to feel the way toward the "evaluation of values" which lies behind these patterns and shows the covert project of the imagination to devaluate an order that the artist himself may consciously *intend* to elevate.

The hunger for materiality by the "eternal" or spiritual in Yeats's poetic and metaphysical world is an imaginatively revealing and finally *inexplicable* hunger in terms of the system Yeats sets up. It is a hunger for unity, of course; but why the spirit world, if ideal, should desire what is inferior is unexplainable unless the categories of superior/inferior are finally relinquished. It is the categories, as Blake saw, which must be transcended, not life, which is itself the central containing form, embracing everything. For Yeats, the embrace is too much that of the noble soul embracing the world as the lord exercises his *droit·de seigneur* in the cottage of the peasant woman he desires. Mme. Blavatsky's restatement of the Hermetic doctrine of correspondence lies behind and parallels the Yeatsian mind: "What is below is like that which is above, and what is above is similar to that which is below, to accomplish the wonders of one thing . . . *unite together the power of things inferior and superior.*"[37] Behind this doctrine lies the project implicit in the making of such a unity between unequal, though corresponding, levels: "Each earthly thing reflects something in heaven. We are surrounded by kinships, secret accords, cosmic 'sympathies,' 'friendships.' Whoever knows them can control nature, the inferior being unable to do otherwise than submit to the superior."[38]

Yeats's belief in reincarnation is but the logical extension of the view that the soul is separate from the body, the soul of a higher order and immortal, but somehow, for all of that, an author in search of a character, seeking a bodily form to give it power and life. Thus the poet's creation of emblematic characters and images is like the process of reincarnation in a single life, unearthly soul seeking an earthly form, a hopelessly medieval soul with hopelessly modern appetites. The "Eternal Beauty" which, from the beginning of Yeats's poetic canon, chooses to suffer with and in the world, reveals something which can only be called patronizing in that choice:

> Weary and kind one lingered by His seat;
> He made the world to be a grassy road
> Before her wandering feet.
> ("The Rose of the World," p. 12)

Position is everything in this image; the world is *beneath* beauty's feet, a personification that has a peculiar reversing effect on the human form it chooses as its vehicle. To pursue the aristocratic parallel, it is as if God, the lord of the universal manor, were sending out the beautiful lady of the house to succour and bring gifts to the sick peasants, with the paradoxical effect of offering them comfort in an image that reminds them of their own lowliness. The poet, by identifying with the archetype of eternal beauty may elevate himself, but only at the price of reducing the value of the common life of man which he must share. And behind beauty of this sort, as both Blake and Beddoes saw, lurks the spectre of dominion, an interior feudalism which has its corollary in the social world: "the inferior being unable to do otherwise than

---

37. Moore, *The Unicorn*, p. 104.
38. *Ibid.*, p. 112.

submit to the superior." But the power of the superior is revealed as unreal; it is only the power the master draws from the servant's submission, a power which he ends by worshipping and which imprisons him: "For a Spectre has no Emanation but what he imbibes from deceiving a Victim;/Then he becomes her priest and she his Tabernacle" (*Jerusalem*, Pl. 65, p. 701). "Players and painted stage took all my love,/And not those things they were emblems of" ("The Circus Animals' Desertion," p. 185). At the last, then, only Blake's conception of imaginative language will suffice to account for all three artists, for however they thought they were using language, their language is their life, the imaging of how their valuation of their own parts allowed them to experience the world, their images having an existential identity with their consciousness of the relative freedom or captivity of the life of their own creative being.

The parallels drawn throughout this chapter between poets of a pluralistic Western society and the "healers" of preliterate societies are not, of course, intended as identities, but rather as analogies drawn for their usefulness in clarifying the structural constants, the social context, and the common healing purpose of imagination. The obvious difference in social function between these poets and their non-Western parallels is in itself illuminating, for it suggests the relative isolation of imagination in Western society since the eighteenth century, the bifurcation and stratification of the reality men experience, and the inability of such a society to find healing in the work of its most imaginative members, and the complementary difficulty of those creative individuals to find social forms for their own development.

Blake, despite the structural similarity of his vision to that of the prophets considered earlier, did not assume the prophet's mantle in his society; on the contrary, he was treated with indifference or contempt and was generally considered to be mad. And "though in fancy Blake could equip his blacksmith with a thousand sons working with him as he rolled 'furious his thunderous wheels from furnace to furnace, tending diligent,' in reality he could not find the 'brethren' to whom he appealed."[39] His canon remained closed to those for whom he spoke, in part because of the enormous intellectual exertion required to understand the created characters of the private archetypal drama of his coherent and radical world view. The privacy of his creation is a symptom of a lack of social moorings for a vision necessarily achieved in isolation from the debased language and rationalized conceptual system of his own day. Perhaps one of the explanations for the

39. David V. Erdman, *Blake: Prophet against Empire. A Poet's Interpretation of the History of His Own Times* (Garden City, N.Y.: Doubleday and Company, Anchor Books, 1969), p. 331.

originality of his vision was his own lack of formal schooling, which kept him from early emotional attachments to and subsequent imprisonment in the preconceptions of his society; but even as this freed him it condemned him to irrelevance for the very independence and idiosyncrasy that made his vision possible. Blake's irrelevance in his own time is the tragedy of health in a society that shared neither a sense of health, a quest in search of it, nor a symbolic language to serve it. Thus he remains atypical, ouside the central development of the literary tradition, and yet, paradoxically, from our vantage point he provides a key to unlocking its mysteries.

Beddoes was an exile, also considered mad in his own day; his contemporaries in England were at great pains to explain away his work as personal aberration. Yet the very rejection of Beddoes by his contemporaries suggests his identification with a malevolence which they wished to banish from their consciousness. The question, of course, was whether his society was properly ridding itself of the illness Beddoes represented, or protecting itself from the recognition of its own illness and division which Beddoes, in extreme form, embodied. At any rate, in our own society, with its greater awareness of the contradictions inherent in the kind of society emerging in Beddoes' day, the grotesque and absurdist art he prefigured has become a dominant mode, as the demonic—the desire to kill where there seems no cure—has become an all too apparent historical reality.

The poet, in general, in his search for wholeness, is like the shaman, insofar as he seeks the cure for self and social division within a traditional framework. In this sense, Yeats resembles the shaman, seeking to restore the lost soul of his society to its spiritually destitute present by the heroic struggle to reanimate a past synthesis. But Yeats's idiosyncratic art, formed of esoteric occultism, Irish lore, Blakean studies, and Pateresque aesthetics, is a synthesis beyond the reach of the Irish people whom Yeats dreamed of as sharing his dream. For the very tradition to which he bore allegiance and which he sought to restore has become separate from the actual, everyday life of his time, an elitist position which made him significant only for an elite who shared his conflicts and desires—the poetic voice, finally, not of revitalization but of reaction. The greatness of his art lay in the tension embodied between the celebration and the critique of a point of view. Yeats, the ironic poet, reveals that the shamanistic function, the power to cure within a traditional order, is impossible as long as that order is not oriented to both human needs and social reality.

"The need of his times works inside the artist without his wanting it, seeing it, or understanding its true significance. In this sense he is close to the seer, the prophet, the mystic."[40] Blake, Beddoes, and Yeats, who take us from the end of the eighteenth to the beginning of the twentieth century, in their deep imaginative response to their lives, acquaint us with the deepening malaise of order in their times; three archetypal responses to a crisis of order in Western society, a crisis to which the uncommon eye responded much before the common eye had perceived it. The crisis has deepened in our own day, deepened to the point where uncommon and common eye begin to meet, as they have before in deep historical crisis, and these imaginative responses to crisis—the ironic conservative, the nihilist-absurdist, and the revolutionary-apocalyptic—continue to share out the Western imagination, but with an increasingly deep communal response, so that the problems which once vexed only an intellectual elite or were inarticulate among great masses of men now have broad reverberations in growing segments of the larger community. Each of these three responses could be developed into categories enlarged by their twentieth-century parallels; however, this study will turn in its concluding discussion from the alternative responses of Beddoes and Yeats to the more positive response to order-crisis with which it began.

It takes enormous courage and imaginative freedom to maintain form-seeking moral energy in the face of a collective which provides no archetypal props for the artist's imagination; the risks of the creative imagination are greater than at other times—the twin risks of falling into the maelstrom of inhuman creative forces (as in Michel Bernanos' *The Other Side of the Mountain*, where the mythic quest goes wrong as the human protagonists slowly and horribly ossify in the midst of a carnivorous, humanlike landscape), or falling backward, like Yeats, into the old myths which, though once charged with vitality, are now the fixed and frozen forms of an embodiment anchored in past time—for "even the numinosum and the divine are mortal in the contingent form which can be apprehended by man."[41] These forms are properly mortal, for no system, no archetypal paradigm which pretends to transcendent validity, has anything but a splitting and alienating effect on the human mind unless that transcendence is fully embodied in a contingent and historically present form, and thus must be "mortal" to be felt fully as final and eternal. Apocalyptic thought feels that its own vision is the culmination of history precisely because it contains and explains the history of a cultural moment so completely that all error seems doomed and all that can be imagined seems fully and freely contained within its

40. Eric Neumann, *Art and the Creative Unconscious*, trans. Ralph Manheim (Princeton, N. J.: Princeton University Press, 1971), p. 97.
41. *Ibid.*, p. 92.

ideal form. Then begins a new period of elaboration of that which seems finally given. "Finally" is of course a word meant here only as it feels to those who share the apocalyptic vision; another epoch will overthrow it; but man is a timebound creature, and his only escape from time, as T. S. Eliot said, is through time. Eliot's vision of "the still point of the turning world" is, however, like Yeats's in that it is time past and time present; the future for him is unimaginable (except in terms of revivifying the past and past structures), and thus his remains a conservative vision, a singing of bones, a certain kind of earthly hope burned away. Like Yeats he celebrates tragic defeat: "We have taken from the defeated/What they had to leave us—a symbol:/A symbol perfected in death."[42]

But there is another symbol that can be "taken from the defeated," one which invests a debased materiality and a dispossessed humanity with a new and common significance, a vision of the future which is a symbol perfected in life. We turn, then, to examine the pragmatic and poetic vision of Karl Marx, against the paradigm of apocalyptic vision, discovering among its adherents the "sons of Albion" and in its reversed and renewed image of society one of the great themes of our own age.

42. T. S. Eliot, "Little Gidding, III," in *Collected Poems*, p. 206.

3/THE STORM'S EYE
Karl Marx and Vision in a Troubled World

—then the slave groans in the dungeon of stone, The
captive in the mill of the stranger, sold for scanty hire.

Blake, *Jerusalem*

The apocalyptic poet is not, by definition, the prophet; the
imaginative process is the same, but it is finally the response of the
collectivity which defines the prophet. Religion, said Santayana, is the
poetry in which we believe; this distinction within identity is the one
that is honored here. But, however distinct, as Santayana saw, the two
are one in that they share the same source, celebrate the same humanized life force, follow the same structural principles in the creation of
unified vision or mythic embodiment of micro/meso/macrocosmos (i.e.,
individual, society, universe).[1]

The individuation process, as Jung describes it, ends with unitary
or religious vision, and is not, despite some evolutionary claims for its
recent development, the sole possession of modern man, of the artist/
visionary isolated in the mass and struggling against the collective
inheritance for his own Self. In all societies, both traditional and
complex, stable and disordered, there are creative people, souls in crisis,
who carry within them the need to struggle through to "wakeness," for
whom internal unity is an imperative that makes disunity a visible and
painful experience, and who bear within them the creative seeds of
evolved consciousness.

It ought to be added here that this "poetential," at least, is in
everyone; for most members of a viable social order, however, the
collective and institutionalized form of myth, as in religion, and its
elaboration in art, seems to mediate the series of maturational transformations adequately. Where the creative force is stronger, for whatever

1. This particular terminology comes from Joseph Campbell's *The Masks of
God: Creative Mythology* (New York: Viking Press, 1968), p. 6.

135

reason, the collective and received embodiments serve not as full container, but, in part, as counterpoint against the inner forces. The struggle with the Angel, as it has sometimes been characterized in the West, is thus the creative individual's struggle with the collective archetype in the name of its power in *him;* the successful struggle ends, not in the destruction of the Angel (which would be a kind of psychic death), but in a winning of the powers of collective archetype to those of his own being, which both strengthens the Self and reverences the archetype, whose full embodiment must always be in the integrated development of the individual *within* a human group. Thus a viable social order and vision does not make these souls quiescent, but assigns to them the role of shaman, holy man, or poet, whose imaginative labors are used as communal resources by individuals passing through crisis or conflict who require active transformational guides; and by the community at large during its seasons of regular change, its great occasions, its time of danger, disease, or heightened conflict.

The creative process, then, is at work in every community and is the sum total at any moment of the present action of individual imagination at work on the collective inherited store of image systems, which of course offer much greater possibility for variation in complex and pluralistic societies. These image systems or structures, despite mental inertia and the vested interests of priestly dogmatists, are not themselves fixed forms, but processes so slow and of such long duration that they appear fixed, even while individual adaptations work to alter them over time. Then too there is process within process, for the structures themselves are built of myths, which are stories embodying the humanized unfolding of the seasons of cosmic, social, and personal life. At times, however, as has been repeatedly shown, mutation replaces slow evolution; the structure of myth undergoes abrupt and radical transformation out of the pressures of actual changes the old structure cannot account for or contain, or out of the confrontation of seemingly incompatible mythic descriptions of reality accompanying the collision of peoples with incompatible or opposing interests. It is here that the individuation process cannot go forward without the crystallization of new archetypal structures, where it is impossible for the imagination to find individual wholeness without simultaneously imagining a new order for society. At this moment, lesser or more personally blighted imaginations may powerfully reflect the disorder, defend themselves against it, or succumb to it; the great and fortunate imagination may go beyond disorder to a new vision of a reunified, rehumanized self and world.

In the statement that ends the previous paragraph, the phrase that introduces it must be underlined: *At this moment.* What is wanted in reading man's visionary history is not some messianic fervor, nor the demand that imaginative works be judged in their approximation to apocalyptic-millennial vision, but, rather, respect for *the moment* —social, historical, personal—in which the vision is embedded and out of which it grows. Apocalyptic vision is always the operation of imagination *at the extreme,* a response by creation of a new synthesis to radical dislocation and the threat of psychic annihilation. Consideration of this kind of imaginative response, however, not only relocates imagination in its social matrix but gives us a context for thinking about works of imagination, about their healing purpose, and enables us to judge imaginative visions by the transparency with which they both embody and evaluate a particular relation between man and world, the experience of life which is always conditioned by the way in which life is viewed. The active element in this "viewing" or ordering of the self and world is, as has been shown, precisely the imagination, which is not a mere passive recorder but an active participant in altering this order in the direction of man's deepest needs.

It is clear from the three poets studied in the previous chapter that the imagination cannot always effect the "cure" it desires and may remain symptomatic and diagnostic in the grotesque or artificial embodiments it produces. In both Beddoes and Yeats, though in different degrees, it was suggested that the attachment to dead forms of the ideal destroys or inhibits the quest for harmonious vision and regeneration. This failure is instructive, for it reminds us that societies, too, do not inevitably find revitalization, but may end in disintegration or stagnation. The latter consequence succeeds in defensively holding back the enormous forces or transformational elements whose uprush disorders the mind but also offers the possibility of forming it again in living materiality. The former reflects the inability either to restrain these rebellious forces or to order them by taking their side, and so condemns itself to be torn apart—like Orpheus dreaming of his dead Eurydice—by the passions which demand a living attachment to contain them. In a society whose original vision is no longer related to its actual situation nor guides its actions, its ideal formulations become a frozen mask unrelated to the naked reality of its actions, or, in more radical disorder, its actions end by destroying the very words and images which once conveyed order and humanity, and language itself seems no longer to signify. The return of these libidinal forces where human forms are dissolved is terrifying; when embodied archetypes and viable social forms no longer control human powers, then those powers are given over to the non-human world in a negative reversal of the sympathetic animism of myth and poetry that humanizes the world. In this reversed world of terror, a world become alien, the non-human natural or mechanical takes over the human attributes or powers, while the human figure ossifies, drowns in, or is dismembered by the powers over which the mind, like society, has lost control. That much of modern art, as of modern history, is a record of this process hardly needs documentation.

What Mario Praz has called "the Romantic agony," the dismemberment of the isolated poet by the very muse who inspires him, is symptomatically related to the nostalgia of Romanticism, to its often melancholy obsession with past forms and a glory which seems gone from the waking world, and especially from society. Deeply related to the Romantic's victimization by ungovernable but somehow animating powers was his awareness of his isolation, his alienation from the society of his day being not so much willful self-aggrandizement as the intuitive recognition that the creative, attached human being was being closed out of an increasingly atomized and inhuman social order. Too often the artist attached this rejection to a mystique about the artist as a privileged consciousness; only in the twentieth century was there a development of the idea that the alienation of the artist was more properly understood as one of the symptoms of the alienation of man, that the artist was not the sole possessor but rather the articulator of a humanness that society increasingly opposed. Alienation thus became the catchword for the condition of man in the war-torn, power and production crazed world of the twentieth century. The recognition of a common solitude among men becomes the origin of a new relation among men; increasingly, the artist is seen not as different from other men but as one of their subversive agents in an order which denies them all equally.

In the following quotation, the Mexican poet and thinker Octavio Paz reflects, from his own national perspective, this current of thought:

> . . . although alienation is more basic to our character than our individual traits, it is now a condition shared by all men. We Mexicans have always lived on the periphery of history. Now the center or nucleus of world society has disintegrated and everyone—including the European and the North American—is a peripheral being. We are all living on the margin because there is no longer any center.[2]

Our condition is common because our culture is now a shared one:

> All of today's civilizations derive from that of the Western world, which has assimilated or crushed its rivals. . . . Communists and bourgeois democrats brandish opposing ideas, but those ideas have a common source and are phrased in a common language which both sides understand. The contemporary crisis is not a struggle between two diverse cultures, as the conservatives would have us

---

2. Octavio Paz, *The Labyrinth of Solitude: Life and Thought in Mexico*, trans. Lysander Kemp (New York: Grove Press, 1961), p. 170.

believe, but rather an internal quarrel in a civilization that no longer has any rivals, a civilization whose future is the future of the whole world.[3]

In meditating on Mexicanism, the young writer, says Paz, is led to realize that he is meditating on "a much vaster theme: the historical alienation of dependent peoples and of mankind in general."[4] As Paz contemplates the solitude of the Mexican, cut off from his Indian past by Spanish conquest, from Spanish culture by his adoption of the liberal ideology of the Enlightenment and the French Revolution, and from both by the only partially achieved populist Mexican Revolution at the beginning of this century, he discovers in his people's condition that of modern humanity—the orphan, as he says, of its own history. In Europe, as in Mexico, the growth of awareness in this century has been of "orphanhood," a demolition of the past tied inextricably to a growing sense of other men, of what Paz calls "the outstretched hands of other solitary beings."[5] It is only in the discovery of solitude that "the longing for a place,"[6] implicit in the experience of that solitude, puts men back on the mythic quest for a lost center that "opens the doors of communion."[7] At the extreme of solitude, then, myth reappears.

Contemporary man has rationalized the myths, but he has not been able to destroy them. Many of our scientific truths, like the majority of our moral, political and philosophical conceptions, are only new ways of expressing tendencies that were embodied earlier in mythical forms. The rational language of our day can barely hide the ancient myths behind it. Utopias—especially modern political utopias (despite their rationalistic disguises)—are violently concentrated expressions of a tendency that causes every society to imagine a golden age from which the social group was exiled and to which man will return on the Day of Days . . .

Every moribund or sterile society attempts to save itself by creating a redemption myth which is also a fertility myth, a creation myth. Solitude and sin are resolved in communion and fertility. The society we live in today has also created its myth. The sterility of the bourgeois world will end in suicide or a new form of creative participation. This is the "theme of our times," in Ortega y Gasset's phrase; it is the substance of our dreams and the meaning of our acts.[8]

3. *Ibid.*, p. 172.
4. *Ibid.*, p. 171.
5. *Ibid.*, p. 194.
6. *Ibid.*, p. 208.
7. *Ibid.*, p. 211.
8. *Ibid.*, p. 212.

There is, then, not only the reappearance of redemptive myth, but, this time, of a collective dream which is no longer the abstraction of comparative mythology but a truly international mythic drama—one that pits the "proletariat" or, more broadly construed, "alienated man" against "the sterility of the bourgeois world." The existentialist hero of postwar Europe, and of France in particular, was a modern mythic embodiment—alienated man in an absurd world choosing freedom, a myth that embodied the modern Western sense of being the orphan of its own past, an orphanhood embraced as the condition of a conscious and concrete existence. But the existentialist hero left one abstraction intact—and that was freedom; the need to make it concrete transformed that hero into another man, one who found himself once again implicated in history. If the intellectual odyssey of Jean-Paul Sartre as a primary creator of the image of existential man may be taken as a prototypal modern Western journey, it is possible to see his more recent Marxism as the exercise of an existential freedom that has chosen its content, a choice that transforms radical solitude into the possibility of radical solidarity and social renewal, and that leaves behind the Romantic individualism of existentialism which defined the isolated man as totally self-creating, as if neither history nor society existed. It is this Marxist myth, to which so many have committed their freedom, to which we now turn. The "redemptive vision" of Karl Marx cannot be questioned in terms of its theoretical power as an adequate description of historical or economic reality without considering it as a new mythic description of the world, whose worldwide communal response marks it as a legitimate "prophecy"—not a prediction in the sense of the physical sciences but a prophecy in the sense of articulating the discontent of an age and empowering a new vision of man and society.

To have said this is to raise the question of the adequacy of any social theory that does not begin with an imaginative response to a lived experience, that does not intend to close the gap in understanding which refuses to let people (in the words of Richard Wright) believe in what their life has made them feel. For if prophecies are to some extent "self-fulfilling," that is, since men—unlike the phenomena of the physical sciences—live in a social world of their own creation, which they continually modify, then the way in which they conceive their situation is finally inseparable from the direction in which that situation may develop and change. Thus the response of a great mass of mankind to a new world view becomes one of the positive measures by which the descriptive power of that view may be authenticated. To insist on "neutrality" in the observation of the human world is to accept the given arrangements of a society as final, to see it as so many social "scientists" presently do, as a homeostatic mechanism requiring only internal adjustments to keep it operational—a view which is finally far from neutral with its implicit allegiance to the *status quo*. Thus neutrality in human descriptive sciences is an illusion (or a symptom of a society which is bereft of human attachments); a valuation of human institutions is built into the observation of them. An ahistorical description of society, and its complement—an *intra*personal view of psychic disorder, is always in part an apology for the present system and a falsification of what is in fact an historical and *inter*personal reality. An attempt at a truer description of society requires a consideration of the creative element in human affairs, which demands a philosophical decision about the values which impel change and the direction in which men seek to move the world in response to their evaluation of their present situation. The study of history, as Lucien Goldmann has said, is the search for human values; the imaginative response of men, particularly in moments of crisis which are pregnant with new arrangements, is an index to the kinds of values by which, however imperfectly, they modify and even radically restructure their reality. If, as Goldmann says, "philosophy really tells us something about the nature of man, then every attempt to destroy it necessarily obstructs the understanding of human reality. In this case, the human sciences will have to be philosophical *in order to be scientific.*"[9]

"An ideology," writes Lewis Feuer in his introduction to a collection of Marxist writings, "is a myth written in the language of science."[10] To which might be added that all myths are equally ideologies, and that while traditional myths were written in the language of religion, modern myths are written in the language of science, because they are more conscious and base themselves on an awareness that man and the natural world, our actual existence, are the source and ultimate measure of our ideas rather than some absolute or supernatural realm which has been recovered as our own projection. All ideologies, whether couched in the language of theology or science, are defined as myths because they are essentially a judgment of history and an embodiment of a set of ideal relations among men that is the measuring rod of that judgment; the ideology of Karl Marx can only be understood and its influence explained if it is seen that his description of the economic and social relations of men—drawn from empirical evidence (from "men, not in any fantastic isolation or abstract definition, but in their actual, empirically perceptible process of development under

9. Lucien Goldmann, *The Human Sciences and Philosophy*, trans. Hayden V. White and Robert Anchor (London: Jonathan Cape Ltd., 1973), p. 22.

10. Lewis S. Feuer, Introduction to Karl Marx and Friedrich Engels, *Marx and Engels: Basic Writings on Politics and Philosophy* (London: Collins, Fontana Library, 1969), p. 22.

definite conditions"[11]), derives both its method and its form from a humanistic premise, one that simultaneously restores to man his materiality, and to materiality its human meaning.

This role of Marx as moral diagnostician and social prophet is hardly surprising if we consider the impact of Marx's thought over the last hundred years. No mere student of political economy, as Marx described himself, could have inspired such a movement were there not implicit in his doctrine a prescription for change and a *telos*: an ideal of a morally perfect world.[12]

But the ability of a teleology to organize a system is common to all theories that embrace such a notion and does not ensure their adoption by society; what is socially significant in Marx's teleology is the convincing quality of its inevitability, precisely because it is predicated on the actual material situation, a situation described in a way which both diagnoses concretely the contradictions and articulates the felt needs of his time while promising that the present situation must *necessarily* be overcome and produce the desired end. The power of Marx's synthesis, then, rests on its non-theistic and humanistic reworking of the ultimately religious idea of the "unity of opposites" as the fulfillment of human life. He believed that man had fallen into division but would be whole again; he "established '*Aufhebung*' (the transcendence of alienation) as a concept denoting ontological necessity."[13] But it is the extremely concrete way in which he understands "alienation" and its "transcendence" that makes his theory an effective instrument of genuine social change. The coherence of Marx's system, its ability to generate response by enunciating a new world view along with the assurance of its inevitable victory, turns on its reciprocal materialization of what had been "purely" philosophical concepts and its humanization of what had seemed "merely" material relations.

Perhaps the best way to approach the Marxist synthesis is to follow its growth in his own mind, for once constructed the system is so coherent and its parts so mutually dependent that it nearly defeats the mind's attempt to find a starting point in regard to it. As Marx built his system, he selected major elements from the philosophic, political, and economic theories of his time, theories which, taken fully and separately, appear irreconcilable, but which Marx, drawing selectively from them all, fused into a new vision which overcame their contradictions in a way that seemed simultaneously to numberless people to

11. Marx and Engels, "The German Ideology," *Basic Writings*, p. 289.
12. Jerome Balmuth, Introduction to *Marxist Social Thought* (New York: Harcourt, Brace & World, 1968), p. xxvii.
13. István Mészáros, *Marx's Theory of Alienation* (London: Merlin Press, 1972), p. 113.

solve the contradictions of their own existence. In this fact lies the exoneration of Marx from the charge of grandiosity in claiming to have unified philosophy with the actual world, for the ability of his world view to find converts did not depend on philosophical sophistication, though without it the Marxist view would never have found its completed form.

The earliest and most decisive influences on Marx were double: the idealist philosophic-historical construction of Hegel's system and the actual climate of revolutionary hopes in which he came of age. His formative years in the Germany of the late 1830's were spent among the "Young Hegelians," "who saw themselves living in a general atmosphere of crisis and impending catastrophe,"[14] and who found the refutation of Hegel's conservative quietism in his own description of history as a dialectical progression marked by revolutionary periods where the contradictions of a preceding age produced their own negation in a radically new synthesis. Thus they wished to use the critical weapons he had given them for what they called the "realization of philosophy," the democratic reform of the still feudal and absolutist Germany which, as the young Marx said, had shared in all the restorations of Western Europe and none of its revolutions, and which was, of all these nations, the most philosophically advanced and the most politically backward. The subsequent suppression of the liberal press by the Prussian government drove many of the would-be reformers back to purely theoretical discussions, but drove others—Marx among them— into exile to continue the fight from abroad. As a matter of fact, the gathering of the forces of reaction could only encourage a man of Marx's temperament, who felt revolution crackle in the air as it grew more oppressive: "Let the dead bury and mourn their dead. In contrast, it is enviable to be the first to go alive into the new life; and this shall be our lot." In this same letter of 1843 he wrote of Germany: "It is only its own desperate situation that fills me with hope."[15]

During this same period Marx read and absorbed the insights of Feuerbach's *Preliminary Theses for the Reform of Philosophy*, which was to give him his strategy for the demystification of Hegel by turning Hegel's own critical categories against him. Feuerbach, in an earlier book on Christianity, had already given an account of religion as the alienation of man's own powers and capacities by their projection onto a supernatural being; in his *Theses* he extended this argument to Hegelian philosophy, asserting that Hegel's view was merely a rationalist's religion that reversed the real order of things with its identifi-

14. David McLellan, *Karl Marx: His Life and Thought* (London: Macmillan & Company, 1973), p. 35.
15. Quoted in *Ibid.*, p. 63.

cation of an Absolute Spirit as the ultimate source of history and the material world. According to Hegel, history had been the evolution of this Spirit, or Idea, working unconsciously through man; in the final development of self-consciousness in his own philosophy, the Spirit becomes conscious of itself, and through cognition recovers the world as its own objectification, thereby closing the hostile gap between subject and object, negating the object whose very presence had set a limit to and thereby negated the infinite freedom of the subject. In this Absolute Knowledge, as Hegel called it (actually a rather mad solipsism), the spirit simultaneously knows itself as it knows the world to be its own materialization; the object world is dissolved in subjectivity in the identity of subject and object which is the Absolute Spirit in full possession of itself. This, for Hegel, was the transcendence of alienation—alienation being one of his key concepts which expressed the loss of self through its objectification, a loss which is only overcome in full consciousness of that objectification as such. But for Feuerbach, Hegel's philosophy is not the cure but rather a symptom of alienation, for like religion it projects an Infinite—which is really an abstraction from the collective life of finite human beings—and gives to its own creation an illegitimate ontological status, thereby alienating man from his own free being which seems merely the predicate of an Absolute Being. Hegel, according to Feuerbach, had simply reversed reality: thought arises from being and not the other way around. Thus philosophy must begin where all thought begins—with man's actual, finite life, with his material and sensuous existence. The significant relation of man is to other men; Feuerbach ends with a humanism that asserts that man overcomes his alienation when he discovers his identity with other men in a loving I-Thou relationship.

Marx, while concurring in the humanistic reversal of Hegel's categories, departs somewhat from Feuerbach's standpoint, for he feels that Feuerbach remains too abstract in his discussion, rescuing an *abstract, generalized* man from an abstract Absolute; if thought is the predicate of being, then thinking must begin with man's particular being in the world—that is, in his political, and ultimately his economic relations with other men at any moment in time. Marx's desire to politicize Feuerbach's reversal of Hegel's idealism comes first; it was the influence of the socialist and communist theories which he met in full force in Paris, where he settled in the fall of 1843, together with his reading there of English political economy and French political history, that convinced him that economic relations lay at the center of human history, and that in them lay the key to man's alienation and to the way to transcendence of that alienation. If the necessity to demystify Hegel seems a peculiar obsession in these philosophers, it must be remembered that his dialectic of history was a revolutionary view to which we have now become so accustomed that, like all thought paradigms which have been absorbed, its source has become shrouded and its conclusions have come to seem self-evident. Yet it was Hegel who first

> conceived of history as it were in two dimensions: the horizontal, in which the phenomena of different spheres of activity, occurring among different peoples belonging to the same stage of development, are seen to be broadly interconnected in some unitary pattern, which gives each period its own individual "organic," recognizably unique character; and the vertical dimension, in which the same cross-section of events is viewed as part of a temporal succession, as a necessary stage in a developing process, in some sense contained and generated by its predecessor in time, which is itself seen already to embody, although in a less developed state, those very tendencies and forces whose full emergence makes the later age that which it ultimately comes to be.[16]

This sense of history as a totality, interrelated in all its parts, tied to the notion of its evolution (which included the organic necessity of revolution in the process) as a *purposive activity,* made it possible to see all systems as historically contingent but without the loss of all values in an overriding relativism, for if a common purpose could be discerned behind all of history's contingent manifestations, then human history became intelligible and meaningful at the same stroke. The flaw in Hegel's system, however, was precisely that he attributed that purposive activity to an Absolute Spirit, historically manifest in the Spirit of various ages and nations, which he felt had come to its culmination in his time and in his system. When Marx rescued this historicism from the mystical, when he gave its purpose a human source, he destroyed it as a determinism and established it as a radical instrument of change, in which man is seen as both the creator and the end of his own history. It was Marx who came to see all aspects of human activity in an age as reciprocally determining each other, rather than as reciprocally determined and united by non-human Spirit; man's purpose, which lay behind this history, could only be sought in the material existence through which he—by his very nature—must realize himself.

For Marx, as for Hegel, history and consciousness were converging; for Hegel, this convergence was the swallowing of objective history by developed self-consciousness; for Marx, on the contrary, consciousness would lose its separateness in material action with which it was becom-

16. Isaiah Berlin, *Karl Marx: His Life and Environment,* 3rd ed. (London: Oxford University Press, 1963), pp. 46–47.

ing coincident. What consciousness perceives and humanity suffers point to a single outcome—all it needed now was time:

> On our side the old world must be brought right out into the light of day and the new one given a positive form. The longer that events allow thinking humanity time to recollect itself and suffering humanity time to assemble itself the more perfect will be the birth of the product that the present carries in its womb.[17]

For Marx the gestation period of his own vision of futurity, of humanity "consciously bringing its old work to completion," ended in Paris with the writing of the so-called *Economic and Philosophic Manuscripts of 1844*. The Paris Manuscripts, child of the cross-fertilization of German philosophy, French political theory, and English economics, first published in German only as recently as 1932 and much discussed since then, reveal—by clarifying the original synthesis as it took form—the deep unity of Marx's thought, the later development of which is but an elaboration in more and more concrete detail of this first formulation, what I. Mészáros has called a system *"in statu nascendi."* In them, for the first time, economics and philosophy become indissoluble, for it is here that Marx makes explicit the exact identity of the alienation of *man* with the alienation of *labor,* the synthesizing principle which reconciles heretofore irreconcilable systems.

It is well to remember at this juncture that Marx was living at a time when vast social changes were being wrought by the Industrial Revolution, when the relation of social forms to means of production was, therefore, becoming increasingly transparent; the awareness of this relation was responsible for the liberal optimism about scientific and technological process as productive of human progress and happiness as well as the new socialist belief that only a redistribution of society's wealth could counteract the destructive social tendencies at work in the new exploitative and rapacious industrial forces it saw gathering. Preceding what turned out to be the abortive revolutions of 1848, there was a growing excitement among intellectuals and working men alike that coming events would see the completion of the liberation begun in the French Revolution, a belief which generated both invective against the *status quo* and visions of utopian solutions to mankind's ills. Sharing in this climate, but suspicious of enthusiasm that did not rest on a firm empirical and philosophic base, Marx turned to the study of history and economics, refracted always through the teleology of his fundamental Hegelianism. It was this teleology, resting on a firm material base, that gave to his predictions the ring of certainty, that changed the utopian "ought to be" into the prophetic "will be." The

17. Quoted in McLellan, *Karl Marx*, p. 64.

key lay in seeing that Hegel's doctrine was a mystification of the actual relations of civil society, whose shape was determined in turn by economic relations:

> The outstanding achievement of Hegel's *Phenomenology* and of its final outcome, the dialectic of negativity as the moving and generating principle, is thus first that Hegel conceives the self-creation of man as a process, conceives objectification as loss of the object, as alienation and as transcendence of alienation; that he thus grasps the essence of *labor* and comprehends objective man—true—because real man—as the outcome of man's own labor.[18]

Thus Marx sees, with Hegel, man's self-creation as a process of his "objectification," the creation of himself through labor. But labor, for Hegel, had been—as Marx said—"abstractly mental labor," a mental act whereby consciousness objectifies itself in an object which is only recovered through cognition when, as was said, the thinking self knows the object as its own creation, its own alienated self, and thereby overcomes alienation by the illusory dissolution of the objective world. But the resolution of a problem by the dissolution of one of its sides is no solution; Hegel negates, not alienation, but man's objective nature, his *reality*, for as Marx says, "a being that does not have its nature outside of itself is not a natural being and has no part in the natural world."[19] For Marx, Hegel's subject-object identity is "alienated self-consciousness," a reflection of the existent world where man's labor necessarily involves him in alienation, for reasons which Hegel does not see. According to Marx, objectification need not be automatically alienating; in fact, labor is "self-genesis"—man has his human existence precisely in the necessary and natural act of objectification, his trans-action with nature whereby through his productive activity man creates his "inorganic body," the objectification of himself in which he has his being. Man is nothing else but his activity—"as individuals express their life, so they are."[20] If, then, man's productive activity is the "mediator" with nature and other men that is the substance of a truly human existence, how has it come to pass that productive activity has become identified with his alienation, has become, in fact, the negation of his humanity? "Hegel's standpoint," says Marx, "is that of modern political economy." For both, "Labor is man's *coming-to-be-himself* within alienation, or as *alienated* man."[21]

18. Karl Marx, *Economic and Philosophic Manuscripts of 1844*, ed. Dirk J. Struik, trans. Martin Milligan (London: Lawrence & Wishart Ltd., 1973), p. 177.
19. Quoted in McLellan, *Karl Marx*, p. 127.
20. *Marxist Social Thought*, p. 115.
21. Marx, *Economic and Philosophic Manuscripts*, p. 177.

This contradiction is explained by the fact that it is not productive activity *per se* but *its present historical form*, the capitalist mode of production, that has made labor synonymous with estrangement. It is precisely because man has his being in his life activity, in production, because "free, conscious activity is man's species character," that the deformation of the productive process is the loss of his "species character," the loss of his humanity. In *The German Ideology*, written with Engels in 1846, Marx would explore the historical development of the estrangement of labor through the growth of the productive forces, and with them, the division of labor; in the *Manuscripts* he was concerned with describing what that estrangement of labor meant in human terms, how it was identical with the self-estrangement of man, and how they would be overcome together.

In this reformulation of Hegel, two things happen together. First, idealism is overcome, that is, the traditional devaluation of the material world in relation to a higher spirit; and pattern is returned to the material life from which it had in the first place been abstracted. Second, a redemptive humanism is reinstated, for by attributing the "alienating" aspects of human life to a present, and perishable, form of production relations—the ruthless competition, egoism, and exploitation of the capitalist system—they become contingent and not essential characteristics of human nature; they are in fact equated precisely with man's alienation from his real nature. This latter article of Marxist faith was responsible, in large part, for the ability of Marxism to inspire action and embody hope, and marks it as millennial thought. It is this belief that evil will disappear with a particular manifestation of it that marks all apocalyptic-millennial vision; in this lies both its diagnostic perception of the particular inhuman forms which oppress a society, and through that very perception the reawakening of an image of human wholeness which the present order betrays. Thus it is consistent to believe in that wholeness as assured by the destruction of the present order of things; such historical innocence marks a period of social change, directs and empowers it.

To return to Marx's demystification of Hegel: for Hegel, every object, by setting a limit to the self, was perceived as the subject's negation; freedom, for Hegel, who perceives the self as infinite, is the absence of everything that is non-self, of everything that imposes finitude. Thus, the search for knowledge becomes "that voyage into the open, where nothing is below or above us, and we stand in solitude with ourselves alone."[22] This solipsistic inflation of the self, until it inhabits the void, is a project whose horror is revealed in the metaphor; this "overreaching of the intellect," as Marx called it, is precisely the

22. Quoted in Robert C. Tucker, *Philosophy and Myth in Karl Marx*, 2nd ed. (Cambridge: Cambridge University Press, 1972), p. 54.

indication of the intellect's helplessness in the objective world, of that distance—in Germany, in particular—of philosophy from the world of practical action. It is also an indication, as was said, of the inability of the objective world to express and embody "free conscious activity"— hence the idealist's rejection of that world. The Paris Manuscripts analyze at length what had gone wrong with man's objectification of himself; how, under the present mode of production, his productive activity resulted not in his self-creation but his self-negation:

> In the sphere of political economy this realization of labor appears as *loss of realization* for the workers; objectification as *loss of the object* and *bondage to it;* appropriation as *estrangement*, as *aliena-tion.*[23]

This alienation has several interconnected forms: the alienation of man from the product, or object, of his labor; the alienation of man from himself; and finally, the alienation of man from nature— specifically, from his human or "species" nature, thus alienating man from man. In the first instance, what ought to be labor's realization in the creation of a product becomes, because of the capitalist's appropria-tion of it, his congealed power, possessed by another as the material power that is used to control him. Thus his product becomes an alien, hostile thing which embodies not his mastery but his bondage. Second, the laborer loses himself not only in his product but in the *"act of production,* within the *producing activity,* itself,"[24] for not only does the worker's activity belong to another, but it constitutes the restric-tion of his powers rather than their free and manifold expression. In the early capitalism which Marx took as his model, the laborer worked inhumanly long hours for the barest necessities of life; his labor was often the monotonous repetition of a mindless act; he had become the mere appendage to a machine he had no scientific understanding of, in a process he could not fully comprehend—another way in which mental and physical activity had become divided:

> . . . in his work, therefore, he does not affirm himself but denies himself, does not feel content but unhappy, does not develop freely his physical and mental energy but mortifies his body and ruins his mind. The worker therefore only feels himself outside his work, and in his work feels outside himself.[25]

Finally, since labor for Marx is the mediation between man and nature and man and other men, "estranged labor estranges the *species* from man."[26]

23. Marx, *Economic and Philosophic Manuscripts,* p. 108.
24. *Ibid.,* p. 110.
25. *Ibid.*
26. *Ibid.,* p. 112.

The whole character of a species—its species character—is contained in the character of its life activity; and free, conscious activity is man's species character. Life itself appears only as a means to life.[27]

In changing the "life of the species into a means of individual life,"[28] man has only an abstract individual life, abstract because the individual denies his real life in getting his living, and ,so has no *real* existence. And, "In fact, the proposition that man's species nature is estranged from him means that one man is estranged from the other, as each of them is from man's essential nature."[29] Put less abstractly, the competition engendered by the capitalist system, in the perverse freedom of the market—which is really the negation of freedom by turning men into commodities and by its tendency toward ever greater monopoly—turns man against man in the bloody war of all against all. Thus Marx sees capitalistic society as predicated on the most antisocial of laws, which it attempts to elevate to the status of eternal laws of nature in support of its own system. Marx, as a matter of fact, reversing the Social Darwinists, accused Darwin of reading into nature's evolution the ruthless competition of the civil society in which he lived. Man, after all, in creating his society, is in control of the variable sense attached to the concept of what constitutes the "fittest."

For Marx, man's essential nature, from which he has become estranged, is not some abstract human essence but his creative and conscious activity—physical and mental—expressed in the production of the man-made world (*"humanized* nature"). This essential nature, real only insofar as it is expressed and objectified in productive activity (hence only presently actual in its estranged form) is by definition social: "Activity and mind, both in their content and in their *mode of existence* are *social; social* activity and *social* mind."[30] Human production is by its nature social; every individual product is equally a social product. The notion of the independent producer as the starting point of human history is, says Marx, "one of the unimaginative fantasies of eighteenth-century romances;"[31] in fact, he says, the further back one goes in human history, the more communal is the productive process. Even the solitary thinker is engaged in a social action, for the stuff of thought—language—is itself a social creation. Society is the individual's

27. *Ibid.*, p. 113.
28. *Ibid.*, p. 112.
29. *Ibid.*, p. 114.
30. *Ibid.*, p. 137.
31. Karl Marx and Friedrich Engels, *The German Ideology*, ed. C. J. Arthur (London: Lawrence & Wishart Ltd., 1970), p. 124. This quotation is from the supplementary texts: Marx, "Introduction to a Critique of Political Economy."

being, just as the individual is society's: "*as* society itself produces *man as man,* so is society *produced* by him."[32]

The Marxian critique of society is motivated by society's failure to realize man's potentialities. For while man actualises his being in social life, he is also hampered by it. Man is social by nature. One must "above all avoid postulating 'society' once more as an abstraction confronting the individual. The individual is a social being . . . individual life and the life of the species are not different things. . . ."[33]

The relationship is always reciprocal: individuals, acting upon each other and the material world create society, actions which in turn are formed by the historical action of society on them—the dialectic of man as a "real individual social being" who is "the centre of reference of the essential unity between the individual and the species."[34] For as Marx was to write several years later, man "is not only a social animal, but an animal that can individualise himself only within society."[35]

The *human* essence of nature first exists only for *social* man; for only here does nature exist for him as a *bond* with *man*—as his existence for the other and the other's existence for him—as the life-element of human reality. Only here has what is to him his *natural* existence become his *human* existence, and nature become man for him. Thus *society* is the unity of being of man with nature—the true resurrection of nature—the naturalism of man and the humanism of nature both brought to fulfillment.[36]

The resurrection of nature in a human body—social man mirrored in the objective man-made world (man's "inorganic body") in which he recognizes and is united with himself: this is the dream of the poetic imagination made actual, the marriage, in Blake, of Albion and Jerusalem, man and the city of his works. This marriage is consummated with "*Communism* as the *positive* transcendence of *private property,* as *human self-estrangement,* and therefore as the real *appropriation of the human* essence by and for man."[37]

This communism, as fully developed naturalism, equals humanism, and as fully developed humanism equals naturalism; it is the *genuine* resolution of the conflict between man and nature and between man and man—the true resolution of the strife between

32. Marx, *Economic and Philosophic Manuscripts*, p. 137.
33. George Lichtheim, *Marxism: An Historical and Critical Study*, 2nd ed. rev. (London: Routledge and Kegan Paul, 1964), p. 43.
34. Mészáros, *Marx's Theory of Alienation*, p. 333 n.
35. Marx and Engels, *The German Ideology*, p. 125.
36. Marx, *Economic and Philosophic Manuscripts*, p. 137.
37. *Ibid.*, p. 135.

existence and essence, between objectification and self-confirmation, between freedom and necessity, between the individual and the species. Communism is the riddle of history solved, and it knows itself to be this solution.[38]

"Such a consummation is metaphysical, and indeed ultimately religious";[39] yet it is precisely because Marx reversed the meaning of transcendence from the old religious notion of transcendence of the finite and human to transcendence of the inhuman and fulfillment of finite human needs that this metaphysical solution becomes *practical*— dependent as it is on the changing of production relations in society, that theory is united to practice and human values appear once again as active agents in the newly affirmed material world. Thus the interpreters of Marx who would illegitimately partition his system by positing two Marxes, an early philosophical humanist and a later empirical economist, ignore the clear evidence that from the moment his synthesis took form in the Manuscripts of 1844, his ethics and his economics were inseparably joined.

The numerous versions of the "young Marx versus mature Marx" (or the other way round) approach have something in common. This is: an effort to oppose political economy to philosophy or philosophy to political economy and use Marx as a supporting authority in favour of such pseudo-alternative. Broadly speaking those who want to evade or reject the vital—and by no means speculative— philosophical problems of freedom and the individual, side with the "mature political economist" or "scientific" Marx, whereas those who wish the practical power of Marxism (which is inseparable from its demystification of capitalist economy) never existed exalt the "young philosopher Marx".[40]

Among Marx's critics, one of the tendencies is to attack him on the grounds of his unprovable philosophic standpoint, the other is to attack him for being a crass materialist, unconcerned with "higher" moral and spiritual considerations. The fascinating paradox in these opposite points of attack is resolved precisely by the presence of both these heretofore split systems in Marx's thought, and the inability of such critics to transcend the dualism which he himself overcomes.

The unity of mental and material in Marx's thought is nowhere more evident than in his notion of the *inevitability* of transcendence of alienation, which arises from his equation of human alienation with the alienation of labor under the capitalist system and from Hegel's "con-

38. *Ibid.*
39. Lichtheim, *Marxism*, p. 44.
40. Mészáros, *Marx's Theory of Alienation*, p. 227.

viction that the totality of the world is an ordered whole which the intellect can comprehend and master."[41] And that inevitability is synonymous not with determinism—but ultimately with man's freedom, his own self-creation. The first question to be raised here is how does the philosophic recognition of man's self-estrangement through capitalist labor result in its transcendence? Here Hegel's dialectic of historical change joins the study of economics and history to reveal to Marx that capitalism, like every other system evolved in man's struggle to wrest his human existence from nature, creates its own contradiction with which it struggles until both are negated in a higher synthesis which resolves their contradictions. The development of industrial capitalism depended upon the creation of its eventual negation—a laboring force, the proletariat, whose impoverishment was the necessary consequence of the enrichment of the owners. In *The Holy Family,* written with Engels and published in 1845, Marx makes his attack on German abstract and "spiritualized" philosophy consistent with his sympathetic description of the impoverished laborer's condition:

> But Not To Have is not a mere category, it is a most disconsolate reality; today the man who has nothing is nothing, for he is cut off from existence in general and still more from a human existence. . . . Not To Have is the most desperate *spiritualism,* a complete unreality of the human, a complete reality of the dehumanized, a very positive To Have, a having of hunger, of cold, of disease, of crime, of debasement, of all inhumanity and monstrosity.[42]

Thus the spiritualism of the philosopher in the empty heaven of his mind and the worker in the crowded hell of his life are complementary; both will lose that negative spiritualism together in what becomes not merely the amelioration of social and economic inequity, but something far more grand: the unity of philosophy and reality:

> Where then is there the *positive* possibility of German emancipation? In the formation of a class with *radical chains* . . . a class which is the dissolution of all classes, a sphere of society which has a universal character because its sufferings are universal, and which claims no *particular right* because the wrong committed against it is not a *particular wrong* but wrong *as such.* . . . When the proletariat declares the *dissolution of the existing social order* it does no more than proclaim the *secret of its own existence,* for it constitutes the *effective* dissolution of order. . . . As philosophy finds its *material* weapons in the proletariat, so the proletariat discovers its

41. Lichtheim, *Marxism,* p. 35.
42. Quoted in Stanley Edgar Hyman, *The Tangled Bank: Darwin, Marx, Frazer and Freud as Imaginative Writers* (New York: Grosset & Dunlap, 1966), p. 89.

intellectual weapons in philosophy. . . . *Philosophy* is the *head* of this emancipation, and the *proletariat* its *heart.* Philosophy cannot realise itself without abolishing the proletariat, and the proletariat cannot emancipate itself without realising philosophy.[43]

The universal Idea of Hegel, whose unfolding was the logic of history, is transformed into man, incarnate in the proletariat, whose emancipation from capitalist chains overturns the orders of the world and inaugurates the era of a redeemed humanity living at one with its creation, a humanized nature. Thus the greatest modern Gnosticism gives birth to a material doctrine of redemption: "In the beginning was the Word, and the Word was made flesh."

> Without this central idea, Marxism is just another species of materialist determinism, and this is indeed what the later socialist movement largely succeeded in making out of it. But the transformation was never complete; at the core of the system, however much it might be watered down by its own author and others to suit the positivist fashion of the later nineteenth century, there remained something resembling the original vision of a world made new by a unique event fusing thought and action, theory and practice, philosophy and revolution, into a creative drama of human liberation. It is literally true that apart from this quasi-metaphysical *tour de force* the whole subsequent history of the Marxist movement must remain incomprehensible.[44]

In the proletariat, then, philosophy has found "its material weapons": the negation of the negation, the material force by which human alienation will be overcome. In identifying the striving of the nascent working-class movement with the interests of humanity, and in seeing its wrongs as "wrong *as such,*" Marx gives the apocalyptic imagination's view of reality: a Manichaean description of the world as two factions—the capitalist and the proletarian—one evil, the other good, whose final struggle would result in the overcoming of evil and the coming of a humanistic millennium, the end of what Marx called the "prehistory of society." Lewis Feuer suggests how insightful this simplification was:

> . . . Marx knew of the diverse social universes of aristocrats, high financial bourgeois, industrial bourgeois, working men, students, bureaucrats of all levels, entrepreneurs, thieves, lumpenproletarians, churchmen . . . journalists, peasants. . . . His sweeping simplification did, however, distort social realities, and he mispredicted the evolution of capitalist societies. . . . And yet this bold simplification has been another source of Marx's perception of

43. Quoted in Lichtheim, *Marxism*, p. 53.
44. Lichtheim, *Marxism*, p. 54.

social truth. For wherever conditions are such that a large group of men feel themselves exploited by another, their perception of society will tend to be in Marx's dualistic terms . . . . always the consciousness of exploitation has tended to create an image of the social world in which the basic class division is between the oppressors and the oppressed, the exploiters and the exploited.[45]

With a kind of poetic exactitude, Marx drew out of his world its own perception, or at least the perception of a part of it, that part whose championship was, for him, the defense, in the long run, of the whole of humanity. In this lay another common element of chiliastic vision, so familiar by now, that the lowest of humanity—the "suffering servant"—shall be raised up, and mankind with it. "Marxism," writes Feuer, "was the first social creed in the world's history to declare unequivocally that history henceforth was going to be made by the lowliest, the working class."[46] In fact, of course, crisis vision by its very nature has always elevated the lowest to a redemptive role: the mission of Jesus was to the "people of the earth"—the lowest strata of Jewish society in his day; Thomas Münzer's was to the German peasantry whom he raised in revolt against the princes. The apocalypse in Marx's thought is, of course, the prophesied violent revolution which will overthrow the existing order; further, the communist hereafter has, in its particular form, all the characteristics typical of such visions—a world of abundance, amity, and equality, free of coercion and of divisions both inner and outer, a world whose basic unity is that wholeness central to Marx's thought: the unity of the mental and the material, of man and his work. There would be a period of transition, for something of the old is always preserved in the new; but later,

> In a higher phase of communist society, after the enslaving subordination of the individual to the division of labour, and therewith also the antithesis between mental and physical labour, has vanished; after labour has become not only a means of life but life's prime want; after the productive forces have also increased with the all-round development of the individual, and all the springs of co-operative wealth flow more abundantly—only then can the narrow horizon of bourgeois right be crossed in its entirety and society inscribe on its banners: "From each according to his ability, to each according to his needs!"[47]

This passage was written in 1875 and bears witness to the unfaded presence in Marx's mind of his millennial hopes for humanity.

45. Feuer, Introduction to *Marx and Engels: Basic Writings*, p. 13.
46. *Ibid.*, p. 21.
47. Marx, "Critique of the Gotha Programme," *Marx and Engels: Basic Writings*, p. 160.

The reference in this passage to "the enslaving subordination of the individual to the division of labour" is another central concept in Marxist thought, one which is fully explored in its historical development in *The German Ideology* of 1846, which contains perhaps the fullest enunciation of Marx's doctrine of historical materialism. This doctrine was already implicit in his materialist inversion of Hegel, restated years later, in 1873, in *Capital*:

> My dialectic method is not only different from the Hegelian, but is its direct opposite. To Hegel the life process of the human brain, i.e., the process of thinking, which, under the name of "the Idea," he even transforms into an independent subject, is the demiurgos of the real world, and the real world is only the external, phenomenal form of "the Idea". With me on the contrary, the ideal is nothing else than the material world reflected by the human mind and translated into forms of thought.[48]

If this were so, then the systems of thought and belief of all the ages of man had been the reflection of their actual material relations, the production relations of their society. This conception of economic infrastructure as the determinant of cultural superstructures led Marx to reexamine history through its actual economic relations, and to discover in it a pattern common to apocalyptic modes of thought—a deepening spiral of evil (or divisive error), greatest at the present moment, which is also simultaneously to produce its destruction and usher in a new age and a redeemed humanity. Also consonant with such a visionary interpretation of history is the notion that behind this only apparently downward spiral is an upward one which reveals the hidden purpose in history, a purpose whose achievement is at hand.

The deepening "evil" is, for Marx, the division of labor which is born, paradoxically, out of a liberating purpose—man's attempt to master the natural world, to end his bondage to material *necessity*, and to realize himself in that "free, conscious activity" which is his "species nature." Early man had lived in a system of communal ownership in which, though he enjoyed a high degree of social union, he was the bondsman of nature, most of his life's activity being involved with the satisfaction of man's primary subsistence needs. But, as he began to improve the instruments and mode of production, he necessarily, at the same moment, introduced the division of labor, this division which began to split "mental and material labor"[49] and, by creating a surplus, to give some men the means by which to control others, thereby

48. Marx, Introduction to the Second Edition of *Capital,* in *Basic Writings,* p. 186.
49. Marx and Engels, *The German Ideology,* p. 51.

introducing class struggle as the central fact of historical process. With the higher development of the instruments of production, division of labor had proportionately increased, even while man was preparing the means for his eventual conquest of the stultifying "realm of necessity."

> . . . natural science had invaded and transformed human life all the more *practically* through the medium of industry; and has prepared human emancipation, although its immediate effect had to be the furthering of the dehumanization of man.[50]

Bourgeois society, with its commercial values, had produced the modern industrial means of production which it organized according to its own capitalistic production relations; technology could liberate man from bondage to nature, but not until it was liberated from the alienating grip of private ownership:

> The bourgeois relations of production are the last antagonistic form of the social process of production . . . at the same time the productive forces developing in the womb of bourgeois society create the material conditions for the solution of that antagonism. This social formation brings, therefore, the prehistory of society to a close.[51]

Thus Marx is not a primitivist but resembles rather the Blakean call to a radical innocence on the far side of experience; man would recover his primitive communism, but, with the development of a sophisticated technology for which he had paid so dearly, would enjoy a liberated social and individual existence in which he would be freed not only from the coercion of other men but from the enslavement to nature. Thus, in the end as it was in the beginning, but with a difference so great as to justify the long historical division and struggle which had produced this return to a changed and humanized earth. Marx vacillated somewhat on how complete man's triumph over necessity through technology could be, but he saw the course of development toward that freedom clearly, always viewing industrial production as a means to a human end; freed from the capitalist drive to amass wealth and fill acquired needs, industry and machine technology would fill man's subsistence needs and free him for the creative diversity of action compatible with his manifold and self-creating nature:

> . . in communist society, where nobody has one exclusive sphere of activity but each can become accomplished in any branch he wishes, society regulates the general production and thus makes it

50. Marx, *Economic and Philosophic Manuscripts*, p. 142.
51. Marx, Preface to "A Contribution to the Critique of Political Economy," *Marxist Social Thought*, p. 127.

possible for me to do one thing today and another tomorrow, to hunt in the morning, fish in the afternoon, rear cattle in the evening, criticise after dinner, just as I have a mind, without ever becoming hunter, fisherman, shepherd or critic.[52]

This passage reminds us how poorly Marxism agrees with totalitarianism; the envisioned social harmony is fully in the Western tradition of individuation—but with the understanding that the attempt at affirmation of the individual self without regard to its participation in the world is the negation of the self, a spurious, abstract individuality, for man has a social nature and is only humanly realized as a "social individual."

Marx is revealed here in a rare mood; seldom does he describe in any concrete way the particular social instrumentalities and actual forms of the communist hereafter. He was impatient to the point of intolerance with the "utopian" socialists who produced exact models of an ideal society. This impatience was philosophically consistent, for Marx's historicism made it clear that future systems—utopias—could only be imagined by historically contingent minds and were therefore only the values of the current bourgeois liberalism artificially conceived without their negative and necessary consequences—the good writ large, the evil merely written out. Only when the present contradictions had been actually resolved through the destruction of the capitalist system would a new society begin to emerge whose structure could then take form out of that new situation.

> *Communism* is the necessary pattern and the dynamic principle of the immediate future, but communism as such is not the goal of human development—which goal is the structure of a human society.[53]

Communism may be the riddle of history solved, but that is the "pre-history" in which men have lived to the present. There is in this refusal to construct a programme for a nonexistent society an historical appreciation that a new world view is first and foremost a radical critique of the existing order, a justification and programme first for its dissolution, and only by extension a prophecy for a new society, conceived of as free of the contradictions of private property but inconceivable on its own new, historically yet undeveloped terms. The utopian ambience which, nevertheless, surrounds Marx's expectations for the future is precisely that the clear perception of present wrong as wrong *as such* makes its extirpation seemingly identical with the realization of the ideal, and thus the standpoint of the oppressed

52. Marx and Engels, *The German Ideology*, p. 53.
53. Marx, *Economic and Philosophic Manuscripts*, p. 146.

class becomes the standpoint of humanity. The proletariat is the self-emptying redemptive force; the losing of itself would be the finding of humanity. It is seen, then,

> not simply as a sociological force diametrically opposed to the standpoint of capital—and thus remaining in the latter's orbit—but as a *self-transcending* historical force which cannot help super-ceding *alienation* (i.e., the historically given form of *objectification*) in the process of realizing its own immediate ends that happen to coincide with the "reappropriation of the human essence."[54]

Thus the victory of the proletariat is seen simultaneously as its dissolution, for it exists only in relation to a class of owners; the proletariat therefore disappears with the class it overthrows as it initiates the "classless society," the disappearance of social antagonisms, and the resultant "withering away" of the state which had traditionally mediated those class hostilities. The vision not only transcends class and state but national differences, for with the creation of a world market and the extension of industrialism, the "world historical individual" replaces the local being. Even as this extension of productive activity and exchange to a world scale had enlarged the alien power to which the individual was enslaved, so with the communist revolution will his social connections and the scope of his freedom be enlarged: "the liberation of each single individual will be accomplished in the measure in which history becomes transformed into world history."[55]

The liberation of mankind was conceived by Marx as a material force gathering beneath the surface of bourgeois society; as with so many of his images which make significant metaphors out of actual conditions, this image is literal as well—workers forced to live in the dark cellars of the cities were seen as the underground force which must regain the light of day. Marx's writing is full of references to volcanoes and earthquakes as natural analogies to the revolutionary forces gathering and about to erupt and shake the earth, powers which would be released, not by moral exhortations, but by material conditions:

> No class in civil society has any need or capacity for general emancipation until it is forced by its immediate condition, by material necessity, by its very chains.[56]

Much of Marx's later economic analysis, written during his long years in London (1849–1883) and drawn largely from English economic conditions, was designed to show how this emancipating class was being

54. Mészáros, *Marx's Theory of Alienation*, p. 64.
55. Marx and Engels, *The German Ideology*, p. 55.
56. Quoted in Mészáros, *Marx's Theory of Alienation*, p. 221.

formed by the very nature of the capitalist system, in that apocalyptic sense that the awful conditions of the raw industrial capitalism of the England of his day had to worsen, that the growth of that system could only deepen its contradictions—competition creating monopoly, accompanied by worsening crises and the growing "pauperization" of the worker, and his development, thereby, into the force for "general emancipation." As Marx grew older, and away from the revolutionary enthusiasm of 1848, he became more and more convinced that the proletariat was in for an extended struggle, but the consolidation of that force seemed as certain as the worsening of conditions that would accelerate the struggle. To be properly understood, this prophecy must be taken in Blake's sense of the prophet as the man who says "If you go on So, the result is So":

> The visions of the worsening of conditions in *Capital* are not really realistic appraisals of the future, they are dramatizations, what Burke calls "the temporalizing of essence," putting the essence of the present situation as a fated vision of the future (as origin myths put it as a genesis in the past). They demonstrate Burke's "principle of completion," entelechy, the inevitable tendency to perfect terminology by carrying it to the end of the line.[57]

Further, the economic theories of Marx have this prospective impetus because they begin from the recognition of the need for and inevitability of change which rests in its turn on his profoundly partisan humanism and his metaphysical faith in the material unfolding of a realized human freedom in man's self-created and self-creating history. Thus, in reading English political economy against the needs of real human beings, Marx develops out of it its own critique.

There may be theoretical difficulties but there is an imaginative fidelity in Marx's adoption of Smith and Ricardo's "labor theory of value," which he elaborated in his own "surplus value" theory, i.e., profit as the amount of surplus value which the laborer produces but which the capitalist expropriates by paying subsistence wages. Marx himself insists on the central human importance of the labor theory of value:

> The recent scientific discovery, that the products of labor, so far as they are values, are but material expressions of the human labor spent in their production, marks, indeed, an epoch in the history of the development of the human race.[58]

In his adoption of this notion, Marx not only applied it more consistently and drew out its implications in his surplus value theory, but extended its meaning. Ricardo

57. Hyman, *The Tangled Bank*, pp. 129–30.
58. Quoted in *ibid.*, p. 127.

had treated embodied labour as the regulator of exchange values, but had not troubled to define the concept of value itself. For Marx, the quantity of labour incorporated in products does not determine their value; it *is* their value; commodities are congealed labour.[59]

However he had to strain his logical ingenuity to maintain these concepts, he never deserted them. Lichtheim suggests that it was Marx's desire for an invariable criterion for the value of goods that led him to cling to the labor value theory; it would seem, however, more than coincidental that what this theory offered in addition was something deeply compatible with Marx's humanistic materialism, that is, a *human* criterion of value by which to measure and reanimate the material world.

Essentially, "value" for Marx has nothing to do with economics. It is an intrinsic property of commodities representing the amount of workers' blood that has gone into them.[60]

As earlier myths had humanized the natural world, so Marx humanized man's new environment, the world of production, of factory-made commodities. Since capital, which included the technological instruments of mass production, could inevitably be read back to surplus value—the value stolen by the capitalist from the worker's wages—human labor, in an age of machines, was kept in the center of the perception of the productive process. Marx restored human value and the human body to the abstract impersonality of modern economics and mass production, drawing out the implications of his original theory of the identity of human alienation with the alienation of labor, of man with his objectification in the outer world.

Is value the money exchanged for goods in the market? No. Real value is the human energy expended in their making; the object becomes transparent, behind it appears a living man at work. The human presence once again animates a dead world, and profit, according to the surplus labor theory, becomes theft, its quantitative value absorbed in the qualitative loss it represents in the lives of men. Profit, like the commodity, becomes something alive—a living reproach. Always in Marx's thought man is inseparable from what he makes, as he will be in reality when history is fulfilled. Thus the labor value and surplus labor theory in humanly determining the value of commodities, reveal the value judgment behind them; "a problem for Marx was never simply a theoretical question."[61]

59. Lichtheim, *Marxism*, p. 173.
60. Hyman, *The Tangled Bank*, p. 128.
61. Lichtheim, *Marxism*, p. xviii.

> *Capital* admits freely that some commodities embodying labor
> values are unsalable, that with others 'the price realized may be
> abnormally above or below the value'. For the most part, however
> it either ignores demand and market price, or assures us that shifts
> in production eventually adjust them to reflect real value, that is,
> labor value. Labor value is an oddly idealistic conception for so
> materialistic a thinker . . .[62]

Yet by now it should be obvious just how consistent Marx is in the
idealistic cast of his materialism; more, how only the overcoming of the
old dualism adequately accounts for his visionary doctrine.

In his historical materialism Marx finds human values incarnate in
social (economic) history; in his communistic prophecies he finds ideal
value incarnate in the proletariat; in the same way, he finds human
beings incarnate in the things they make. In all his thought, he poetically reverses the process of abstraction by refinding and giving immediacy to the material realities out of which abstractions are made. Thus,
the demystification of mystical consciousness is simultaneously the
human repossession of material reality, the awakening from a long
dream to make it actual, for "the world has long dreamt of something
of which it only needs a fully developed consciousness in order to
realize it."[63]

> In its mystified form dialectic became the fashion in Germany
> because it seemed to transfigure and to glorify the existing state of
> things. In its rational form it is a scandal and abomination to
> bourgeoisdom and its doctrinaire professors because it includes in
> its comprehension and affirmative recognition of the existing state
> of things, at the same time also, the recognition of the negation of
> that state, of its inevitable breaking up; because it regards every
> historically developed social form as in fluid movement, and
> therefore takes into account its transient nature not less than its
> momentary existence; because it lets nothing impose upon it and
> is in its essence critical and revolutionary.[64]

Here is an obvious and central contradiction of Marx's thought: on the
one hand, "every historically developed social form . . . in fluid movement"; on the other, the projection of a millennial social form which,
by abolishing class struggle, seems to destroy the very motor of social
change. Engels wrote the following about Hegel, but his words seem
equally applicable to Marx:

62. Hyman, *The Tangled Bank*, p. 128.
63. Quoted in McLellan, *Karl Marx*, p. 77.
64. Marx, Introduction to the Second Edition of *Capital*, in *Basic Writings*,
p. 187.

With all philosophers it is precisely the "system" which is perishable; and for the simple reason that it springs from an imperishable desire of the human mind—the desire to overcome all contradictions. But if all contradictions are once for all disposed of, we shall have arrived at so-called absolute truth—world history will be at an end. And yet it has to continue, although there is nothing left for it to do—hence, a new, insoluble contradiction.[65]

The contradiction arises because Marx thinks at two very different levels of abstraction. The first level of abstraction is self-conscious thinking about both thinking and social forms in general, Marx theorizing about how conceptual models are made. These models, he says, are drawn from the conditions of actual life, and thus are as mortal as the conditions which produce them. On the second, less distant level of abstraction, Marx is himself making a model for reality, and in so doing is bound by the same constraints as all theorists; he must adhere to the material before him, define the dilemma in terms of his own perception, and resolve it on the same grounds. He cannot simultaneously be a detached theorist about model making and a model maker without involving himself in contradiction. The new social model he makes, of course, has its limits as described by the first level of abstraction; it too is bound to the particulars as it perceives them, is timebound, and will be superseded. But the model cannot, for that very reason, supersede itself; nor does the knowledge that all models, like their makers, are mortal remove either the necessity for making models in the first place or the deep sense their inventor has of their finality. When the contradictions in an existent model become apparent, as did the contradictions in the capitalist model to Marx, these contradictions necessarily disappear in a new model which resolves them and thereby completes itself.

Thomas Kuhn in *The Structure of Scientific Revolutions* describes the development of science not as a linear progression but as the replacement of one paradigm by another, when out of crisis created by large and significant anomalies which the old paradigm could not account for, a new paradigm—in what is called scientific revolution— takes shape. New paradigms, according to Kuhn, are called up only by crises, and old paradigms, however poorly they fit new data, are never relinquished except in favor of a new one. Scientists will tend endlessly to modify an old theory until a new one is available, for it is not possible to design an experiment without a model—in science or in society:

65. Engels, *Ludwig Feuerbach and the End of the Classical German Philosophy*, in *Basic Writings*, p. 243.

Once a first paradigm through which to view nature has been found, there is no such thing as research in the absence of any paradigm. To reject one paradigm without simultaneously substituting another is to reject science itself.[66]

A new paradigm, Kuhn asserts, is in no way a logical progression from the one it replaces:

The transition from a paradigm in crisis to a new one from which a new tradition of normal science can emerge is far from a cumulative process, one achieved by an articulation or extension of the old paradigm. Rather it is a reconstruction of the field from new fundamentals, a reconstruction that changes some of the field's most elementary theoretical generalizations as well as many of its paradigm methods and applications. . . . When the transition is complete, the profession will have changed its view of the field, its methods, and its goals.[67]

Kuhn quotes Herbert Butterfield's description of this process as "picking up the other end of the stick," producing changed relationships among old data in a way analogous to new and often inverted social relationships that emerge from new myths. The abrupt appearance of these new paradigms is also analogous to a phenomenon that has been observed repeatedly as typical of prophetic visions:

More often no such structure is consciously seen in advance. Instead, the new paradigm, or a sufficient hint to permit later articulation, emerges all at once, sometimes in the middle of the night, in the mind of a man deeply immersed in crisis. What the nature of that final stage is—how an individual invents (or finds he has invented) a new way of giving order to data now all assembled—must here remain inscrutable and may be permanently so.[68]

Despite their resemblances, there is a fundamental and obvious difference between the invention of a new scientific paradigm and that of a social model. For the social model is a special kind of paradigm—a myth, which is not a value free description of nature, but a normative and prescriptive embodiment of a set of relations seen as ideal from the perspective of a particular historical setting. By its very nature, myth—as the embedding of process in a dramatization of a vision of ideal human order—must have a teleology, a sense of unfolding design, of where process is tending. Myth is pattern given *human* meaning, and Marx's theorizing about how previous societies had made their myths—

66. Thomas S. Kuhn, *The Structure of Scientific Revolutions*, 2nd ed. (Chicago: University of Chicago Press, 1970), p. 79.
67. *Ibid.*, p. 85.
68. *Ibid.*, p. 90.

despite the contradiction it brought to his work—did make of him a very special, conscious and open-ended sort of mythologist. Not that he was conscious of himself as a mythmaker; he would certainly have hated the label. But because he knew how myths are made, his own myth was completely anthropological, seeing man as a being whose setting was not raw nature but his own humanly determined relation to nature, i.e., his culture. Thus Marx does not, as earlier mythologists had been wont to do, read back into nature the ethical or purposive designs which are human in origin, and whose relations to a larger nature are problematic at best. It was Marx's followers, actually following Engels and not Marx in this respect, who attempted to ascribe "natural laws" to the dialectic progression Marx found in human history. "Marx," writes Lichtheim, "wisely left nature (other than human nature) alone";[69] it was Engels, on the other hand, who made "dialectical materialism" into a "universal 'science' of the 'laws' of *nature* and history," a "cast iron certainty"[70] which fits better for the justification of institutionalized systems (as it indeed has come to serve the Soviet system), and destroys the radical tension of Marx's humanistic dialectics. In fact, it imported a distinctly non-human meaning (another alien abstraction) into a system of thought that begins by denouncing such intellectual maneuvers.

> One may say that the originality of Marx's standpoint consisted precisely in this: while the French materialists had entangled themselves in an insoluble problem by postulating a human nature passively dependent on the environment, and then superimposed upon this depressing picture an optimistic doctrine of progress, Marx pointed out that the key to the desired transformation lay in man's ability to rearrange the world of which he formed part.[71]

Lichtheim makes clear that Engels lost the new balance of Marx's thought, reverting to what was really only an updated form of the old materialism, and that his debt to Hegel in this respect also differed from Marx's:

> Marx had been attracted to Hegel's philosophy because its emphasis on the constitutive activity of mind presented him with the key to his own concept of material activity (*praxis*), wherein consciousness reappears as the specifically human form of natural existence. For Engels the stress lies on Hegel's conceptual machinery whereby material motion is invested with logical certainty. What really fascinates him is Hegel's determinism: his ability to

69. Lichtheim, *Marxism*, p. 247.
70. *Ibid.*, p. 246.
71. *Ibid.*, p. 252.

make it appear that nature (and history) follow a pre-ordained course.[72]

"History," wrote Marx, "does not use man to achieve its own ends, as though it were a particular person; it is merely the activity of man pursuing his own objectives."[73] Engels' appeal to an objective reality external to man somewhat depletes Marxism as a mythic, imaginative construct uniting matter and consciousness:

> Where the youthful Marx had envisaged a unique historical occurrence which enables mankind to comprehend history as its own creative act, Engels presents an evolutionary pattern which in the nature of things can never come to an end, and thus cannot yield up any definite meaning. History as a comprehended totality can "come to itself" by coming to a climax. Nature is immortal almost by definition, and its study—as Engels never tires of stressing—discloses no finality, but at best an endless approximation to a constantly receding limit. To assimilate the historical process to that of nature consequently means doing away with the idea of a decisive historical act that reveals the *meaning* of history.[74]

There is an apparent contradiction here between the immortality of change in Engels' version, which appears at first less static than the teleological version of Marx, which seems to freeze history at some future point. In fact, looked at more closely, the opposite is true. For the meaning that is lost by losing a sense of design is an imaginative, human loss, the sense of human history as self-creating and self-fulfilling. To see fulfillment in a future event is to give present action a meaning that inaugurates change in the direction of that fulfillment. "The philosophers," wrote Marx, "have only *interpreted* the world . . . the point, however, is to *change* it." To see human affairs as determined by natural laws is to make man a creature manipulated by the material world, hence, in fact, by other men; rather than to see the material world as a place constantly remade by man. The social consequences of this difference in view would seem self-evident. Given the imaginative wholeness of his approach to human history, it is not surprising that intrinsic to Marx's method of exposition is the constant use of imagery, the evaluative embodiments that energize his economic analyses and reveal the sympathies of the man behind them. Stanley Edgar Hyman, in his treatment of Marx as an imaginative writer, points out numerous examples of grotesque images which cluster into a powerful, poetic denunciation of capitalism's deformation of human existence. Hyman

72. *Ibid.*, p. 253.
73. Quoted in McLellan, *Karl Marx*, p. 134.
74. Lichtheim, *Marxism*, pp. 250–51.

gathers the images from *Capital* of vampires, ghouls, and other demonic monstrosities that personify capital and its agents living off the blood of labor; of giants, ogres, and cyclopean horrors for the machines of the new industrial age; and the images of life "crystallized, congealed, petrified," representing money and commodities which are the "alienated ability of mankind." And it is "living labor (that) must seize upon these things and rouse them from their death-sleep."[75] Just as the labor of living men is congealed in commodities, and man dehumanized, so his inhuman machines take on a monstrous life from the men they feed on: "a mechanical monster whose body fills whole factories, and whose demon power, at first veiled under the slow and measured motions of his giant limbs, at length breaks out into the fast and furious whirl of his countless working organs."[76]

The language here is Blakean, and a similar belief fuels it: the belief that as error increases it will reveal itself in the ugliness of its true nature, and, further, bring about its own destruction. The image of tearing away veils which Hyman finds a dominant one in Marx, "of exposing beautiful temptresses as the loathly hags they are,"[77] is also reminiscent of Blake. In the *Communist Manifesto of 1848* in a variation on this theme, Marx writes:

> The bourgeoisie, wherever it has got the upper hand, has put an end to all feudal, patriarchal, idyllic relations. It has pitilessly torn asunder the motley feudal ties that bound man to his "natural superiors," and has left remaining no other nexus between man and man than naked self-interest, than callous "cash payment." It has drowned the most heavenly ecstasies of religious fervour, of chivalrous enthusiasm, of Philistine sentimentalism in the icy water of egotistical calculation. It has resolved personal worth into exchange value and, in place of the numberless indefeasible chartered freedoms, has set up that single, unconscionable freedom—free trade. In one word, for exploitation, veiled by religious and political illusions, it has substituted naked, shameless, direct, brutal exploitation.[78]

What is curious about this quotation is that the veil of illusion is not one that the capitalist world throws over its own actions, but one which, in its "naked self-interest," it tears off the old world. There is here something like Blake's faith in the self-revelation of error—but something more, a peculiar ambivalence about those old illusions, as if

75. Quoted in Hyman, *The Tangled Bank*, p. 135.
76. Quoted in *ibid.*, p. 134.
77. *Ibid.*, p. 135.
78. Marx and Engels, *Manifesto of the Communist Party*, in *Basic Writings*, p. 51.

there was something of decency and dignity in the deceit, something illusion honored that bourgeois society has lost. Nakedness for Marx seems equivalent not to truth *per se*, but to some ugly and sordid truth; it has a brutal connotation suggestive of victimization, of man's helplessness when stripped of his humanity and dignity. In the communist society of the future, presumably, nakedness and veils will disappear together in the genuine production of the "living flowers" of a materialized humanity:

> Criticism has plucked the imaginary flowers from the chains not so that man may bear chains without any imagination or comfort, but so that he may throw away the chains and pluck living flowers. The criticism of religion disillusions man so that he may think, act, and fashion his own reality as a disillusioned man comes to his senses; so that he may revolve around himself as his real sun.[79]

Man's coming to his senses is meant by Marx quite literally; "the forming of the five senses is a labor of the entire history of the world down to the present."[80] Man must be freed from "the sense caught up in crude practical need," a " 'crudity' [which] is not a fatality of *nature*; on the contrary, under the conditions of capitalism this crudity is *artificially* produced by superimposing on all physical and mental senses 'the sheer estrangement of all the senses—the sense of having.' "[81] This acquisitive sense demands that man deny both his social and his sensuous nature in order to enlarge his hoard, and so makes impossible the forming of the *"human* sense" which "comes to be by virtue of its object, by virtue of *humanized* nature."[82] Always in Marx there is this reciprocity between human powers and their materialization. To set aside the old idealist notion that to actualize essence in material action is necessarily to degrade it is the Marxist axiom that *without its materialization one cannot speak properly of essence at all.*

Yet there is in the two longer quotations above none of that positivistic sense that modern, economic man has outgrown his illusions and can now cynically see men as they are, but rather the sense that men are not meant to be "naked" in their relations with each other, objects for use, as they are in an exploitative society. For Marx, what the positivist capitalist calls "realism" about man's nature is in fact only a mirror of the particular economic arrangement of his own society, whose "nexus" of "naked self-interest" is not a nexus in the social sense at all, but its negation—institutionalized division, semantically

79. Quoted in McLellan, *Karl Marx*, p. 90.
80. Marx, *Economic and Philosophic Manuscripts*, p. 141.
81. Mészáros, *Marx's Theory of Alienation*, p. 292.
82. Marx, *Economic and Philosophic Manuscripts*, p. 141.

hiding under "the illusion that competition is the ostensible absolute form of free individuality."[83] A "social" myth which gives selfishness, greed, expediency, and exploitation the seal of nature (Social Darwinism) and the sanction of God (the Protestant ethic) is an unveiling of all previous myths, revealing their actual motives by making them explicit. But after discovering the omnipresence of exploitation behind previous social myths, Marx does not succumb to cynicism. For Marx's critique of the capitalist system is inextricable from his imaginative creation of a new social paradigm which rests on a humanistic faith that both shapes it and permits it to eventuate in real action in the world, in part by undermining both the "scientific" and the "moral" buttresses of the capitalist world view, in part by adherence to a creative historicity which assures men that, as Brecht put it, "long is not forever." Marx's model of society not only promises liberation of the poor from their masters, but already liberates them from their master's myth, i.e., the sense of the sinfulness of the poor by which the Protestant ethic made them appear responsible for their own exploitation. Marx makes this explicit when he retells in *Capital* the myth of "primitive accumulation" which "plays in political economy about the same part as original sin in theology":

> In times long gone by there were two sorts of people: one, the diligent, intelligent, and above all, frugal elite; the other, lazy rascals, spending their substance, and more, in riotous living. The legend of theological original sin tells us certainly how man came to be condemned to eat his bread in the sweat of his brow, but the history of economic original sin reveals to us that there are people to whom this is by no means essential. Never mind! Thus it came to pass that the former sort accumulated wealth and the latter sort had at last nothing to sell except their skins. And from this original sin dates the poverty of the great majority that, despite all its labour, has up to now nothing to sell but itself, and the wealth of the few that increases constantly although they have long ceased to work. Such insipid childishness is every day preached to us in the defense of property.[84]

For this "insipid childishness" Marx substitutes the actual history of "conquest, enslavement, robbery, murder—briefly, force,"[85] the development of capital—the ownership of the means of production separated from the labor force—out of earlier feudal relations of production, and behind this process and propelling it inexorably, his own conception of "original sin," the division of labor.

83. Quoted in McLellan, *Karl Marx*, p. 298.
84. Marx, *Capital*, in *Basic Writings*, p. 202.
85. *Ibid.*

Thus it is the feelings of inferiority—both natural and moral—which an oppressive society breeds in its victims that Marx destroys; it is an immobilizing guilt that he attacks. Mankind, he once wrote, needs only to recognize its errors to have them forgiven. This helps to explain why, in the desolation which modern man has made of his reality, Marx's vision has, to so many, seemed to enunciate in a palatable modern form man's best hope about himself, a hope reborn at the moment it once again becomes desperate:

> It is possible that what we call "sin" is only a mythical expression of our self-consciousness, our solitude. I remember that in Spain during the civil war I had a revelation of "the other man" and of another kind of solitude: not closed, not mechanical, but open to the transcendent. . . . I believed and still believe that "the other man" dawned in those men. The Spanish dream was broken and defiled later, not because it was Spanish but because it was universal and, at the same time, concrete, an embodied dream with wide, astonished eyes. The faces I saw have become as they were before they were transformed by that elated sureness . . . they are the faces of coarse and humble people. But the memory will never leave me. Anyone who has looked Hope in the face will never forget it. He will search for it everywhere he goes, among all kinds of men. And he will dream of finding it again someday, somewhere, perhaps among those closest to him. In every man there is the possibility of his being—or, to be more exact, of his becoming once again—another man.[86]

"An embodied dream with wide, astonished eyes"; this is the moment of revitalization, when vision finds a living body in the world, the materialization of the ideal which, as the last two chapters suggested, is the project of the imagination; which is why a dead and disincarnate ideal, unified with the embodiment of another age, can only appear to the imagination as a ghost, something detached and artificial like a "robe of speculative cobwebs, embroidered with rhetoric,"[87] something so intrinsically detached that it can only by art be hammered into unity with a recalcitrant material world. In apocalyptic dreams, materiality bursts forth and finds once again a contemporary human embodiment. As Jung wrote:

> These archetypal images belong to humanity at large and can crop up autochthonously in anybody's head at any time and place, only needing favourable circumstances for their reappearance. The suitable moment for this is always when a particular view of the world

86. Paz, *The Labyrinth of Solitude*, pp. 27–28.
87. Marx and Engels, *Manifesto of the Communist Party*, in *Basic Writings*, p. 76.

is collapsing, sweeping away all the formulas that purported to offer final answers to the great problems of life. It is, as a matter of fact, quite in accord with psychological law that . . . when a religion glorifying the spirit disappears, there should rise up in its stead a primordial image of creative matter.[88]

It is possible to extend Jung's insight here and suggest that it is always with "a primordial image of creative matter," like the volcanoes and tidal waves that usher in apocalypse, that a new order begins, or, seen another way, with which an old one ends or is transformed. It is as if the old forms that contained matter dissolve and matter reappears—first as raw material in motion, then as new forms that crystallize and take shape—human shape if the process is complete. All genuine apocalyptic myth unites spirit and matter—in fact, cannot imagine them, as Marx could not, as separate; oppositely, a hollow order is always simultaneously a religion of detached spirit and a worship of dehumanized material force, depending on which side of the split order is focused on. But, on the "last day," as apocalyptic imagination sees it, the dead will be raised, which is to say—metaphorically—body will be reunited to soul, man to his community, past to future, "heaven" to earth.

Frank Kermode in *The Sense of an Ending* describes the reappearance in modern imaginations of what he calls the *aevum,* the medieval word used to describe that time which is neither profane earthly temporality nor eternity, but which partakes of both—a moment when temporality seems to open into eternity and to be timeless, while it remains but a moment. For the medieval theologian it was the angels who lived in the *aevum*; a way both of resolving the nature of angels, midway between human and divine, and of banishing this subversive psychic state from the experience of the run of men. This sense Kermode relates to an experience of society in crisis, as in the time-between, when ending and beginning are somehow co-present. It corresponds quite exactly to the sense of the chiliast in his timeless *now*, when everything is being overturned and made new.

Apocalyptic vision overcomes, then, the sense of time and tragedy, but the tragic is, perhaps always, reborn on the far side of vision. Once this historic moment of apocalyptic vision is past, and the golden age seems no longer an imminent event, but past, and only distantly future, and time seems to be wearing out the order, even as it is annually renewed, then the tragic vision again becomes central, even as religion, then, may center on the image of the hanged or dismembered rather than the risen god. Atlantis sinks back into the sea; the new Jerusalem

88. C. G. Jung, *The Spirit in Man, Art and Literature,* in *The Collected Works of C. G. Jung* (New York: Pantheon Books, 1966), 15: 9.

disappears in distant clouds. In a stabilized society, which means individuation can be imagined within and against the confines of the archetypally given, we can expect the confrontation of the limits of order by the heroic individual, a confrontation that must always end with the reaffirmation of those limits. If the social order becomes too recalcitrant, not sufficiently susceptible of renewal, if the fully human individual continues to outgrow the old structure, then the tragic vision may begin to color the Comic structure of rebirth and societal integration in which it is set, to bleed, as it were, over the lines, so that the tragi-comic or ironic vision may begin to replace the tragic, as both the limits of the old system and the possibilities of renewal within it are called into question. If disorder deepens, then the ironic may deepen into the demonic or grotesque vision, the "gods" of imagination becoming primordial material and oceanic force as they are reabsorbed into the solution of the unconscious, and the forms that make the humanization of reality possible are deformed or totally disorganized, releasing inhuman powers. Then apocalyptic vision may be reborn, destroying alike the social order and its mythic embodiment, but heralding, at the same time, new myth and new social order. Thus apocalyptic vision typically denies the sense of tragedy in its triumph over the old limits, as its eschatological vision celebrates the victory of the liberated libidinal figure, who, joined by the higher forces which are released by "the forgiveness of sins" from their role as censor, becomes transformed into man-god or culture hero, who overcomes the order of the world as it is and so is reborn and redeemed—and society with him.

Thus is born again "the apocalyptic world, the heaven of religion . . .the categories of reality in the forms of human desire, as indicated by the forms they assume under the work of human civilization."[89] When the crisis myth is new it breaks the power of the old mythic formulations, overcomes limits, binds the forces of disorder into new order, making self and world eternally young. Thus the focus is not on an aging, chastened Oedipus and a once again healthy Thebes, but on a risen and resplendent god-hero, a Prometheus unchained, his victory synonymous with the returned health of the collective. Both put out the eyes of worldly sight, but the second sight they restore sees different things. Society's second sight sees what it is and what it needs: stable order produces the tragic vision, distinct from the Comic or redemptive vision within which it is set; distorted order produces the ironic, and later, the demonic vision, confounding tragedy and comedy in an increasingly dark vision; crisis society may produce again the

89. Northrop Frye, *Anatomy of Criticism* (Princeton, N.J.: Princeton University Press, 1957), p. 141.

redemptive vision, and with it the possibility of the society's revitalization.

The development of Greek drama and art is a compressed paradigm of this process: the *Oresteia* of Aeschylus sets the tragedy in the context of redemptive vision—forgives Orestes, turns the savage Furies into the civilizing Eumenides, and institutes in Athens, through the agency of a merciful Athena, the reign of a just social order. It ends with a vision of the chthonic forces under the hill on which sits the human court of the Areopagus presided over by Athena—the proper ordering of parts in a single ideal human civilization. With Sophocles, tragedy dominates the stage, the fate of Oedipus already heavy with irony. By the late fifth century, when the order had become increasingly imperial and corrupt, the plays of Euripides move from the tragic to the ironic, and the demonic—ambiguously and properly associated with the divine—forces the gates of the ordered city. In the *Medea*, the revenge theme or Furies return in the person of Medea, oppressed female and despised alien, intimate of Hecate, goddess of earth's chthonic forces, who kills her children by Jason, the Jason who embodies the smug and cold opportunist that Athenian power had become. For this unnatural crime of killing her own children Medea is not punished but is carried off in the sun god's chariot, out of Jason's reach. By betraying human nature, the play suggests, Athens had made nature inhuman and vengeful, and had thereby been the agent of destruction of its own progeny, its future life. Following Euripides' time came the Athenian defeat and the agonized, tormented imagery of the Hellenistic period: the Laocöon statue pushing the limits of tortured, fettered expression; the human figures of the Pergamum temple tangled with monsters, one figure attempting to crawl out of the design, his stone knee on the step leading to the altar of the distant god. With the loss of Greek power and failure of nerve came the great upsurge of orgiastic and Orphic mystery cults, a crisis cult phenomenon which was eventually to feed, under the imperial power of Rome, along with the eschatological vision of the Messianic Jews, into the redemptive vision of early Christianity.

These paradigmatic imaginative responses to social situations may quite possibly have their parallels among the preliterate societies, with changed mythic emphasis to mirror the society's changing fortunes. Without written history and documents, obviously, it is possible only to surmise about the origin, or creative moment, of different forms of expression. Nevertheless, as in our own tradition, the mythic and artistic store of these societies runs the gamut of imaginative expression, reflecting not only a sense of order but also an awareness of nature's mischief, of disorder, disharmony, and the absurd. Few observers of these societies any longer entertain the notion that their people live in a timeless psychic state, a notion sometimes wishful, sometimes insulting—depending on whether that state is conceived as the zenith of psychic wholeness or the nadir of magically fogged perception. The African has a fund of cruel humor, where he sees himself as the butt of larger forces—in short, a highly developed sense of dark irony; his art forms show a large admixture of the grotesque. His life, like that of all human beings, is hedged with taboos; his "uncontrolled eroticism" is largely the projection of the white man's fantasy. His occasional orgiastic dancing speaks of his everyday repression; his liberation comes only in frenzied bursts. Awareness plagues him, too, with division; his enormous dread of public shame bespeaks his primal fear of separation from himself, of becoming a guilty object in his own eyes. Expectedly, myths of the "fall" are general throughout Africa; it is usually through the agency of a woman that God has been angered and withdrawn himself, as in the myth of the Nuba of Sudan which tells that the sky was once close to mankind, but a woman, resenting the pressure of its proximity, thrust her spoon through it and caused the sky to retire to the great distance at which it, and God, stands today. Many of these stories suggest that hard work and trouble were the result of man's angering God and thereby causing his withdrawal, that there was a Golden Age when God lived among men and life was better.[90] Thus the original tragedy, man's fall and separation from deity, is a central myth, accompanied by the postponed reunification when the culture hero will appear again, together with the restored connection between divided realms.

As long as a social order and the mythic order which incarnates its values are relatively viable and stable, then tragedy—whether it be individual or collective—is a statement that keeps vision alive; however distant men may feel from it, a given order remains the background of their actions and the standard against which they may be measured. There is, even in the bleakest tragedy, a vision of man that is protected; but when the artist, in drawing from his age its own image, sees the human image distorted or shattered, then the tragic perception is no longer possible. In the *Iliad*, which is both epic and tragic, when Achilles, in the name of his own passionate but too narrow loyalty to his dead friend, attempts to disfigure the body of Hector, the gods themselves intervene and preserve Hector's body unblemished—as the imagination intervenes to protect the human form from its mutilation by tyrannous force attached to dead or disincarnate ideals.

Marxism, as has been suggested, was such an imaginative attempt

90. Geoffrey Parrinder, *African Mythology* (London: Paul Hamlyn, 1967), pp. 94–95.

to humanize and unify a dehumanized and atomised modern world of markets, commodities, and technology; "Things," as Georg Lukács wrote, "become animated poetically only through their connection with human destinies."[91] Though Marx's thought is timebound, and many of its assurances have been outdated, both by changes it has wrought and by changes it did not foresee, the continuing argument against it as well as its constant revision by its twentieth-century adherents in both the Western and the non-Western world, suggest that its core remains significant and that it has passed into the very fabric of modern society, conditioning the way in which this century sees itself. By now, Marxism has its own complex tradition, woven of its inter-action with real events which have altered it, even as it influenced them.

The influence of Marxist thought on industrially underdeveloped nations began during his own lifetime; it was later extended (first by Rosa Luxembourg) to focus more sharply on imperialism as a central expression of the capitalist accumulation of "surplus labor," cheap resources, and more recently, the opening of consumer markets among those whose human and natural resources it had earlier exploited. The critique of capitalism struck an immediate chord among colonized peoples who suffered expropriation on a national scale, and it continues to suggest alternative social and political-economic structures to those nations who, almost the day after their independence movements were victorious, found themselves in the grip of a new national bourgeoisie which co-opts the language of national unity while serving its own private interests at the expense of the nation by acting as the agents of the former capitalist rulers. Frantz Fanon, for instance, while insisting on the need for Africans to develop their own values and style apart from existing models, takes a fundamentally Marxist view in his pre-scription for the remedy of widespread poverty, hunger, and social ills:

> Capitalist exploitation and cartels and monopolies are the enemies of under-developed countries. On the other hand the choice of a socialist regime, a regime which is completely oriented towards the people as a whole and based on the principle that man is the most precious of all possessions will allow us to go forward more quickly and more harmoniously, and thus make impossible that caricature of society where all economic and political power is held in the hands of a few who regard the nation as a whole with scorn and contempt.[92]

91. Georg Lukács, *Marxism and Human Liberation: Essays on History, Culture and Revolution*, ed. E. San Juan, Jr. (New York: Dell Publishing Co., 1973), p. 123.
92. Frantz Fanon, *The Wretched of the Earth*, trans. Constance Farrington (Harmondsworth, England: Penguin Books, 1973), p. 78.

When Marxism began to be exported to these nations, the question of whether the bourgeois stage in development could be skipped became a central issue; the affirmative answer to this question bespeaks the power of Marx's synthesis, which led, in dissimilar circumstances, not to its refutation but to its preservation through adaptation. Thus, a doctrine growing out of a developed bourgeois society undergoes adaptation in countries where the bourgeois stage of development is not consistent (as it was in European history) with national interest, but becomes merely subservience to the interests of the capitalist power of richer nations. Further, as with the notion of a second coming, the non-Western Marxists continue to expect the inevitable destruction of capitalism—this time through the cutting off of its imperialist tentacles, with resultant crisis and social upheaval and with their own peoples replacing the Western proletariat as the vanguard of a world socialist society. What becomes clear from these permutations is the manner in which the idea of a new world order grows within its own methodological assumptions, and the pattern of that growth may continue to be questioned—in the manner of Marx—by the real lives of real men. As the Cuban poet Heberto Padilla wrote:

> But it's true, old Marx,
> that History is not enough.
> > > Important occasions,
> > > man makes them.
> > > It's a real, live man who does it,
> Who masters it, who will fight.
> History by itself does
> > nothing, dear friends,
> > > It does absolutely
> > > nothing.[93]

There is something in Marx's method, explicit in the early writings, that speaks of an imaginative restoration of reality which Marx holds in common with many of the literary artists of modernity, the insistence on sensuous experience as the point of departure for any understanding or critique of the human situation. In *The Holy Family*, in criticizing the detached idealism of the "Young Hegelians," Marx writes:

> Here Critical Criticism is not against love alone, but against everything living, everything which is immediate, every sensuous experience, any and every *real* experience.[94]

93. Heberto Padilla, "'Important Occasions,'" trans. Paul Blackburn, *The New York Review of Books* 16, no. 10 (June 3, 1971): 5.
94. Quoted in Hyman, *The Tangled Bank*, p. 89.

The mythic imagination in modern literature makes its reappearance, similarly, in the context of a similar affirmation of everyday, sensuous experience: the synthesizing of time and space typical of the "multiple and multivalent reflections of consciousness"[95] in much of modern literature crystallizes in and through the random moments of such everydayness. This radical realignment of fiction, which makes central what had always seemed outside the great events and patterns with which literature and myth concerned itself, is, in its way, analogous to that elevation of the sensuous, material world in Marx to a determinative role in human consciousness and history. It is this analogous development in art and social thought that suggests to us a common direction of positive vision in our own age. It represents the healing countercurrent to all the violent division which threatens the social life of man with its own suicide. In this regard, it would seem worth quoting at some length the analysis which Erich Auerbach gives to this development in fiction which seems simultaneously to dissolve order and to refind it in an unaccustomed place:

> But the method is not only a symptom of the confusion and helplessness, not only a mirror of the decline of our world. There is, to be sure, a good deal to be said for such a view. There is in all these works a certain atmosphere of universal doom: especially in *Ulysses*, with its mocking *odi-et-amo* hodgepodge of the European tradition, with its blatant and painful cynicism, and its uninterpretable symbolism—for even the most painstaking analysis can hardly emerge with anything more than an appreciation of the multiple enmeshment of the motifs but with nothing of the purpose and meaning of the work itself. There is often something confusing . . . something hostile to the reality which they represent. We not infrequently find a turning away from the practical will to life, or delight in portraying it in its most brutal forms. There is hatred of culture and civilization, brought out by means of the subtlest stylistic devices which culture and civilization have developed, and often a radical and fanatical urge to destroy.
>
> . . . in the process something new and elemental appeared: nothing less than the wealth of reality and depth of life in every moment to which we surrender ourselves without prejudice. To be sure, what happens in that moment—be it outer or inner processes—concerns in a very personal way the individuals who live in it, but it also (and for that very reason) concerns the elementary things which men in general have in common . . . In this unprejudiced and exploratory type of representation we cannot but see to

95. Erich Auerbach, *Mimesis: The Representation of Reality in Western Literature*, trans. Willard R. Trask (Princeton, N. J.: Princeton University Press, 1973), p. 551.

what an extent—below the surface conflicts—the difference between men's way of life and forms of thought have already
lessened. The strata of societies and their different ways of life
have become inextricably mingled. There are no longer even exotic
peoples. . . . Beneath the conflicts and also through them, an economic and cultural leveling process is taking place. It is still a long
way to a common life of mankind on earth but the goal begins to
be visible. And it is most concretely visible now in the unpreju-
diced, precise, interior and exterior representation of the random
moment in the lives of different people. So the complicated
process of dissolution which led to fragmentation of the exterior
action, to reflection of consciousness, and to stratification of time
seems to be tending toward a very simple solution. Perhaps it will
be too simple to please those who, despite all its dangers and
catastrophies, admire and love our epoch for the sake of its
abundance of life and the incomparable historical vantage point
which it affords. But they are few in number, and probably they
will not live to see much more than the first forewarnings of the
approaching unification and simplification.[96]

The Western imagination seems now to have come full circle since the
age of exploration and cultural contact opened. At first, Western man
responded to his contact with alien cultures by rejection and by
reinforcement of his own sense of cultural superiority. Later, a more
open cultural relativism tended to turn cultural contact into icono-
clasm, to use comparative mythology as a rational tool for undermining
all mythic thought, in particular the old beliefs of the changing Western
world. This led not only to religious and cultural demolition at home,
but to a counter tendency to romanticize an exotic primitivism abroad.
More recently, through closer acquaintance and deeper reflection on
what are by now more digested experiences of multiplicity, the modern
mind increasingly finds congruencies and commonness, as the writer
and the comparative mythologist alike find resemblances in the mythic
structures of mankind's cultures which tend, rather than to invalidate
myths, to validate them anew at a psychic and existential level. And
this discovery coincides with a changed reality—"differences between
men's ways of life and forms of thought have already lessened." Thus as
myth is read back to the common sensuous and psychic experiences of
men, as men in fact become more alike, mythic interpretations of the
world emerge which dissolve the old local and hierarchical structures in
the radical democratization of reality. "And when one day our human
kind becomes full-grown, it will not define itself as the sum total of the

96. *Ibid.*, pp. 551–53.

whole world's inhabitants, but as the infinite unity of their mutual needs."[97]

In reviewing all that has been said about cultural order, crisis of order and abrupt change, and its imaginative counterparts, the interaction of collective and individual has, hopefully, been clarified, and a tentative answer to an old argument suggested—an argument which has been raised again in our age between advocates of religious transformation and those of Marxist revolution. The popular Marxist point of view states that radical social change precedes individual transformation, and that only in a new society will men live more harmoniously with themselves and each other. The religious belief is that first must come a change in the souls of men; then, and only then, will the orders of the world be changed and a more just society be established. If the foregoing discussion about the role of vision in radical social change has validity, then it would seem that the Marxist position is here opaque to its own origins. For the Marxist doctrine combines analysis of economic conditions and prescriptions for change with an apocalyptic-millennial vision, and it is only through belief in this vision of a new world order—which is also a refutation of the old one—that men are both directed and empowered to take the action which can in fact change the orders of the world. Thus the transformation of inner man, here, as in other such movements, has preceded the political act; human imagination has proposed what man disposes.

Nor is this the imposition of a new direction from "above," but one which arouses active response precisely because it arises from and answers to the needs of the actual situation in which men find themselves. The vision is not, like fantasy, an attempt to escape contradictions, but, achieving a full awareness of these contradictions, attempts to ripen reality, to achieve their resolution. As Marx wrote:

> mankind always sets itself only such tasks as it can solve; since looking at the matter more closely, it will always be found that the task itself arises only when the material conditions for its solution already exist, or are at least in the process of formation.[98]

Thus Marx's monism—or imaginative mode of thought—his sense that reality is a unitary, organic whole, its parts reciprocally dependent, makes vision for him the consciousness of an emerging new set of relations; nor does a new world view really exist apart from the attempt

97. Jean-Paul Sartre, Introduction to Fanon, *The Wretched of the Earth*, p. 23.

98. Quoted in McLellan, *Karl Marx*, p. 239.

to realize it. "In revolutionary activity," he writes, "change of self coincides with change of circumstances."[99]

> When communist *artisans* associate with one another, theory, propaganda, etc. is their first end. But at the same time, as a result of this association, they acquire a new need—the need for society—and what appears as a means becomes an end.[100]

This is reminiscent of that ritual renewal, discussed in the first chapter, when activities prescribed by the myth-dream reunite a people and restore a sense of self-worth and of action, so that acting on the myth is itself transformational and does not depend, ultimately, on an actual utopian outcome. For utopia activates the process—if it loses its prospective function, it becomes something other—a bulwark against change, stasis. In fact, as the vision is absorbed through the action of man and the passage of time, the changed way of regarding the world gives meaning and direction to action, preserves a kind of utopian tension without the messianic enthusiasm or the necessity of literal belief in a millennium. As the contemporary Marxist Mészáros says:

> What gives sense to human enterprise in socialism is not the fictitious promise of a fictitious absolute (a world from which all possible contradiction is eliminated forever) but the *real* possibility of turning a menacingly *increasing* trend of alienation into a reassuringly *decreasing* one. This itself would already be a qualitative achievement on the road to an effective, practical supercession of alienation and reification.[101]

Once a sense of human creative action and possibility is restored, and its direction clarified, it becomes increasingly possible to accept the necessary and tragic limitations in all possibilities.

The ability of the human imagination to make the world new, to imagine itself beyond division into a self and a society made whole, is both the refutation and the vindication of authority, the authority of the spiritual and cultural traditions of human life expressed alike in religion and art. To hold to the authority of tradition without seeing its source and renewal in recurrent visions of apocalypse is to accede to some sense of revelation, entering history at a given moment, finally and fully given, on which only commentary is possible. To focus one's sight on the vision of apocalypse is to begin to understand the nature of "revelation," how and why it does enter history at a given moment—the conditions that precipitate it, the imaginations that produce it, and the communities that embrace or reject it. The study of apocalyptic vision,

99. Quoted in *ibid*.
100. Marx, *Economic and Philosophic Manuscripts*, p. 155.
101. Mészáros, *Marx's Theory of Alienation*, p. 249.

therefore, vindicates the visions of the past, their efficacy in inspiring confidence, renewing dignity, reordering reality; and, at the same time, it asserts the possibility of the recurrence of this kind of revelation, or transformation, in souls and societies whose need produces them. Thus apocalyptic vision offers us both the source and the criticism of institutionalized symbol systems, and especially the criticism of frozen or degraded ones. Imagination is the guide through the symptoms it reveals in the forms of the grotesque, which precisely by being grotesque are revealed as symptoms of malaise; finally, the crisis imagination reveals its health and works its cure by creating new images of fertility, beauty, and wholeness on the far side of a necessary destruction.

Blake may have been the first Western artist to fully and explicitly identify the human imagination with the "divine," but he was only the first of what has become a long line. This was an identification many of the Romantics flirted with, but without the sense of commonality, of social order, which the freed imagination finds at the extreme of disorder and solipsism; society and self being, in the end, indivisible. The Romantics more often felt the creative force in nature, but missed its form, precisely because they were turned away from human society and from that humanized nature given shape by the love and arts of man. In apocalyptic vision there is neither a vague pantheism nor a mysticism which uses image as a way to get to the "Imageless"; it celebrates not mystery so much as created order, a living structure in which man feels, quite simply, at home. Visionary imagination is equally impatient with positivism and mysticism, neither drowning in actuality without significant form nor losing itself in pure light. The illumination that is the culmination of vision does not lose the human shape in light, but finds it there, as Blake saw "one Sun/Each morning, like a Newborn Man," as Marx saw man revolving "around himself as his real sun."

Increasingly, modern thinkers tend to restore this insight, to identify the synthesizing, creative faculty in man with what had traditionally been regarded as religious power, to understand the imagination's power to play Samson to its own Philistine and Daphne to its own Apollo. Thus it reproves both the mind's tyrannous literalism and the intellect's possessiveness, putting the power of matter and the design of intellect to its own imagistic forming purpose.

The basic paradigm of apocalyptic vision, discovered repeatedly in this study, is fundamentally simple, seeming almost negligible when extracted and abstracted from the living embodiments of it in achieved vision. At the end, then, it is necessary to recall to mind the many visions that have been examined throughout, refraining from a restatement of their own pattern stripped of particulars, recalling them rather in the deep dimensionality of their simultaneous embodiments. Otherwise, there is the danger of being left at the last with some theoretical skeleton of vision, a gaunt anatomy swinging, Beddoesian fashion, on the gibbet of the mind.

Let us remember, then, the constant recurrence of these similar patterns of vision in response to extreme crisis, and the substantial evidence for the transformational powers attendant upon such visions in both individuals and societies. In the midst of storm, imagination, refusing to consent to life's dissolution, provides a glowing center of illumination when the old center will not hold—at first, like Queequeg holding the lantern aloft in the midst of a squall:

> There, then, he sat, holding up that imbecile candle in the heart of that almighty forlornness. There, then, he sat, the sign and symbol of a man without faith, hopelessly holding up hope in the midst of despair.[102]

And out of that hopeless holding, out of its own despair, may come the unlooked for aftermath:

> Till gaining that vital centre, the black bubble upward burst, and now, liberated by reason of its cunning spring, and, owing to its great buoyancy, rising with great force, the coffin lifebuoy shot lengthwise from the sea, fell over and floated by my side. Buoyed up by that coffin, for almost one whole day and night, I floated on a soft and dirge-like main.[103]

Thus, like Queequeg's coffin, the primal past breaks from the vortex, the "dead" rise to restore the living, the forces of man's deepest past rise to sustain him from the very sea that would drown him; lower and upper world, dark racial unconscious and bright intellect join in new consciousness; the "I" becomes "we" as the "imbecile candle" takes on intelligible meaning:

> Within its vital boundary in the mind,
> We say God and the imagination are one . . .
> How high the highest candle lights the dark.
>
> Out of this same light, out of the central mind,
> We make a dwelling in the evening air,
> In which being there together is enough.[104]

But once again the imagination sets the limits to its own vision: Queequeg's coffin is empty, Ishmael remains an orphan—survivor but

102. Herman Melville, *Moby Dick* (San Francisco: Rinehart Press, 1957), p. 223.
103. *Ibid.*, p. 566.
104. Wallace Stevens, "Final Soliloquy of the Interior Paramour," *The Palm at the End of the Mind* (New York: Random House, 1972), pp. 367–68.

not saviour. The past he clings to is the dead shell of a primitive past, alien, somehow not his own, and Melville's vision remains that of the Romantic and isolate artist. The community is not reborn here with the man, though the human form is rescued from the maelstrom by its very solitude, its refusal of false social forms, against a better day. Melville's vision, though echoing the forms that always mark the imagination's attempt at unity, speaks of the symptoms of social and personal malaise beyond which it could not go. And it is apocalyptic vision against which such large but yet partial visions may be read—not by way of judging them inferior, but to explain the pain which is a function of what remains to be seen.

The apocalyptic imagination, then, becomes our guide to the workings of imagination at large, because, representing imagination at the extreme, it embodies the fullest expression of man creating an order that makes him whole, that rediscovers the collective nature of his individual humanity and connects it to the world in a vision that embodies the past, transforms it by accomodation to selected aspects of the present, and projects a future which mirrors this resolution, and which thereby seems eternal, both because it contains past and future in the present and because its very resolution gives to it the quality of finality. Apocalyptic vision thus embodies the sense of "eternal return" with the fullest humanism:

> Thus every revolution tries to create a world in which man, free at last from the trammels of the cold regime, can express himself truly and fulfill his human condition. Man is a being who can realize himself, can *be* himself, only in a revolutionary society. And that society bases its hopes on man's own nature, which is not something given and static, but rather consists in a range of possibilities that the regime has suppressed or mutilated. How can we tell that man is possibility, frustrated by injustice? The mythic notion of a Golden Age enters here: at some moment in history, in some part of the world, there was once a society that permitted man to express and realize himself. It prefigured and prophesied the new society which the revolutionary proposes to create. Almost all utopias suppose the previous existence, in some remote past, of a Golden Age that justifies revolutionary action and makes it viable.[105]

Imaginative revolution is, then, equally resolution, seeming both original and final to its adherents, the certainty accompanying vision a function of its totality; its configuration is large enough to draw everything into its orbit. Thus, collectively, the vision gathers the winds around the storm's eye; it draws its followers in ecstatic movement

105. Paz, *The Labyrinth of Solitude*, p. 143.

around it, even as, individually, the vision collects the heretofore broken parts of the self into a single entity. This is the moment of the imagination's triumph—not the moment of the greatest art, but the moment when myth and reality merge, which is the end of art. Seen from outside, it must always be ephemeral; from within, eternal. Such are the states of imagination which bring body to language: the words we use are but signs of the state we are in. In the state embodied by apocalyptic vision, language is returned, and returns us, to the world which seems, now and then, our proper home.

BIBLIOGRAPHY

Abbot, C. Colleer. "The Parents of Thomas Lovell Beddoes." *Durham University Journal* 3 (June 1942): 159–75.

Abell, Walter. *The Collective Dream in Art: A Psycho-Historical Theory of Culture Based on Relations between the Arts, Psychology, and the Social Sciences.* New York: Schocken Books, 1957.

Adams, Hazard. *Blake and Yeats: The Contrary Vision.* Ithaca, New York: Cornell University Press, 1955.

Altizer, Thomas J. J. *The New Apocalypse: The Radical Christian Vision of William Blake.* East Lansing: Michigan State University Press, 1967.

Alvarez, A. *The Savage God: A Study of Suicide.* New York: Random House, 1972.

Auerbach, Erich. *Mimesis: The Representation of Reality in Western Literature..* Translated by Willard R. Trask. Princeton, New Jersey: Princeton University Press, 1973.

Banton, Michael, ed. *Anthropological Approaches to the Study of Religion.* New York: F. A. Praeger, 1966.

Barnett, Homer G. *Innovation: The Basis of Cultural Change.* 1st ed. New York: McGraw-Hill, 1953.

Beddoes, Thomas Lovell. *The Letters of Thomas Lovell Beddoes.* Edited by 973 (leading article).

Beddoes, Thomas Lovell. *The Letters of Thomas Lovell Beddoes.* Edited by Edmund Gosse. London: Elkin Matthews and John Lane, 1894.

———. *The Poetical Works of Thomas Lovell Beddoes.* Edited, with a memoir, by Edmund Gosse, 2 vols. London: J. M. Dent and Company, 1890.

———. *The Works of Thomas Lovell Beddoes.* Edited by H. W. Donner. London: Oxford University Press, 1935.

Berlin, Isaiah. *Karl Marx: His Life and Environment,* 3rd ed. London: Oxford University Press, 1963.

Binswanger, Ludwig. *Being-in-the-World; Selected Papers of Ludwig Binswanger.* Translated by Jacob Needleman. New York: Basic Books, 1963.

Blake, William. *Blake: Complete Writings.* Edited by Geoffrey Keynes. London: Oxford University Press, 1969.

———. *Poems of William Blake.* Edited by W. B. Yeats. London: George Routledge and Sons, Ltd., n.d.

Bloom, Harold. *Blake's Apocalypse: A Study in Poetic Argument.* Ithaca, New York: Cornell University Press, 1963.

———. *Yeats.* London: Oxford University Press, 1970.

———. ed. *Romanticism and Consciousness.* New York: W. W. Norton and Company, Inc., 1970.

Blunden, E. "Beddoes and His Contemporaries." *Times Literary Supplement* (December 13, 1928), p. 973.

Bronowski, J. *William Blake and the Age of Revolution.* New York: Harper and Row, 1969.

Burridge, Kenelm. *Mambu: A Melanesian Millennium.* London: Methuen and Company, 1960.

_____. *New Heaven, New Earth*. New York: Schocken Books, 1969.

Butt, Audrey J. "The Birth of a Religion." In *Gods and Rituals*, edited by John Middleton, pp. 277–435. Garden City, New York: The Natural History Press, 1967.

"(Mr.) Buttle's Review." *Blackwood's Edinburgh Magazine* 80, no. 392 (October 1856): 447–49.

Campbell, Joseph. *The Hero with a Thousand Faces*. Cleveland: World Publishing Company, Meridian Books, 1956.

_____. *The Masks of God: Creative Mythology*. New York: The Viking Press, 1968.

Carroll, Paul. *The Poem in Its Skin*. Chicago: Follett Publishing Company, 1968.

Chew, Samuel. "The Nineteenth Century and After (1789–1939)." In *A Literary History of England*, edited by Albert C. Baugh, pp. 1256–58. New York: Appleton-Century-Crofts, Inc., 1949.

Church, Richard. "Beddoes: The Last of the Alchemists." *The Spectator*, no. 142 (February 1929): 188–89.

Cohn, Norman. *The Pursuit of the Millennium*. New York: Harper and Row, 1961.

Coxe, Louis O. "Beddoes: The Mask of Parody." *Hudson Review* 6 (Summer 1953): 252–65.

Danzig, Allan. "An Unexpected Echo of Beddoes in Frost." *Notes and Queries* 10 (April 1963): 150–51.

Deaux, George. *The Black Death*, pp. 145–222. London: Hamish Hamilton, 1969.

Devereux, George. "Dream Learning and Individual Ritual Differences in Mohave Shamanism." *American Anthropologist* 59, no. 6 (December 1957): 1036–45.

_____. *Reality and Dream: Psychotherapy of a Plains Indian*. Garden City, New York: Doubleday and Company, 1969.

_____. 'Shamans as Neurotics." *American Anthropologist* 63, no. 5, part 1 (October 1961): 1088–90.

Donner, H. W. "Echoes of Beddoesian Rambles." *Studia Neophilologica* 33 (1961): 219–64.

_____. *Thomas Lovell Beddoes: The Making of a Poet*. Oxford: Basil Blackwell, 1935.

_____. "Thomas Lovell Beddoes to Leonhard Tobler: Eight German Letters." *Studia Neophilologica* 35 (1963): 227–55.

_____. ed. *The Browning Box or The Life and Works of Thomas Lovell Beddoes as Reflected in Letters by His Friends and Admirers*. London: Oxford University Press, 1935.

Donoghue, Denis. *William Butler Yeats*. New York: The Viking Press, 1971.

Eiseley, Loren. *The Invisible Pyramid*. New York: Charles Scribner's Sons, 1970.

Eliade, Mircea. *The Forge and the Crucible: The Origins and Structures of Alchemy*. Translated by Stephen Corrin. New York: Harper and Row, 1971.

_____. *The Myth of the Eternal Return*. Translated by Willard R. Trask. New York: Pantheon Books, 1965.

_____. *The Sacred and the Profane*. Translated by Willard R. Trask. New York: Harper and Row, 1961.

Eliot, T. S. *Collected Poems 1909–1962*. New York: Harcourt, Brace & World, Inc., 1963.

––––. *Selected Essays of T. S. Eliot* pp. 25–100, 100–199 passim. New York: Harcourt, Brace & World, Inc., 1960.

Elliott, Robert C. *The Power of Satire: Magic, Ritual, Art*. Princeton, New Jersey: Princeton University Press, 1970.

Ellmann, Richard. *Yeats: The Man and the Masks*. New York: E. P. Dutton & Co., Inc., 1948.

Erdman, David V. *Blake: Prophet against Empire. A Poet's Interpretation of the History of His Own Times*, rev. ed. Garden City, New York: Doubleday and Company, Anchor Books, 1969.

Evans-Pritchard, E. E. *Theories of Primitive Religion*. Oxford: Oxford University Press, Clarendon Press, 1965.

Fanon, Frantz. *Dying Colonialism*. Translated by Haakon Chevalier. Harmondsworth, England: Penguin Books Ltd., 1970.

––––. *The Wretched of the Earth*. Translated by Constance Farrington. Preface by Jean-Paul Sartre. Harmondsworth, England: Penguin Books Ltd., 1973.

Fiedler, Leslie. *Waiting for the End*. New York: Stein and Day, 1964.

Fletcher, R. *English Romantic Drama, 1795–1843: A Critical History*. 1st ed. New York: Exposition Press, 1966.

Freud, Sigmund. *Beyond the Pleasure Principle*. In *The Major Works of Sigmund Freud*, pp. 639–63. Chicago: Encyclopedia Britannica, Inc., 1952.

––––. *The Interpretation of Dreams*. 3rd ed. New York: The Macmillan Company, 1913.

––––. *On Creativity and the Unconscious*. New York: Harper and Row, 1958.

––––. *Totem and Taboo*. Translated by A. A. Brill. New York: Random House, 1918.

Frye, Northrop. *Anatomy of Criticism*. Princeton, New Jersey: Princeton University Press, 1957.

––––. *Fearful Symmetry: A Study of William Blake*. Princeton, New Jersey: Princeton University Press, 1969.

––––. *The Stubborn Structure: Essays on Criticism and Society*. Ithaca, New York: Cornell University Press, 1970.

––––. *A Study of English Romanticism*. New York: Random House, 1968.

––––. ed. *Blake: A Collection of Critical Essays*. Englewood Cliffs, New Jersey: Prentice-Hall, Inc., 1966.

Garcia Lorca, Federico. *The Poet in New York*. Translated by Ben Belitt. New York: Grove Press, 1955.

Gennep, Arnold van. *The Rites of Passage*. Translated by Monika B. Vizedom and Gabrielle L. Caffee. London: Routledge and Kegan Paul, 1960.

Georges, Robert A., ed., *Studies on Mythology*. Homewood, Illinois: The Dorsey Press, 1968.

Goldmann, Lucien. *The Human Sciences and Philosophy*. Translated by Hayden V. White and Robert Anchor. London: Jonathan Cape Ltd., 1973.

Gomme, A. H., ed. *Jacobean Tragedies*. London: Oxford University Press, 1969.

Good, Donald William. "Thomas Lovell Beddoes: A Critical Study of His Major Works." Ph.D. Dissertation, Ohio State University, 1968.

Hallowell, A. Irving. *Culture and Experience*, chaps. 4, 13, 17, 19, and 20. Philadelphia: University of Pennsylvania Press, 1955.

Harrex, Anne. " 'Death's Jest-Book' and the German Contribution." *Studia Neophilologica* 39 (1967): 15–37.

Hassan, Ihab, ed. *Liberations: New Essays on the Humanities in Revolution*. Middletown, Connecticut: Wesleyan University Press, 1971.

Heath-Stubbs, John. *The Darkling Plain*, pp. 37–46. London: Eyre and Spottiswoode, 1950.

Heidegger, Martin. *Poetry, Language, Thought*. Translated by Albert Hofstadter. New York: Harper and Row, 1971.

Hoffer, Abram; Osmond, Humphrey; and Smythies, John. "Schizophrenia, A New Approach. *The Journal of Mental Science* 100, no. 418 (January 1954): 29–45.

Hoffman, Daniel. *Barbarous Knowledge: Myth in the Poetry of Yeats, Graves, and Muir*. London: Oxford University Press, 1967.

Hogbin, H. Ian. "Pagan Religion in a New Guinea Village." In *Gods and Rituals*, edited by John Middleton, pp. 41–75. Garden City, New York: The Natural History Press, 1967.

Howarth, R. G. "Beddoes' Last Poem." *Notes and Queries* 193 (November 1, 1947): 475.

———. "Two Poems of Beddoes." *Notes and Queries* 193 (September 20, 1947): 410–11.

Hoyt, Charles Alva. "Studies in Thomas Lovell Beddoes." Ph.D. dissertation, Columbia University, 1961.

———. "Theme and Imagery in the Poetry of Thomas Lovell Beddoes." *Studia Neophilologica* 25 (1963): 85–103.

Hyman, Stanley Edgar. *The Tangled Bank: Darwin, Marx, Frazer and Freud as Imaginative Writers*. New York: Grosset & Dunlap, 1966.

Inglis, Judy. "Cargo Cults: The Problems of Explanation." *Oceania* 27, no. 4 (June 1957): 249–63.

Janov, Arthur. *The Primal Scream, Primal Therapy: The Cure for Neurosis*. New York: Dell Publishing Co., 1970.

Jensen, Adolf E. *Myth and Cult among Primitive Peoples*. Translated by Marianna T. Choldin and Wofgang Weissleder. Chicago: University of Chicago Press, 1966.

Johnson, Hiram Kellogg. "Thomas Lovell Beddoes: A Psychiatric Study." *The Psychiatric Quarterly* 17 (July 1943): 446–69.

Jones, Le Roi. *Tales*. New York: Grove Press, 1967.

Jung, Carl Gustav. *The Collected Works of C. G. Jung*. 2nd ed. Translated by R. F. C. Hull, vols. 1, 7, 15; Bollingen Series 20. New York: Pantheon Books, 1970 (1), 1966 (7, 15).

Kaplan, Bert, ed. *Studying Personality Cross-Culturally*. New York: Harper and Row, 1961.

Kayser, Wolfgang. *The Grotesque in Art and Literature*. Translated by Ulrich Weisstein. Bloomington: Indiana University Press, 1963.

Kermode, Frank. *The Sense of an Ending*. New York: Oxford University Press, 1967.

Kolakowski, Leszek. *Toward a Marxist Humanism: Essays on the Left Today*. Translated by Jane Zielonko Peel. New York: Grove Press, 1968.

Krader, Lawrence. "A Nativistic Movement in Western Siberia." *American Anthropologist* 58, no. 2 (April 1956): 282–92.

Kuhn, Thomas S. *The Structure of Scientific Revolutions*. 2nd ed. Chicago: University of Chicago Press, 1970.

La Barre, Weston. *The Ghost Dance: Origins of Religion*. Garden City, New York: Doubleday and Company, 1970.

––––––. "Materials for a History of Studies of Crisis Cults: A Bibliographic Essay." *Current Anthropology* 12 (February 1971): 3–44.

––––––. *The Peyote Cult*. New Haven: Yale University Press, 1938.

Laing, R. D. *The Divided Self*. New York: Penguin Books, 1959.

––––––. *The Self and Others*. London: Tavistock Publications, 1961.

Lanternari, Vittorio. *The Religions of the Oppressed: A Study of Modern Messianic Cults*. Translated by Lisa Sergio. New York: New American Library, 1965.

Lawrence, D. H. *Apocalypse*. New York: The Viking Press, 1971.

Lawrence, Peter. *Road Belong Cargo: A Study of the Cargo Movement in the Southern Madang District, New Guinea*. Manchester, England: Manchester University Press, 1964.

Leach, Edmund, ed. *The Structural Study of Myth and Totemism*. London: Tavistock Publications, 1967.

Lévi-Strauss, Claude. *Structural Anthropology*. Translated by Claire Jacobson and Brooke G. Schoepf. Garden City, New York: Doubleday and Company, 1967.

––––––. *Totemism*. Translated by Rodney Needham. Boston: Beacon Press, 1962.

Lichtheim, George. *Marxism: An Historical and Critical Study*. 2nd ed. rev. London: Routledge and Kegan Paul, 1964.

Lienhardt, Godfrey. *Social Anthropology*. London: Oxford University Press, 1966.

Linton, Ralph. "Nativistic Movements." *American Anthropologist* 45 (1943): 230–40.

Lowie, Robert H. *Primitive Religion*. New York: Liveright, 1924.

Lucas, F. L. "Death's Jester." *Life and Letters* 5 (October 1930): 219–45.

––––––. "The Strange Case of Dr. Beddoes." *Life and Letters* 4 (January 1930): 55–73.

Lukács, Georg. *Marxism and Human Liberation: Essays on History, Culture and Revolution*. Edited by E. San Juan, Jr. New York: Dell Publishing Co., 1973.

McFarland, H. Neill. *The Rush Hour of the Gods: A Study of the New Religious Movements in Japan*. New York: Harper and Row, 1967.

Macfarlane, Alan. *Witchcraft in Tudor and Stuart England*, pp. 147–252. New York: Harper and Row, 1970.

McLellan, David. *Karl Marx: His Life and Thought*. London: Macmillan & Company, 1973.

Malinowski, Bronislaw. *Magic, Science and Religion*. Garden City, New York: Doubleday and Company, 1954.

Bibliography 189

Mannheim, Karl. *Ideology and Utopia: An Introduction to the Sociology of Knowledge.* Translated by Louis Wirth and Edward Shils, pp. 192–263. New York: Harcourt, Brace & World, Inc., 1936.

Marcuse, Herbert. *Five Lectures: Psychoanalysis, Politics and Utopia.* Translated by Jeremy J. Shapiro and Sherry M. Weber. London: Allen Lane, The Penguin Press, 1970.

Maritain, Jacques. *Creative Intuition in Art and Poetry.* Cleveland: World Publishing Company, Meridian Books, 1954.

Marwick, M. G. *Sorcery in Its Social Setting: A Study of the Northern Rhodesian Cewa.* Manchester, England: Manchester University Press, 1965.

_____. ed. *Witchcraft and Sorcery.* New York: Penguin Books, 1970.

Marx, Karl. *Economic and Philosophic Manuscripts of 1844..* Edited by Dirk J. Struik. Translated by Martin Milligan. London: Lawrence & Wishart Ltd., 1973.

Marx, Karl, and Engels, Friedrich. *The German Ideology.* Edited by C. J. Arthur. London: Lawrence & Wishart Ltd., 1970.

_____ *Marx and Engels: Basic Writings on Politics and Philosophy.* Edited by Lewis S. Feuer. London: Collins, Fontana Library, 1969.

_____. *Marxist Social Thought.* Edited by Robert Freedman. New York: Harcourt, Brace & World, Inc., 1968.

Mészáros, István. *Lukacs' Concept of Dialectic.* London: The Merlin Press, 1972.

_____ *Marx's Theory of Alienation*, 3rd ed. London: The Merlin Press, 1972.

Meyerstein, E. H. W. "Thomas Lovell Beddoes." *English* 3, no. 13 (1940): 8–15.

Miller, J. Hillis. *Poets of Reality.* New York: Atheneum, 1969.

Moore, Virginia. *The Unicorn: William Butler Yeats' Search for Reality.* New York: The Macmillan Company, 1954.

Neumann, Erich. *Amor and Psyche: The Psychic Development of the Feminine.* Princeton, New Jersey: Princeton University Press, 1971.

_____. *Art and the Creative Unconscious.* Translated by Ralph Manheim. Princeton, New Jersey: Princeton University Press, 1971.

Newman, Charles, ed. *The Art of Sylvia Plath.* Bloomington: Indiana University Press, 1971.

Nickerson, Charles C. "T. L. Beddoes' Readings in Bodley." *Studia Neophilologica* 36 (1964): 261–65.

"On the Trail of Beddoes. Secrets from the Vanished Browning Box." *Times Literary Supplement*, November 16, 1935, p. 729 (leading article).

Ornstein, Robert, and Spencer, Hazelton, eds. *Elizabethan and Jacobean Tragedy: An Anthology.* Boston: D. C. Heath and Company, 1964.

Paz, Octavio. *The Labyrinth of Solitude: Life and Thought in Mexico.* Translated by Lysander Kemp. New York: Grove Press, 1961.

Pierce, Fredrick E. "Beddoes and the Continental Romanticists." *Philological Quarterly* (1927), pp. 123–32.

_____. *Currents and Eddies in the English Romantic Generation*, pp. 193–95. New Haven: Yale University Press, 1918.

Praz, Mario. *The Romantic Agony.* Translated by Angus Davidson. 2nd ed. London: Oxford University Press, 1970.

190 Bibliography

Radcliffe-Brown, A. R. *Structure and Function in Primitive Society*. New York: The Free Press, 1965.

Radin, Paul. *The Trickster: A Study in American Indian Mythology*. New York: Philosophical Library, 1956.

Review of *Poems* by the late Thomas Lovell Beddoes. Edited by Thomas Forbes Kelsall. *The Athenaeum*, no. 1247 (September 20, 1851), pp. 989–90.

Review of *The Poetical Works of Thomas Lovell Beddoes*. Edited by Edmund Gosse. *The Athenaeum*, no. 3296 (December 27, 1890), pp. 879–81.

Reynolds, Frank, as told to McClure, Michael. *Freewheelin Frank: Secretary of the Angels*. New York: Grove Press, 1967.

Rickword, Edgell. "Thomas Lovell Beddoes." *The London Mercury* 9, no. 50 (December 1923): 162–74.

Róheim, Géza. *Animism, Magic and the Divine King*. New York: A. A. Knopf, 1930.

――――. *Magic and Schizophrenia*. Bloomington: Indiana University Press, 1955.

Sargant, William Walters. *Battle for the Mind: A Physiology of Conversion and Brainwashing*. Garden City, New York: Doubleday and Company, 1957.

Schiller, Frederick. "The Ghost Seer." In *The Works of Frederick Schiller*, translated by Henry C. Bohn, pp. 377–482. London: Henry C. Bohn, 1849.

Scholem, Gershom. "The Holiness of Sin." *Commentary* 51, no. 1 (January 1971): 41–70.

Seboek, Thomas A., ed. *Myth: A Symposium*. Bloomington: Indiana University Press, Midland Books, 1965.

Seiden, Morton I. *William Butler Yeats: The Poet as a Mythmaker*. East Lansing: Michigan State University Press, 1962.

Snow, Royall H. *Thomas Lovell Beddoes: Eccentric and Poet*. New York: Covici-Friede, 1928.

Sorokin, Pitirim A. *Man and Society in Calamity: The Effects of War, Revolution, Famine, Pestilence upon Human Mind, Behavior, Organization and Cultural Life*. New York: Greenwood Press, 1968.

Stanner, W. E. H. "On the Interpretation of Cargo Cults." *Oceania* 29, no. 1 (September 1958): 1–25.

Stokoe, F. W. *German Influence in the English Romantic Period*, pp. 1–19. Cambridge: Cambridge University Press, 1926.

Strachey, Lytton. "The Last Elizabethan." *Books and Characters: French and English*, pp. 235–65. New York: Harcourt, Brace & Company, Inc., 1922.

Sullivan, Harry Stack. *The Interpersonal Theory of Psychiatry*. New York: W. W. Norton and Company, Inc., 1953.

Sundkler, Bengt G. M. *Bantu Prophets in South Africa*. 2nd ed. London: Oxford University Press, 1961.

Swanson, Guy E. *The Birth of the Gods: The Origin of Primitive Beliefs*. Ann Arbor: The University of Michigan Press, 1968.

Symons, Arthur. Review of *The Poetical Works of Thomas Lovell Beddoes*, edited by Edmund Gosse. *The Academy* 40, no. 1005 (August 8, 1891): 128–9.

Todd, A. C. "Anna Maria, The Mother of Thomas Lovell Beddoes." *Studia Neophilologica* 29, no. 2 (1957): 136–44.

――――. "T. L. Beddoes and His Guardian." *Times Literary Supplement*, October 19, 1952, p. 668.

Bibliography   191

Tucker, Robert C. *Philosophy and Myth in Karl Marx*. 2nd ed. Cambridge: Cambridge University Press, 1972.

"Two Unpublished Fragments by Thomas Lovell Beddoes." *Spectator* 148 (February 27, 1932): 286.

Ulam, Adam B. *The Unfinished Revolution: An Essay on the Sources of Influence of Marxism and Communism*. New York: Random House, 1964.

Voget, Fred W. "The American Indian in Transition: Reformation and Accommodation." *American Anthropologist* 58, no. 2 (April 1956): 369–78.

Wach, Joachim. *The Sociology of Religion*. Chicago: University of Chicago Press, 1962.

Wagner, Geoffrey. "Centennial of a Suicide: Thomas Lovell Beddoes." *Horizon* 19 (June 1949): 417–35.

Wallace, Anthony F. C. "Dreams and the Wishes of the Soul: A Type of Psychoanalytic Theory among the Seventeenth Century Iroquois." In *Magic, Witchcraft and Curing*, edited by John Middleton, pp. 171–90. Garden City, New York: The Natural History Press, 1967.

_____. *Religion: An Anthropological View*. New York: Random House, 1966.

_____. "Revitalization Movements." *American Anthropologist* 58, no. 2 (April 1956): 264–81.

Walzel, Oskar. *German Romanticism*. Translated by Alma Elise Lussky. New York: G. P. Putnam's Sons, 1932.

Williams, F. E. *Orokaiva Magic*. London: Oxford University Press, 1928.

Wood, Henry. "T. L. Beddoes: A Survival in Style." *American Journal of Philology*, 4, no. 16 (1883): 445–55.

Worsley, Peter. *The Trumpet Shall Sound: A Study of 'Cargo' Cults in Melanesia*. London: Macgibbon and Kee, 1957.

Yeats, W. B. *The Autobiography of William Butler Yeats*. New York: The Macmillan Company, 1965.

_____. *The Collected Poems of W. B. Yeats*. New York: The Macmillan Company, 1970.

_____. *Selected Poems and Two Plays of William Butler Yeats*. Edited by M. L. Rosenthal. New York: Collier Books, 1966.

_____. *A Vision*. New York: Collier Books, 1966.

INDEX

193

Ricardo, David, 160–61
Róheim, Geza, 9
Romantic: agonies past, 87; agony,
138; animism perverted in Beddoes,
104; ecstasy declining, 82; faith of
Yeats, 124; idealism, 75; images, 85;
imagination, 123; irony, 93; isolate
artist-hero, 105; sadness in Freud,
57; vision of Melville, 183
Romantic, the: as idealism in extreme
form, 76; as target of mockery, 90
Romanticism: in Beddoes, 75, 82;
destructive nostalgia of, 138; disillusionment of, with revolutionary
hopes, 95; divorced from society,
75; English, 75; German, 75, 104
Romantics, the: brief candle of, 49;
compared to Blake, 50; German, and
Beddoes, 96; preceded Beddoes, 73;
repressed evil of, 83; unscientific
animism of, 84

"Sailing to Byzantium," 114
Santayana, George, 135
Sartre, Jean-Paul, 80, 140
Satire, 70–73; as unmasking, 97
Satirist: Beddoes as nihilist-, 74, 91;
satirized, 96
Second Brother, The, 84, 89
Secret Rose, The, 115
Sense of an Ending, The, 171
Shaman: compared with prophet and
priest, 17–18; as institutionalized
dreamer, 7, 136; nature and function
of, 14–17; Yeats as, 132
Shamanism, 6, 14–18
Shelley, Percy Bysshe, 82
Sibylla, 82, 92, 94, 100–101, 104
Smart, Christopher, 49
Smith, Adam, 160
Smohalla, 25
Sophocles, 173
Sorcery, 68–72; as cause of illness, 7,
14; epidemics of, 29; and satirist, 75
Spectre of Urthona, 49

Spiro, Melford, E., 10
Steppenwolf, 79
Structure of Scientific Revolutions,
The, 163–64
Swanson, Guy E., 9

Thanatos: in Beddoes, 76, 96; in Blake
and Freud, 56; in Yeats, 106–7
Tharmas, 54–55, 56, 127
Torrismond, 78–79, 81
Tylor, Sir E. B., 8

Ulro, 79, 101
Urizen, 54–56, 62–63, 64–65, 127,
129

Vailala Madness, 34, 43
Vala, 57, 97
Victorians, 73, 83, 95
Vision, A, 106–7, 124, 125, 129
Voltaire, 46, 66

Wallace, Anthony F. C., 5, 10, 11, 12,
25, 43, 44
Wallis, W. D., 26
Weiss, Peter, 12
Wolfram, 78, 89, 91–94, 97–98, 100–
101, 103–6
Wordsworth, William, 82, 95
Wovoka, 25

Yali, 28–29
Yeats, William Butler, 106–26; compared with Blake and Beddoes, 126–
34
"Young Hegelians," 143, 176

Zevi, Sabbatai, 24
Ziba, 74, 77, 91, 92, 96, 101
"Zoas," 55, 65

THE JOHNS HOPKINS UNIVERSITY PRESS
This book was composed in Baskerville text and
York display type by The Composing Room of
Michigan, Inc., from a design by Patrick Turner.
It was printed on 50-lb. Cream White Bookmark
paper and bound in Holliston Roxite cloth by
Thomson-Shore, Inc.

Library of Congress Cataloging in Publication Data

Wilner, Eleanor.
   Gathering the winds.

   Bibliography: pp. 185–92
   Includes index.
   1. Imagination. 2. Creative thinking. 3. Social
change. I. Title.
BF408.W54   301.2'1   75-9846
ISBN 0-8018-1670-X